AMERICAN LITERATURE READINGS IN THE 21ST CENTURY

Series Editor: Linda Wagner-Martin

American Literature Readings in the 21st Century publishes works by contemporary critics that help shape critical opinion regarding literature of the nineteenth and twentieth centuries in the United States.

Published by Palgrave Macmillan:

Freak Shows in Modern American Imagination: Constructing the Damaged Body from Willa Cather to Truman Capote
By Thomas Fahy

Women and Race in Contemporary U.S. Writing: From Faulkner to Morrison
By Kelly Lynch Reames

American Political Poetry in the 21st Century
By Michael Dowdy

Science and Technology in the Age of Hawthorne, Melville, Twain, and James: Thinking and Writing Electricity
By Sam Halliday

F. Scott Fitzgerald's Racial Angles and the Business of Literary Greatness
By Michael Nowlin

Sex, Race, and Family in Contemporary American Short Stories
By Melissa Bostrom

Democracy in Contemporary U.S. Women's Poetry
By Nicky Marsh

James Merrill and W.H. Auden: Homosexuality and Poetic Influence
By Piotr K. Gwiazda

Contemporary U.S. Latino/a Literary Criticism
Edited by Lyn Di Iorio Sandín and Richard Perez

The Hero in Contemporary American Fiction: The Works of Saul Bellow and Don DeLillo
By Stephanie S. Halldorson

Race and Identity in Hemingway's Fiction
By Amy L. Strong

Edith Wharton and the Conversations of Literary Modernism
By Jennifer Haytock

The Anti-Hero in the American Novel: From Joseph Heller to Kurt Vonnegut
By David Simmons

Indians, Environment, and Identity on the Borders of American Literature: From Faulkner and Morrison to Walker and Silko
By Lindsey Claire Smith

The American Landscape in the Poetry of Frost, Bishop, and Ashbery: The House Abandoned
By Marit J. MacArthur

AMNESIA AND REDRESS IN CONTEMPORARY AMERICAN FICTION

Counterhistory

Marni Gauthier

AMNESIA AND REDRESS IN CONTEMPORARY AMERICAN FICTION
Copyright © Marni Gauthier, 2011.

First published in 2011 by
PALGRAVE MACMILLAN®
in the United States—a division of St. Martin's Press LLC,
175 Fifth Avenue, New York, NY 10010.

Where this book is distributed in the UK, Europe and the rest of the world,
this is by Palgrave Macmillan, a division of Macmillan Publishers Limited,
registered in England, company number 785998, of Houndmills,
Basingstoke, Hampshire RG21 6XS.

Palgrave Macmillan is the global academic imprint of the above companies
and has companies and representatives throughout the world.

Palgrave® and Macmillan® are registered trademarks in the United States,
the United Kingdom, Europe and other countries.

ISBN: 978–0–230–11577–4

Library of Congress Cataloging-in-Publication Data

Gauthier, Marni J.
    Amnesia and redress in contemporary American fiction :
counterhistory / Marni Gauthier.
        p. cm.—(American literature readings in the twenty first century)
    Includes bibliographical references.
    ISBN 978–0–230–11577–4
    1. American fiction—History and criticism. 2. Truthfulness and
falsehood in literature. 3. Memory—Social aspects—United States.
4. Memory—Political aspects—United States. 5. Collective memory in
literature. I. Title. II. Series.

PS374.T78G38 2011
813'.08106054—dc22   2011009879

A catalogue record of the book is available from the British Library.

Design by Newgen Imaging Systems (P) Ltd., Chennai, India.

First edition: October 2011

10 9 8 7 6 5 4 3 2 1

Printed and bound in Great Britain by
CPI Antony Rowe, Chippenham and Eastbourne

For Anna and Nicholas,
May you always have the courage to see and stand for truth

Cover photo: *Robert Carter holds a photograph of his platoon of soldiers taken moments before Shot Hood was detonated on July 5, 1957, at 74 kilotons the biggest atomic shot ever in Nevada. "I was happy, full of life before I saw that bomb, but then I understood evil and was never the same."*

CONTENTS

PERMISSIONS

Portions of chapter 2 were originally published in Nevada Humanities' *Halcyon* 23 (2001). This chapter is reprinted with permission from Nevada Humanities.

Earlier versions of chapters 3 and 4, respectively, were published in the following:

African American Review 39.3 (Fall 2005): 395–414.

Beyond Adaptation: Essays on Radical Transformations of Original Works (© 2010), edited by Phyllis Frus and Christy Williams by permission of McFarland & Company, Inc., Box 611, Jefferson NC 28640; www.mcfarlandpub.com.

Acknowledgments

We write alone, and yet I could not have completed this book in the absence of a number of communities along the way. To their many members, I am most grateful.

In my intellectually formative years, Richard Halpern, Russell Samolsky, and Michael Fitch showed me ways of writing and thinking that benefited me enormously and ultimately made this book better. Jeremy Green and Mark Osteen read early versions of several chapters: their detailed critical responses were invaluable. I thank John-Michael Rivera at the University of Colorado, who, having read an inchoate version of this volume, suggested the need to historicize my study of this new historical novel form. It was this simple but keen insight that put me on the path of exploring truth commissions and numerous forms of global and national redress that ground this project. Years later, Mark Osteen and Jack Matthews graciously read the first drafts of my prologue, which summarized these findings; their comments were invaluable and the encouragement they provided then catalyzed my seeing the book through to its end. As important is their wise and generous mentorship; for their gifts of perspective, advice, and humor, I am deeply grateful.

I am greatly indebted to Anna Brickhouse, who read most of these chapters in one or several forms over a span of years and who taught me so much: approaches to historical and cultural analyses; how to write; how to be a good reader, colleague, and friend. Her generosity of mind and heart and her consistent encouragement and guidance kept me going first at Colorado and then in later years, when we were far-flung and, more than once, I lost my way. I cannot imagine having arrived here without her. Bruce Holsinger, likewise—as generous with his brilliance as with his easy companionship—mentored me at early, key stages.

Providing respite from a heavy teaching and service load, SUNY Cortland awarded me a Drescher Leave that, in one semester, provided the space I needed to engage the project anew and take it to the next level. And my sabbatical leave, which Cortland granted last year, allowed me finally to bring the book to fruition. At various places, fresh readers made time in their schedules to respond to chapter drafts. To Beege Harding, Matt Reiswig, and Kim Stone: many thanks. At its penultimate stage, David Cowart read the entire manuscript; I am so grateful for his generous-minded, sharp review of my work. Thanks to Brigitte Shull and Jo Roberts at Palgrave Macmillan for acquiring my book for the American Literature Readings in the 21st Century series and for seeing it through to acceptance and publication.

Outside academia, Karen LaFace and Andy Getzin's fun friendship was often my lifeline. And similarly, I thank Angela and Zach Shulman, Teresa and Phil Nugent, Beege and Doug Harding, Margaret and Pierre Faber, Susanne Chiang, and JB Brockman: your love and companionship have been my sanity.

Finally I thank my family for their faith along the way: my father, mother, and brother, Roy, Patricia, and Michael Gauthier, and Elizabeth Whitley. More than anyone, Drew Martini provided consistent support in so many capacities: my gratitude to him for being with and alongside me. My children, Anna and Nicholas—born, respectively, at the beginning and middle of my writing this book—have been so patient, loving, and kind. Their sweet smiles, free laughter, and open arms keep me warm and grounded; for the joy and delight they bring, they have my heartfelt appreciation.

Prologue

Increasingly, writers of fiction find themselves in the position of having to tell the truth because the people who are supposed to tell the truth do not.

—*Salman Rushdie*
Step Across This Line *(2003)*

On December 10 and 11, 2006, Iran hosted a government-sponsored conference to assess the scale and validity of the Holocaust. Holocaust deniers and skeptics, including 67 foreign researchers from 30 countries, gathered in Tehran to present their theories about whether six million Jews were indeed killed by Nazis during World War II. Recalling the Iranian president Mahmoud Ahmadinejad's 2005 claim, the assertion that the Holocaust is a "myth"—created to justify the creation of the state of Israel and its occupation of Palestine—opened the conference and echoed in several of the speakers' remarks throughout.[1] Critics across the Western world excoriated "the spectacle in Iran" as "offensive, dangerous," and "predictably a circus of Holocaust denial and racism." Whereas some dismissed the conference as a "monstrous freak show," others exhorted "civilized people" not to "stand by in silent complicity." The conference's call for a "debate" on the Holocaust, notes one editorial, appeals to Western values of reason, logic, and tolerance, masking the fact that "some things are not debatable." Insisting, "The Holocaust is not open to debate. It is undeniable," the journalist then restates the basic facts of the "extermination planned and executed with machine-like efficiency." A recurrent critical response to the conference was that "denying the Holocaust isn't an *opinion*; it's a lie." The conference is a reminder, writes one journalist, of "why history's truths must never be taken for granted or forgotten"; another warns against "sowing seeds of doubt about the heinous historical truth."

The Iran Holocaust denial conference and the international reaction to it reveal a paradox of two cultural phenomena that are emblematic of the legacy of the twentieth century: official denial and historical amnesia on the one hand and public, cooperative attempts at truth telling and redress on the other. This book shows how this dynamic of amnesia and truth telling shapes literary constructions of history, particularly those by Don DeLillo and Toni Morrison—two of our most canonized and popular contemporary novelists—and Michelle Cliff, Bharati Mukherjee, and Julie Otsuka, artists who have attracted critical attention but not achieved such widespread recognition. Although these writers are typically considered in terms of their postmodern narrative strategies, no one has studied how a global culture of truth telling together with such strategies mediates their collective treatment of subjugated histories. By reading this emergent genre of historical fiction in relation to the contemporary era's concern with truth, this project hopes to make four main contributions to American literary and cultural studies: 1) provide a brief history of the historical novel and its twentieth-century forms, through the postmodern historical novel of the 1970s and 1980s known as "historiographic metafiction"; 2) illuminate the dramatic shift in the political and cultural environments of the 1990s with regard to official truth-seeking; 3) identify a corpus of contemporary fiction that, arising from this distinct climate, articulates a politics of truth; and 4) analyze significant exemplars of this new historical novel form that, like its predecessor, challenges realistic mimesis—but does so through unique and resourceful narrations that assert truth claims about the past.

In the case of the Holocaust as in many late-twentieth-century atrocities, from Argentina's Dirty War and the military process of "disappearances" to genocide in the former Yugoslavia, concealment and official denial were an integral part of the collective violence. Yet like the Nuremburg trials, the subsequent Argentinean Truth Commission and Yugoslavian International Criminal Tribunal exposed the secrets of these oppressive regimes and spoke truth to their power. These innovative forums are part of a much larger contemporary tide of exoteric truth telling—from the continuing exhumation of mass graves in Bosnia to the current situation in Spain, where citizens have issued a concomitant call for a truth commission to investigate the atrocities of Franco's dictatorship. As tangible evidence and testimony form the essential framework of such enterprises—filling the cultural need for truth for which the new geopolitical form of truth commissions is established—documentary material vitally informs this new type of historical fiction. Such public truth-avowal projects mark a break with traditions of repressing the historical injustices upon which nations are founded. At the same time, a burgeoning strand of contemporary historical fiction undertakes a correlative determination to excavate and represent the past in ways that counter official history.

Massive violence—and associative denial—punctuates the entire twentieth century. Yet coordinated tenacious efforts at public acknowledgment of "what really happened"—a recurrent and insistent emphasis in the context of criminal tribunals and trials, reparations, and, above all, truth commissions—and ensuing redress for state-sanctioned crimes is a particularly recent phenomenon, unique, in fact, to the 1990s. But it is not only political readers who address what Priscilla B. Hayner, in her 2002 exhaustive study of truth commissions, calls "unspeakable truths." The dialectic of amnesia and truth telling that plays out in the arena of transitional justice manifests across the humanities—in philosophy and ethics, history and anthropology, and popular culture, in the cultural work of novelists and filmmakers, and even in the historical sensibilities of ordinary citizens. In various fields, scholars have told versions of this unfolding story. Hayner, Martha Minow, Robert Rotberg, Dennis Thompson, and others trace the invention of new and distinctive legal forms of response to widespread atrocities that, in Minow's words, is the "more unusual" legacy of the twentieth century "than the facts of genocide and regimes of torture making in this era" (1). Alan S. Rosenbaum and Michel-Rolph Trouillot place in perspective such events as those in Bosnia, Somalia, Rwanda, Cambodia, and Haiti—and the concomitant forgetting of those events—alongside Holocaust discourse and denials. Elie Wiesel, Shoshana Felman, and Dori Laub show how testimony is the literary mode particular to a contemporary "crisis of truth" (in Felman's words) that proceeds from historical and collective trauma. In the wake of public diagnoses of US amnesia by cultural critics from Jean Baudrillard and Gore Vidal to Stephen Bertman, historians Michael Frisch, David Thelan, Roy Rosenzweig, and John Bodnar attempt to uncover the meaning of the past for common Americans. They find that Americans firmly distinguish "history" from "the truth of the past" and contrast "official" and "vernacular" memory. Drawing on this political climate, noted debates about collective memory and these recent social histories of Americans' sense of what constitutes "history," this book illuminates the incongruity between denial and a particularly American forgetting on the one hand and recent international concern with public acknowledgment and official apology on the other.

In the interstices of these two apposite late-twentieth-century phenomena—amnesia and truth telling—a new genre of historical novel develops and performs a vital cultural work: telling the truth in an age of amnesia and redress. In this sense, *Amnesia and Redress* takes up where Linda Hutcheon's and Frederic Jameson's respective seminal studies, *A Poetics of Postmodernism* (1988) and *Postmodernism, or the Cultural Logic of Late Capitalism* (1991) leave off, responding to the subsequent dramatic shift in the global political and cultural environments: the moment when the fall of the Berlin Wall, the rapid end of the Cold War, and the upheaval of many repressive regimes in Latin America, Africa, and Asia create a new set of conditions for what Hayner calls "the turn towards truth." Beginning in the mid-1980s but proliferating in the 1990s on several continents, new governments emerged that, to deal with brutal pasts, launched truth commissions. The 1990s become the decade of truth telling and redress: 23 of 29 such bodies were commissioned in the 1990s, including the most well known in South Africa in 1995, whose stated purpose was to "establish a public record of truth," "preventing amnesia," which raised an international consciousness about truth. Situating the Truth and Reconciliation Commission (TRC) in a broader South African history of reconciliation that indicates "its calling to a faith in words," Erik Doxtader notes its significance to "restorative justice": assessing "the work of truth-telling [and] healing"—which has ensued in so many nations (7). In 1993 and 1994 respectively, the United Nations established the Yugoslavia and Rwanda war crimes tribunals that likewise, say advocates and journalists years after their conclusions, do "produce justice, gather truth, and create needed public acknowledgment."[2]

In a similar vein of historical redress, the late 1990s witnessed a spate of official apologies[3] both abroad and in the United States, wherein holocaust testimonials and reparations claims also multiply and occasion national debate.[4] Throughout the decade, President Clinton issued landmark formal apologies that confess past national crimes, including the May 1997 apology to survivors of the US Public Health Service's secret 40-year study that, from 1932 into the 1970s, withheld proven medical treatment from a group of Tuskegee, Alabama, African American men with syphilis. The first truth commission established by the US Congress, the Commission on Wartime Relocation and Internment of Civilians, published its report entitled *Personal Justice Denied* in 1983. Yet it was not until 1990 that, as a result of that report and the Civil Liberties Act of 1988, President Bush signed letters of apology and checks to each surviving individual of the US internment of Japanese Americans during World War II.[5] In 1994 the US energy secretary instituted the second US truth commission, the Advisory Committee on Human Radiation Experiments, to examine government-sponsored experiments conducted on unknowing medical patients, prisoners, and communities in the United States from the mid-1940s to the mid-1970s. The committee's report provided "unprecedented insight into a murky area of American history," according to one observer.[6] The same year this truth commission was launched, the US government finally declassified Atomic Energy Commission (AEC) documents from 1951 to 1962 that detail the exposure of "downwinders" to nuclear fallout from test bombs and their ensuing cancers, leukemia, and other horrific maladies.

The relation of this broader current of truth seeking—in the wake of long-standing official denial—to a particular body of American historical fiction is nowhere better exemplified than in *Underworld* (1997), Don DeLillo's trenchant excavation of the Cold War era that these recently declassified AEC documents critically inform. The downwinder accounts throughout the novel overlap with extratextual documented oral histories and moreover form a constitutive counterpoint to the denial that surfaces around such "fictional" accounts. The radiation-devastated bodies revealed in *Underworld* are part of the "invisible history" of the Cold War, what a character in an earlier DeLillo novel calls "latent history": "events that definitely took place but remai[n] unseen and unremarked on...Real events that go unrecorded [which] are often more important than recorded events." "The latest secret" about the Cold War atomic bombs is, a contemporary weapons worker in *Underworld* says, "something that's more or less out in the open but at the same time...Secret. Untalked about. Hushed up." In part through its tactical narrative and archival detail of radiation survivors, *Underworld*—along with all the texts this book treats—accomplishes a truth telling not unlike that of truth commissions, which, Hayner explains,

> literally record a hidden history. A truth commission effectively unsilences a topic that might otherwise be spoken of only in hushed tones, long considered too dangerous for general conversation, rarely reported honestly in the press, and certainly out of bounds of the official history taught in schools. In effect, the report of a truth commission reclaims a country's history and opens it for public review. (25)

The United States, with its democratically inspired institutions and history, may seem removed from the many countries "emerging from a dark history," as Hayner puts it, "virtually all" who have "directly confronted th[e] question": "Can a society build a democratic future on a foundation of blind, denied, or forgotten history?" This book shows an intricate dynamic between US "latent history"—from blind spots and official denials to strands of forgotten histories—and several forms of truth telling that together constitute part of the ongoing American democratic experiment.

Amnesia is an unofficial national tradition, which the aforementioned historical truth commissions and presidential apologies have just begun to acknowledge.[7] We are "permanently the United States of Amnesia," as Vidal puts it. "We learn nothing because we remember nothing."[8] Amnesia, notes writer Lev Grossman, is "profoundly American: the second chance, the clean slate, the shot at redemption." Yet at the turn of the second millennium, as Grossman points out, "there's an amnesia epidemic raging at the box office": *The Matrix, Memento, The Bourne Identity, Finding Nemo, Vanilla Sky, The Man Without a Past, The Majestic,* along with even forgettable romantic comedies *Paycheck* and *50 First Dates.* Likewise, the well-documented amnesia that Bertman analyzes in his assiduously researched 2000 book, *Cultural Amnesia,* increases in scope as the century wears on and is particularly acute in its final two decades. Bertman's plethora of sources that testify to "amnesia on a national scale"—a widespread American ignorance of geography and history and both illiteracy and aliteracy—are from the 1990s, the same decade that witnessed the global and national phenomenon of truth telling and redress[9] and that frames the literary truth telling by American writers this book treats.

Quoting historian Michael Frisch, the 1998 book *The Presence of the Past* probes a related—and ultimately telling—paradox:

> The study and understanding of history occupies a paradoxical and problematic place in contemporary American culture. On the one hand, it is widely believed that we face a general crisis of historical amnesia; on the other hand, there is clearly enormous and growing public interest in history, manifest in museum attendance, historically oriented tourism, participation in festivals, and even the media-driven excesses of nostalgia and commemoration of recent historical periods.[10]

In strategic reaction to the "much-publicized jeremiads [that] warned ominously of historical amnesia and historical illiteracy suffocating the nation," Frisch along with a handful of other professional historians formed, in 1989, the Committee on History-Making in America (COHMIA). They dedicated themselves to finding, in contrast, what Americans "*did* know and think about the past...how Americans used and understood the past." By 1994 they had surveyed 1,500 citizens "to uncover popular historical consciousness at its most obvious source—the perspective of a cross section of Americans."

As such, *The Presence of the Past* details two cross-currents of late-twentieth-century American historical consciousness that together are a significant characteristic of the cultural milieu from which the writers treated in this book emerge: ordinary people are deeply engaged with the past but also alienated from the history they have been taught in school and encounter in the media. The survey, the authors claim, reveals "the ubiquitous presence of the past in everyday lives." Yet their overall conclusion—"If the past was omnipresent in these interviews, 'history' as it is usually defined in textbooks was not"—was only to be expected. For in their quest to yield "the richest answers," COHMIA fine-tuned their questions to carefully avoid any mention of "history"—which their pilot survey respondents had said was *"formal, analytical, official or distant"*—and to ask Americans instead about their "knowledge" of and "connection" to "the past"—which, their pilot program found, "was the term that best invited people to talk about family, race, and nation."[11] (Of course, in tailoring the wording of the survey questions this way, COHMIA evaded the very issues of historical amnesia, illiteracy, and core knowledge ignorance to which they were allegedly replying).[12] Despite the fact that the survey was slanted precisely to privilege a personal sense of the past over historical accounts, the authors assert, "This absence of conventional historical narratives and frameworks surprised us."

Nonetheless, the pilot participants' sense of what constitutes "history" anticipates both the final respondents' skepticism toward sanctioned sources of history and the striking distinctions between the national sample and the targeted African American and Native American samples. The survey is a telling indicator not only of American historical consciousness but of the interstitial gap in which the cultural work of the new genre of historical novel occurs: between national history and personal pasts, which are integrally related to that official narrative yet in friction with it. As deeply researched accounts of actual, unheralded citizens who have a contentious relationship to received versions of national history, the literary texts studied here mine the omissions and distortions of such traditional narratives and insist on the truth of their counterhistories. Their stories correspond to the sense of history expressed by the survey respondents, whose "vivid, candid, creative, passionate" responses in which "emotions often ran high" reveal a people who "do not reject all aspects of national history; they simply reject nation-centered accounts they were forced to memorize and regurgitate in school."[13]

The literary counternarrative of "America" that emerges from this corpus of contemporary historical fiction shares a particular affinity, moreover, with that constructed by the African Americans and Native Americans COHMIA surveyed, for whom "a collective voice came easily." Individuals in these groups invoked a "we" that "stands in sharp opposition to the triumphal American 'we': the narrative of the American nation-state—the story often told by professional histori-ans—is most alive for those who feel alienated from it." In other words, those who have been segregated along the nation's way have the most acute sense of its official story. "Indians and black Americans connect their narratives much more explicitly to the American national story than most white Americans do," writes Rosenzweig, "even while they dissent sharply from its traditional formulations" (149). So even as both groups presented their own interpretations of US history, pro-testing with "deep anger" its "lies" and "distortions," they "implic-itly recognized a traditional American narrative that white Americans eschewed" (153). These two opposed strains of history form in fact the predominant characteristic of ethnic novels published in the 1980s, notes Cyrus R. K. Patell in his essay "Emergent Literatures," which finishes the most recent volume of prose writing in *The Cambridge History of American Literature* (CHAL). "Standard national history and ethnic self-history," Patell writes, "tell very different stories, and the book[s] thro[w their] weight behind ethnic self-history." Patell's conclusion itself is an insightful prologue to the cultural milieu from which the writers studied in this book emerge:

> This volume of the CHAL differs significantly from that of its pre-decessors…arising from a cultural moment marked by dissensus, its task [is to] ope[n] up the canon to expansion and redefinition by acknowledging that literary history must be "a multivocal, multifac-eted, scholarly, critical and pedagogic enterprise" driven by the ener-gies of "heterogeneity."[14]

Out of this dissensus, this book identifies one strand—a significant development in the genre of the historical novel—that, in Patell's words, "reflect[s] both new relationships to the dominant main-stream and new configurations within the field of emergent American literature."

For we can recognize versions of this direct, albeit dissenting, engagement with the traditional national narrative in the contem-porary truth-telling historical novel. From colonial-era emergence of the new republic to the US Civil and Cold Wars, the storylines of the American nation-state that the texts herein revise are also those tar-geted by Indian and black Americans, for whom, Rosenzweig explains,

"the arrival of Columbus, the westward movement of European set-
tlers, slavery and emancipation, wars and treaties at home and abroad
add up to an American history in which blacks and Indians have been
oppressed and betrayed by whites, who then depict their actions in
movies and textbooks that lie about Indians and exclude African
Americans." In sum, the intense involvement with familiar narratives
of the national past that surfaced in the COHMIA survey offers a
key insight into the principal projects of the cluster of texts I address
in this study. Although their subjects and even their titles—from
Americana to *Paradise* and *Free Enterprise*—suggest their revisions
of national mythologies, their trenchant engagement with "official
history" mirrors the minority historical consciousness pinpointed by
COHMIA; and their stories reflect the "sophisticated counternarratives of US history" that these groups themselves offered (165).

This distinction between "history" and "the past" along with the
distrust of conventional representations of the nation that *The Presence
of the Past* reveals as perhaps the most strident and common element
yoking the survey groups corresponds to the fundamental divergence
the historian John Bodnar observes between "official memory" and
"vernacular memory" in his 1992 book, *Remaking America*. Based
on 17 case studies of commemorations in the twentieth century, from
monuments, war memorials and reenactments, parades and caravans
to dedications of public gardens and pioneer and other symbols of
civic loyalty, *Remaking America* defines official memory as the expli-
cation of national themes through government-supported institutions
and ceremonies (such as those of the National Park Service), whereas
vernacular memory is expressed through local, grassroots efforts to
commemorate the past. Official US culture promotes interpretations
of the past and present reality that preserve the political interests of
its dominant social and economic class by reducing the power of competing interests and restating reality in ideal rather than complex or
ambiguous terms—that is, through employing symbols of pride and
patriotism. Vernacular culture, in contrast, restates views of reality
derived from firsthand experience in small communities rather than
the "imagined communities" of a large nation.

Just as the COHMIA survey "respondents did not share historians' assumptions about the nation-state"—as one man put it, "my
interest in history is in what one might call vulgar history, ordinary
history, history of people, what people do, not so much what nations
do"—so too does Bodnar observe official and vernacular cultures
increasingly at odds: "Buttressed by periods of war and economic
crises, the political and cultural power of the nation-state grew to

a point in the twentieth century when it distorted all expressions of vernacular memory" (41). Official control of displays of public memory swelled such that "the complex nature of ethnic memory became acceptable only if the public or patriotic stood above the personal and vernacular dimensions" (77). Through the mid-1970s, public memory "remain[ed] a product of elite manipulation, symbolic interaction, and contested discourse" (20).[15]

In the social historians' late-twentieth-century corresponding observations recorded in *The Presence of the Past* and *Remaking America*, the historical-cultural matrix of the contemporary fiction herein begins to become manifest. As the divisive post–Vietnam War period gave rise to postmodernism, with its fragmented and ironized perspective on history, the turn toward truth of the late 1980s and 1990s gives rise to contemporary truth-telling historical fiction. Not surprisingly, both books locate a weakening of national history in the post-Vietnam era. Although the Vietnam "lesson in the futility of war or the mendacity of government" that Thelan notes is by now a familiar one,[16] Bodnar's tracing the effects of the post-Vietnam milieu on expressions of vernacular culture is provocative: "After the widespread discontent and civil disobedience of the 1960s...the cultural power of the nation-state remained but appeared to be less effective" (244). Racial, immigrant, ethnic, regional, and local groups—and others seeking personal identification with public memory—challenge official interpretations of the past and present. "In recent decades, the power of the nation-state has been contested to a greater extent, and public expressions of vernacular memory have become more pronounced" (244, 251).[17] Taken together, these recent studies of American sociohistorical consciousness underscore the last two decades as especially ripe for the issue and reception of complex literary counterhistories of the nation that collectively reveal a tension between national and cultural identities.

Indeed, as public memory emerges from the intersection of—and from the competition between—official and vernacular cultural expressions, so too does the new genre of historical novel. In this sense, the contemporary truth-telling historical novel is not only another reservoir of public memory, but—given Americans' potent distrust of history classrooms and the media as sources of information about the past[18]—it is a salient form of cultural memory highly relevant to our era. As Bodnar points out, "The major focus of this communicative and cognitive process [of public memory] is not the past, [but] serious matters *in the present* such as the nature of power and the question of loyalty to both official and vernacular cultures" (15, emphasis added). This is why identifying the historical moment from which this body of novels arises is paramount for understanding their cultural work of speaking truth in an age of amnesia and redress. Not unlike the public commemorations Bodnar studies, in which official and vernacular cultures vie for power, the vernacular of these novels speaks truth to the abiding power of national subtexts, illuminating actual resistance to official history. However, whereas Bodnar outlines an assimilative process of public memory, wherein official culture preserves aspects of vernacular cultures while still protecting elite interests, the novels in my analysis perform an opposite cultural work, refracting aspects of official culture while writing alternative dimensions of history over it like a palimpsest.

* * *

A rich scholarly as well as political discourse attaches to the concept of truth itself, relevant tenets of which the introductory chapter takes up to establish my theoretical framework. Following a brief overview of the tradition of the historical novel that can be traced over the last two centuries to Sir Walter Scott through its postmodern form, "historiographic metafiction," chapter 1 clarifies the key terms of the book—truth, history, narrative, and nation—and adumbrates distinguishing features of the truth-telling historical novel that the ensuing chapters analyze. As truth commissions fulfill their mandate, or terms of reference given them, by defining the truth that will be documented, so does my opening chapter situate contemporary literary-historical truth claims vis-à-vis poststructuralism and postmodernism. Homi Bhabha's theory on narrating the modern nation provides an overall rubric for exploring these texts' articulation of oppositional voices to the unifying discourse of "nation," enunciations of national identity that are rooted in specific histories of cultural displacement. Likewise, Michel Foucault offers a theoretical framework and vocabulary that are useful to discuss the role that imaginative historical narratives can play in historical discourse and specifically the means by which, through their construction of countermemories, the novels I have chosen to study constitute what Foucault has called "a politics of truth." For the cultural work of this body of contemporary historical fiction has much in common with Foucault's notion of a genealogy that wrests truth from power through its excavation of the archival past and concomitant interpretation. Indeed, the South African TRC's purpose—to "uncover the past," to help "victims become more visible," to "brin[g] the darker side of the past to the fore"—reverberates Foucault's emphasis on bringing subjugated knowledges into play. Like extending the idea of justice in the context of personal injury law to victims of mass violence, understanding the cultural work of literary-historical truth telling in the global context of transitional justice means crossing over different lexicons of value. Notwithstanding the counterhistories the fiction herein asserts, its cultural work is not coequal with that of truth commissions; the fiction addresses psychological questions official truth seeking raises but cannot answer and, in some cases, provides catharsis from the kind of traumatic histories truth commissions attempt to uncover. As Doris Sommer reasons, "The Holocaust cannot be proven by its victims, neither can it be disproved by its skeptics. It haunts us, unspeakably, the way slavery haunts the Americas" (173). In this sense, as chapter 1 elaborates, literature has an especial capacity to convey the fully human truth of historical experience.

I begin my analysis with Don DeLillo's exposure of national mythologies that are ceasing to evoke collective identification and participation—storylines of America, that is, which are ceasing to function as myth—because such ruptured mythologies anticipate the interanimation of center and margin in the forthcoming chapters. DeLillo's simultaneous engagement of national mythologies and the recalcitrant materials of historical experience that fracture them puts him in a productive dialogue with several contemporary women writers of color—who speak from and to such experience and whom critics heretofore have treated discretely. Chapter 2 shows DeLillo's unrecognized direct debt, in *Americana* (1971), to the first written survivor's account of the horrific Bataan Death March of World War II, an event that popular and academic histories of the war have virtually ignored—until just recently. Beginning in 2001, a number of different presses published several discrete Bataan Death March survivor accounts. I draw on the original 1943 testimony (first printed in the *Chicago Sun*) and, similarly, documents from the US atomic testing program, declassified since 1994—which detail downwinders' exposure to nuclear fallout from test bombs—to suggest how unique histories of each of these events informed *Americana* and *Underworld* (1997), respectively. In these related Cold War novels, DeLillo exploits the tension between innocence and violence—the literally malignant legacies of the nation's hot and cold wars—to reveal the way in which official culture is amnesiac by definition.

Indeed, chapter 3 elucidates two cites/sites of memory, forgetting, and nationhood with which Morrison's *Paradise* is centrally concerned: exclusions to "paradise" based on race and gender and African American westward migration in the post-Reconstruction era. Critics have universally recognized Morrison for redressing the limited perspectives of mainstream US history by reclaiming the narratives of African American history, often from a female point of view. Yet I argue that *Paradise* extends this earlier genre of the historical revision, creating a springboard for the novel's metahistorical argument about traditional national history and the politics of truth it involves—an argument, that is, that probes the ways in which truth is linked to systems of power that produce and sustain it.

Michelle Cliff's *Free Enterprise* (1993), the subject of chapter 4, develops the figure of Mary Ellen Pleasant, the savvy black entrepreneur and abolitionist who made her fortune in San Francisco on the heels of the California gold rush, funding John Brown's raid on Harpers Ferry. In revealing Pleasant's unapologetic, myriad uses of capitalism to undermine "the Trade" that thrived by it, the novel rewrites myths informed by the discourse of "free enterprise." The innovative narrative strategies by which Cliff remembers a historically deep inter-American resistance to slavery recontextualize the Civil War not as a nationalist narrative that consolidated the United States but as a transnational slave uprising against imperialism. Like *Free Enterprise*, Mukherjee's *Holder of the World* (1993), the subject of chapter 5, underscores America's implication in a global economy from its inception. But if, through the historical Pleasant, Cliff resituates US abolition within a long and capacious transnational colonialism, Mukherjee imagines a fanciful Hannah Easton—a Puritan-born immigrant's daughter who comes of age as the Salem bibi on the Coromandel Coast—to recast Salem as the major international port for the East Indies in the eighteenth century. Her novel thus repositions the New England experiment in its global Anglophone context, exploiting the Puritan myth of origin by connecting the remotest ends of transnational empire.

By studying two important novels published since 9/11, Julie Otsuka's *When the Emperor Was Divine* (2002) and Don DeLillo's *Falling Man* (2007), the sixth chapter identifies some facets of the post-9/11 literary imagination and begins to chart the evolution of truth-telling historical fiction in this context. DeLillo and Otsuka write against amnesia, in part, by drawing on their personal histories to focus 9/11 and Executive Order 9066 through a single New York and Japanese American family, respectively. With narratives that work psychologically and evocative of visceral memory and trauma, *Falling Man* and *Emperor* trace the way the historically traumatic events at their centers reconfigured the emotional landscape, memory, and perception of those directly affected. Whereas *Falling Man* is a conscious response to 9/11, *Emperor*, a historical novel about internment during World War II, chillingly evokes the post-9/11 political climate—particularly the War on Terror. Drawing on her own family history,

Otsuka portrays a single Japanese American family who in 1942, as a result of Executive Order 9066, is reclassified virtually overnight as enemy aliens and removed to internment camps for more than three years. Prior to President Roosevelt's signing the order, the FBI alleged that many Issei men (first-generation Japanese immigrants) were spies and arrested them in the night yet never accused them of any crimes. This novel provides an uncanny perspective simultaneously on three phenomena: the Guantánamo prison camp, whose detainees are also classified by executive order as "enemy combatants"; the post-9/11 statist culture of fear, prejudice, and intimidation; and the notorious episode of American World War II history that concerns Otsuka.

In the cultural milieu that shapes this book, Otsuka's novel offers a constitutive counterpoint to obscene state abuses of human rights each contemporaneous with its subject and with its publication: the Japanese Imperial Army's incarceration, rape, and abuse of "comfort women" during World War II; and the Bush administration's excesses of the War on Terror in flagrant defiance of constitutional and international law. The "comfort women" system forced sexual slavery of 100,000–400,000 girls as young as 11—who were abducted from Korea, China, and other Asian and Dutch countries that Japan invaded—resulting in the largest, most methodical, and most deadly mass rape of women in recorded history. Japan's half-century of insistent denial followed by the present widespread revelation and acknowledgment of this atrocity is another poignant example of the 1990s phenomenon of truth telling.[19] Likewise, recently declassified memos, communications, and testimonies by detainees and former US military interrogators make undeniably clear that prisoners of the War on Terror were tortured and even killed in US custody, belying the Bush administration's claims that those at the very highest levels of government did not authorize the abuse. The epilogue situates the truth-telling historical novel in relation to the current maelstrom that surrounds this documentary evidence of torture and calls for a federal truth commission to investigate the abuses of the Bush administration. The heated conflict suggests the force of an ongoing dialectic of denial and truth telling, the salience of this new form of the historical novel in the present moment, and fertile ground for the cultural work of such novels in the future. Although incisive historical sources on "comfort women" and the Bush torture program are recently available, the cathartic and psychological dimensions of these experiences constitute, in part, the unrealized cultural work of the emergent genre of truth-telling historical fiction.

CHAPTER 1

Introduction: Contemporary Historical Fiction and a Politics of Truth

Both the current critical attention to history and the abundance of contemporary popular national histories[1] evidence unresolved tensions about the way the nation has been narrated at the very moment when globalization putatively transcends the "nation." (We are reminded daily that the forces of technology, media, multinational capital, and global climate change are erasing national borders.) Yet from the violent nationalist struggles occurring around the globe to the assertion, in precisely the kind of fiction I treat, of counternarratives that figure discrete cultural identities that yet stake claim to American nationhood and mythology, it is clear that the matter of national identity is far from moot. To apprehend these literary-historical inflections of traditional notions of "America," my approach yokes an earlier phase of American studies, from the 1950s to the 1970s, to contemporary developments in the field. American studies had its beginnings in the study of myths and symbols that constitute an American nationality, as Amy Kaplan puts it, "implicitly defined by its internal and social relationships," whereas contemporary approaches examine "America's conceptual and geographic borders [as] fluid, contested, and historically changing" ("Left Alone with America" 15). Early landmark works in American studies document certain national mythologies: Henry Nash Smith, in 1950, elaborates the American West as symbol and myth; R. W. B. Lewis, in 1955, identifies "a native American mythology" of "heroic innocence" (21); Richard Slotkin, in 1973, chronicles the mythology of the American frontier. The historical novels that constitute this book engage these mythologies and at the same time call into question the conceptual and geographic borders that these landmark studies (re)inscribe. To comprehend such complex articulations of American identity, I draw from contemporary theories of nation, narrative, and history, from postcolonial theory, and from diaspora studies, as well as from earlier theories of national mythologies.

For these and other reasons, this historical fiction marks a clear break from the tradition of the historical novels that can be traced over the last two centuries to Sir Walter Scott. Indeed these contemporary novels' focus on radically contentious histories itself distinguishes them from the form of the historical novel popularized in the nineteenth century by Scott and characterized by Georg Lukács in his critical study, *The Historical Novel*, originally published in 1937. For Lukács, Scott's novels embody "the classical form of the historical novel," and "Scott's greatness lies in his capacity to give living human embodiment to historical social types [that are] typical characters nationally." For Scott, "historical authenticity" means "the quality of the inner life, the morality, heroism, capacity for sacrifice, steadfastness etc. peculiar to a given historical age," reflected in "a mediocre hero who sides passionately with neither of the warring camps in the great crises of his time." In contrast to the central figures of the historical fiction this book considers, it is the task of Scott's heroes to bring together what Lukács calls "the extremes whose struggle fills the novel.... In this sense he never creates eccentric figures, figures who fall psychologically outside the atmosphere of the age" (35–36, 60). A contemporary historical novel in the Scott tradition, that is, would never highlight (as does DeLillo's *Underworld*) "downwinders" subject to fallout from test atomic bombs as indicative of the Cold War era, nor (as does Cliff's *Free Enterprise*) black female abolitionists—from the Caribbean as well as the United States—who operated covertly as suggestive of the Civil War era. Neither does Scott concentrate his efforts to represent major, real-life historical figures, such as those that form integral aspects of the plots of some of the novels herein (such as *Underworld*'s J. Edgar Hoover and *Free Enterprise*'s John Brown). Finally, most important for Lukács is Scott's depiction of English society as a series of "ceaseless class struggles"; likewise, a contemporary version of the classical historical novel (such as Philip Roth's *American Pastoral* [1998] for example) would show class as transcendent of other aspects of social marginality (50, 37, 32). Like a good deal of contemporary fiction, the historical novels that comprise this study instead consider the imbrication of class, race, and gender, exploring the mutually constitutive nature of such categories of identity.

The historical novel, of course, has evolved since the nineteenth century. A number of modernist historical novels deal with the ways in which recent history bears on worldviews—wherein a particular historical event is not the explicit subject of the novel but rather the repressed material that determines the stories within it. Edith Wharton's *The Age of Innocence* (1920), Ernest Hemingway's *The Sun Also Rises* (1926), and Djuana Barnes's *Nightwood* (1937), for example, all refract the historical matrix of modernism. Thus the maelstrom of recent events—from US immigration and industrialization to World War I—fundamentally informs the texts even as their narratives refer only obliquely to these developments. Yet the implicit concerns of all three novels are the aftereffects of these forces—from the decline of the aristocracy and the emergence of capitalism, new markets, and new money to the death of romance and the erosion of traditional social structures such as marriage, family, and faith in God. William Faulkner's *Absalom, Absalom!* (1937), in contrast, stands apart from the modernist historical novel that tries to repress recent, traumatic history and instead makes historical process its subject. The historical record in Faulkner's novel is rife with discrepancies and confusion, and all of the narratives that attempt to comprehend the chronicle of the Sutpen dynasty—Miss Rosa's and Mr. Compson's, as well as Quentin's and Shreve's—are not only patently subjective but characterized by willing invention that attempts to fill in the gaps of the story. Barbara Foley—in her history of the Euro-American historical novel from the seventeenth century to late modernism, *Telling the Truth* (1986)—groups *Absalom, Absalom!* together with Virginia Woolf's *Orlando* (1928) and Robert Penn Warren's *All the King's Men* (1946) under a category she calls "the metahistorical novel," which "takes as its referent a historical process that evades rational formulation" (25). The next (and last) chronological phase of the historical novel that Foley identifies is the "Afro-American documentary novel" that "represents a reality submitting human subjects to racist identification" (25). Although Richard Wright's *Native Son* (1940) is the central text from this phase in Foley's analysis, she briefly addresses "Afro-American metahistorical novels" from other periods, the latest of which are those written by Ishmael Reed in the 1970s.

With the advent of postmodernism came a new form of the historical novel, which Linda Hutcheon, in *A Poetics of Postmodernism* (1988), calls "historiographic metafiction":—"well-known and popular novels" that conflate history and fiction in an attendant ironic manner to question the assumptions of historiography (5). Reed's novels are among the dozens Hutcheon considers in her illustrious survey. Like Foley's study, which provides a history of the historical novel form as it has developed through the centuries in Great Britain and in the United States, Hutcheon's *Poetics* traces the lineage of and difference between historiographic metafiction and its precursors. Hutcheon's renowned book grounds the ongoing discussion of the place of history in postmodern fiction, a debate initially staged by Hutcheon and Fredric Jameson. In *Postmodernism, or the Cultural Logic of Late Capitalism* (1991), Jameson argues that within the postmodern novel, fictional and historical figures are indistinguishable such that the novel is in fact "nonrepresentational": the historical referent *disappears* and, consequently, historicity is weakened (22–25). Hutcheon counters that these same narrative techniques *foreground* the "particular nature of the historical referent" by problematizing the nature and status of our information about the past. Hutcheon agrees with Jameson that the postmodern novel inscribes a "crisis in historicity." However, she rejects Jameson's negative judgment of the crisis, interpreting it instead as a beneficial "irony that allows critical distancing" from history (89). Her elaboration of multifarious problems with history (the same ones that poststructuralism raises and which I address later in this chapter) indicates the necessity of this critical distancing. Both Jameson and Hutcheon concentrate on the deconstructive aspects of postmodern narrative innovations in their identification of a crisis in historicity, and both elide the question of truth in the postmodern novel. In concert with Hutcheon, Amy Elias, in *Sublime Desire: History and Post-1960s Fiction* (2001), argues that "what is left to postmodernists is only 'metahistory,' the ability to theorize and ironically desire history," and extends the crisis in history to literature (xvii, xx). Although we both consider "historical fiction in relation to actual debates in the discipline of history itself," Elias correlates "metahistorical romances" to poststructuralism, in explicit debt to Hayden White (x–xvi). Conversely, I illustrate contemporary historical novels that reflect a critical distance from aspects of poststructuralist theory, tracing in them a departure from White's position. Thus Elias's view of post-1960s fiction that cannot access history "through discovery and imagination" (xvii) differs essentially from the imaginative and resourceful project of the novels I treat, as my definition of counterhistory elaborates.

In this key sense and others, *Amnesia and Redress* is distinct from these and other standard literary-critical accounts of postmodernism, such as Brian McHale's *Postmodernist Fiction* (1987) and *Constructing Postmodernism* (1992), David Cowart's *History and the Contemporary Novel* (1989), and Elizabeth Wesseling's *Writing History as Prophet* (1991). Moreover (with the exception of Elias, whose study extends to the 1990s), all of these books focus on the first wave of postmodern experimentalism—fiction, that is, dating from the late 1960s to primarily the 1970s and early 1980s. Jameson, for example, considers several artistic mediums from this time period, from painting to architecture, illustrating his argument about literary postmodernism through E. L. Doctorow's *Ragtime* (1974), the novel that provides the fictional common ground of the Jameson-Hutcheon debate. Only my first chapter briefly treats a text from this era, DeLillo's *Americana* (1971); like *Ragtime*, *Americana* deconstructs the nostalgic idea of an American past as innocent. Yet the means by which the two novels accomplish this, and their approach to historical referentiality as related to this project, differ significantly. Indeed, the principal features of *Ragtime* that inspire Jameson's critique (and Hutcheon's praise) of it mark *Americana*'s specific departures from it and highlight it as a forerunner of truth-telling historical fiction that came to fruition in the 1990s.[2]

As my prologue suggests, I am concerned not with postmodernism per se but with a new corpus of contemporary historical fiction that, following the dramatic political and cultural shifts of the late 1980s and 1990s, emerges to articulate a politics of truth. It is thus perhaps no coincidence, then, that the historical novels on which I focus mark a departure from postmodern fiction that came of age from the late 1960s through the early 1980s and simultaneously reflect a critical distance from aspects of poststructuralist theory, which also had its heyday in the same time period. My project seeks to add an important but overlooked dimension to the larger critical conversation about contemporary historical fiction. Unlike the novels considered by the significant scholarly works to which I have referred, the contemporary historical fiction I treat here concerns itself with the distinctive truth claims of the historical referents that its arguably postmodern narratives deploy. Like Foley's "documentary novel," it "locates itself near the border between factual discourse and fictive discourse, but it does not propose an eradication of that border" (25–26). Yet at the same time that it "graft[s] onto its fictive pact some kind of additional claim to empirical validation," it also "raises the problem of reference for explicit consideration" (41). Rather than construct a faithful historical "type," as does the traditional historical novel, or merely problematize the nature and status of our information about the past, as does historiographic metafiction, the texts that the following chapters examine present counterhistories to received versions of the American past.

More recently than the book studies cited earlier, scholars such as David W. Price and Nancy J. Peterson have taken issue with

Hutcheon's assessment of postmodern novels as primarily deconstructive. In *History Made, History Imagined* (1999), Price studies world
novelists from Carlos Fuentes to Mario Vargas Llosa and Michel
Tournier who "try to *think* history"; that is, their novels "engage
the poetic imagination in an attempt to construct, not discover, the
truth of the past" (11). In *Against Amnesia* (2001), Peterson studies
women writers who "produc[e] counterhistories" and whose fiction
and poetry Peterson describes "as *postmodern histories* rather than as
historiographic metafiction" (10). In that the literary counterhistories
this book examines make truth claims about the past, *Amnesia and
Redress* shares affinities with this newer scholarship. Neither Price nor
Peterson, however, examines the historical novel tradition; neither is
Price—unlike Peterson—"concerned with the so-called postmodern
novel"; instead he shows how the novels that concern him illuminate the philosophical writings of Vico and Nietzsche (11–12, 15).
Moreover, Price's book, like most studies of postmodern fiction,
describes it (to borrow Peterson's words) "as a game that men, usually
white men, play" (10). Although Price's, McHale's, Cowart's, and
Wesseling's books analyze dozens of novels among them—many of
them historical—only five are by women writers. In similar propor-
tion, Elias's extensive study of over 30 novels includes five by women.
Although most of the novels that comprise *Amnesia and Redress* are
by women writers of color, I did not choose them for that reason
but for their cultural work of truth telling that, along with DeLillo's
historical novels, writes within and against postmodernism. Yet in
that Peterson, by contrast, focuses on "postmodern histories written solely by women of color" to "reconceptualiz[e] postmodernism
so that the narratives and issues of concern to women and minority fiction are no longer seen as eccentric but as fundamental to the
postmodern condition," my book is indebted to hers. For I take as
given Rafael Pèrez-Torres's "multicultural postmodernism" on which
Peterson insists and which *Against Amnesia* deftly elaborates (11). At
the same time, though Peterson's working "theory of postmodernism
that problematizes, but does not deny historical reference" provides a
compelling corrective to much postmodern theory (primarily by and
about male writers), I am less invested in theorizing the postmodern
than in situating a distinctly contemporary literature—particularly a
new development in the historical novel—beyond the postmodern.
Indeed, although the novelists I write about have been described as
postmodern, I find that label misleading with respect to my central
argument regarding their historical truth claims. Lois Parkinson
Zamora's comparative study of US and Latin American fiction, *The*

Usable Past (1997), contends that minority literature "does not reflect 'the disappearance of a sense of history'" but instead uses the tension between "historical truth and narrative truth" as a "primary source of their narrative energy" (41). With *Against Amnesia*, *Amnesia and Redress* underscores this argument and yet suggests that although this type of narrative energy—grounded by imaginative engagement of historical research—may primarily occur in literature of "marginalized racial and ethnic writers" (Peterson 11), it is not exclusive to it.

In one sense, the contemporary truth-telling historical novel is in the tradition of an American history that, as Bodnar notes, "is replete with examples of minority groups mounting spirited defenses of their own versions of the past and resisting pressures to acquiesce to nationally dominant traditions" (43). It is not only minority groups, however, that historically have issued such revisions to national traditions and mythologies. Herman Melville is one example of a canonized nineteenth-century writer who attempted to disabuse his audience from their prejudices of slavery, race, and national character. Like the later defenders of vernacular cultures whom Bodnar addresses, whose cultural expressions were "inherently threatening or oppositional" (246), Melville's stories that dissented from standard interpretations of reality bore authority in part because he drew from his firsthand experience abroad on the high seas. Whereas the women writers around which this study is organized obtain such cultural authority in part by drawing on their own ethnically inflected histories, DeLillo's philosophy as a writer echoes Bodnar's sense of vernacular culture and articulates the cultural work of the contemporary truth-telling fiction. "The writer," says DeLillo, "is the man or woman who automatically takes a stance against his or her government. There are so many temptations for American writers to become part of the system and part of the structure that now, more than ever, we have to resist. American writers ought to stand and live in the margins, and be more dangerous" ("Seven Seconds" 45–46).

But I do not categorize the corpus of historical novels as a new genre merely for their inherently oppositional stance—their bold use of a neglected or alternate historical archive and their ensuing inscriptions of countermemories to juxtapose against and alongside those narratives that comprise our recognizable national mythologies. Indeed, it is these novels' *means* of making the past present, along with their uncommon mining of the historical archive, that definitively contributes to the new form they invent and most importantly to the cultural work they perform. Their counterhistorical perspectives and concomitant strategies can be understood in terms of

"particularism"—the "codependent term" to universalism that Doris
Sommer introduces to literary studies in her 1999 study of minority women writing in the Americas, *Proceed with Caution* (ix–x).
"Particularism is a word I borrow," Sommer explains, "from historians to name cultural embeddedness in experience and circumstance"
(273). "Particularist writing," then, involves "a variety of rhetorical
moves [that] hold readers at arm's length…in order to propose something different than knowledge. Philosophers have called it acknowledgment. Others have called it respect" (xi).

In this sense, through unconventional and often complex
narratives—what some call "postmodern"—the texts that occupy me
in these chapters inscribe an epistemological resistance within the telling of the event itself. Like particularist books, these historical novels
(to borrow Sommer's words) "detain" the reader, requiring "something besides the epistemological desire that drives readers towards
data…before they can do their productive work" (xi). Referring to
Beloved to illustrate particularism, Sommer points out that "Toni
Morrison holds back readers who demand to know a story but will
not witness it" (9). Likewise, the historical fiction to which I turn my
attention invites readers to perceive rather than to merely consume
the story. By digging, as Sommer puts it, "a trench between telling
and what is told" (163), these novels demand the reader's imaginative
stepping into the narrative and thereby—through unique readerly
experiences of the past—transmute obscure histories into memories.
Walter Benn Michaels offers a complementary reading of *Beloved* as
a "historicist" novel. It "is historical in that it's about the historical
past; it's historicist in that—setting out to remember 'the disremem-
bered'—it redescribes something we have never known as something
we have forgotten and thus makes the historical past a part of our
own experience" (6). As in *Beloved* (which is not only perhaps the
earliest but an exemplary novel heralding this truth-telling historical
novel genre), history for the novels taken up by *Amnesia and Redress*
involves the effort to make the past present—not merely to transmit
an unknown or vague history but to transform that past into a memory experienced and possessed.

Finally, these novels' approaches to the dark histories at their
core evoke a current understanding of literary testimony—a "performative speech act," Shoshana Felman calls it, that, through the
"breakage of the words," "enacts" the horror rather than reporting
the event.[3] Although Felman cites the poetry of Paul Celan wherein
such "breakage" occurs, to continue with the example of *Beloved*, I
submit the chapter in which the three women's consciousness—their

"unspeakable thoughts" and indeed their very identities—interweave and mesh as an example of such breakage. In Felman's words, such "sounds testify" by "disrupting" "conscious meaning." As this "breakdown" of meaning occurs, readers become "ready to be solicited" by the "experience" to which the writer testifies (37–39). The current "crisis of truth…proceeding from contemporary trauma" that frames this book study has "brought the discourse of testimony to the fore of the contemporary cultural narrative, way beyond the implications of its limited, restricted usage in the legal context" (6). That testimony is the generally privileged genre of our incongruous times, says Elie Wiesel—the literary "mode par excellence" of our era, writes Felman—is helpful to apprehending the testimonial mode as it manifests in the contemporary truth-telling historical novel.

Indeed, no book has interpreted the truth claims of a contemporary historical fiction—beyond postmodernism—on epistemological and narrative bases, identifying a new literary movement as a distinct phenomenon of recent global and national history. Nor has a particular body of American historical fiction been recognized in relation to a broader current of official truth seeking—which itself is part of the contemporary crisis of truth—and as an important development in both the history of the novel and the evolution of the historical novel genre. Drawing then on this political climate, along with recent social histories of Americans' sense of what constitutes "history" and noted debates about collective memory, *Amnesia and Redress* illuminates the incongruity between the recent international concern with public acknowledgment and official apology—and denial and a particularly American forgetting.

I   THE MODERN NATION-SPACE

My consideration of the ways in which these texts' contest the conceptual territory of America draws on Homi Bhabha's concept of the nation as narration, "the complex strategies of cultural identification and discursive address that function in the name of 'the people' or 'the nation' and make them the immanent subjects of a range of social and literary narratives" (*Location* 140). Whereas Benedict Anderson, in *Imagined Communities*, traces the origins of national consciousness from the sixteenth century to the early nineteenth century, Bhabha locates "the emergence of the later phases of the modern nation, from the mid-nineteenth century, [which] is also one of the most sustained periods of mass migration within the West and colonial expansion in the East." Beginning with this period, "the nation fills the void left in the uprooting of communities and kin, and turns that loss into the language of metaphor," transferring the "meaning of home and belonging…across those distances, and cultural differences, that span the imagined community of the nation-people" (*Location* 139–40). Given that the nation thus becomes "home" for peoples whose identities are rooted in various histories of migration—from without as well as within the nation's borders—Bhabha conceptualizes "an *inter*national culture, based not on the exoticism of multiculturalism or the *diversity* of cultures, but on the inscription and articulation of culture's *hybridity*" It is thus the "inter"—"the *in-between* space—that carries the burden of the meaning of culture. It makes it possible to begin envisaging national, anti-nationalist histories of the 'people'" (38–39). Bhabha revises Anderson's concept of the nation as an "imagined community" that expresses its national public identification in "unisonance."[4] Instead, modern national discourse by definition articulates a culture's hybridity.

In this vein, through its empirical and imaginative resuscitation of the materials and perspectives of social marginality, the contemporary historical fiction that *Amnesia and Redress* considers rewrites events integral to American history. From *Paradise*'s ex-slaves fleeing the post-Reconstruction South to form a more perfect union in the mythical American West to *Holder*'s excavation of sources that show the rich economic and cultural ties between Puritan Massachusetts through the revolutionary era and precolonial India, each novel in this study revisions a national antinationalist history of America. That their titles are in many cases metaphors or metonyms of the United States suggests this project: for example, "Americana," "Paradise," "Free Enterprise." And yet my concern is not the discourse of nationalism. Rather, like Bhabha—who attempts "to write the Western nation as…a form of living the locality of culture…against the historical certainty and settled nature of that term [nationalism]"—I consider these novels' assertions of cultural—or local—identity as discrete and yet indissoluble from national identity. "This locality," explains Bhabha, is "more mythological than ideology; less homogeneous than hegemony…; more hybrid in the articulation of cultural differences and identifications than can be represented in any hierarchical or binary structuring of social antagonism" (*Location* 140). My analysis of a heterogeneity of localities that express a national hybrid culture bears on the politics of canon formation in the last decades, which has resulted in the reversal of the positions of margin and center within the academy. The segregation of American literary studies crystallizes this view: our students enroll either in courses in the white male canon (such as "American

Masterpieces") or in ethnic literature courses; departments of English, ethnic studies, and women's studies are autonomous, though all three study literary, historical, and cultural texts that often overlap. American literary studies have eagerly embraced the textual productions of historically marginalized groups such that, as Henry Louis Gates observes, "the margins have truly taken center stage" (300).

Yet what underlies the academic understanding of the binary relationship between center and margin is a tenuous assumption that the margin is a mere countervoice. One premise that informs *Amnesia and Redress* is that center and margin, despite their seeming mutually adversarial positions, share a dependence on mythic notions of what constitutes America. (Nowhere is this more evident than in Barack Obama's 2008 presidential candidacy, whereby the dominant narrative of his and Michelle's rise to international prominence played out as a familiar version of the American dream.[5]) For all the texts in my inquiry critique and rewrite myths that underpin America: myths of innocence, including the American West as "virgin land"; myths of America as paradise; myths informed by the discourse of "free enterprise"; and myths of American exceptionalism and Puritan origin.[6] Indeed, by considering DeLillo together with such artists as Morrison, Cliff, Mukherjee, and Otsuka, *Amnesia and Redress* responds to the call articulated by Gates for a "comparative American literature"—that is, a conversation among different voices that places "Anglo-American literature" among "ethnic" literatures (293). The type of counternarrative that informs *Amnesia and Redress* can be understood in relation to Bhabha's "renam[ing] the postmodern from the position of the postcolonial"—a way of rethinking history and nation with which my project shares a theoretical affiliation (*Location* 175). This inherently political approach seeks to "extend a new collaborative dimension, both within the margins of the nation-space and across boundaries between nations and peoples." It recasts the center-margin binary as a mutually informative and transformative relational matrix. As Bhabha notes, "A range of contemporary critical theories suggest that it is from those who have suffered the sentence of history—subjugation, domination, diaspora, displacement—that we learn our most enduring lessons for living and thinking. . . . the affective experience of social marginality—as it emerges in non-canonical cultural forms—transforms our critical strategies" (172). In this context, the meaning of *culture*—"how culture signifies"—transmutes from a relatively fixed set of characteristics to something quite fluid and vernacular—or, in Bhabha's words, "enunciatory": "My shift from the cultural as an epistemological object to culture as an enactive, enunciatory site opens up possibilities for other 'times' of cultural meaning...and other narrative spaces....My purpose in specifying the enunciative present in the articulation of culture is to provide a process by which objectified others may be turned into subjects of their history and experience" (178). Through such noncanonical expression, that is, the voice of social marginality shifts from an object- to a subject-position of self-expression and autonomous cultural definition.

My central argument concerning the cultural work of these contemporary historical novels—their truth telling, their revising nationalist histories and mythologies, their (re)making national mythic history, their speaking truth to power—corresponds to this sense of "culture as a strategy of survival" (*Location* 172). I suggest that the new cultural forms to which Bhabha alludes—which invent "other" times and narrative spaces—include the historical fiction with which *Amnesia and Redress* is concerned. Although each text I examine intentionally rethinks, as Bhabha puts it, "the terms in which we conceive of community, citizenship, nationality, and the ethics of social affiliation" (174), it is perhaps not coincidental that the least canonical authors I include, Michelle Cliff and Bharati Mukherjee, create multidimensional narratives in which the past, present, and future interpenetrate—in order to portray figures with transnational and diasporic identities. As my chapters detail, Cliff's *Free Enterprise* and Mukherjee's *Holder of the World* incarnate the synchronic "meanwhile" that Bhabha identifies as the iteration of the sign of the modern nation-space. Through its collective textual analysis, *Amnesia and Redress* discusses in the concrete the cultural forms about which Bhabha speaks in the abstract. The texts that I study extend the speculations of theorists like Bhabha; at the same time, the theoretical writings help to illuminate certain aspects of the texts under discussion.

Countermemory, Counterhistory

The contemporary historical fiction herein realizes a unique relationship between narrative and history that, while it renders countermemories to accepted histories of the national past, is not immediately discernable. Like most historical fiction, these novels do not state explicitly what aspects of their stories derive directly from historical documents and what aspects are products of the author's imagination. Yet they are strategic in their deployment of historical referent and even misleading. They present storylines that may appear purely fictional, when in fact they are appropriated directly from archival historical sources—sources that are neither documented nor even alluded to within the pages of the texts. Each novel suggests in its own way that it makes claim to the historical record, yet none reveals the often extensive research that informs the work. For example, the first chapter of Cliff's *Free Enterprise* invokes two nineteenth-century black abolitionists— and the specific historical contexts of their appearance on which the remainder of the novel turns: "In her mood of reminiscence, Annie could see Frances Ellen Watkins Harper tilted over a lecture in 1858, speaking on 'The Education and the Elevation of the Colored Race,' advocating a Talented Tenth." After a verbal exchange with Harper, "from the floor of the Tremont Temple" (in Boston), "another, older woman" passes her calling card to Annie, which reads:

> Mary Ellen Pleasant
> 1661 Octavia Street
> San Francisco
> California. (12–13)

Here and elsewhere, the novel raises a question that, in one way or another, all the novels in this study raise: What is the relationship of actual historical events to this imaginative construction?

That is, these texts consciously put the reader in a situation that, in fact, is akin to her relationship to all historical narrative: unsure of its degrees of fact, truth, and fiction. A character in *Underworld*, for instance, spreads "rumors" about the citizens who live "down-wind" of the Nevada test site that detonated hundreds of nuclear explosions during the atomic testing period of the Cold War and who were exposed to fallout from the bombs. They suffer from "multiple myelomas, kidney failures," cancers, birth defects, "great red boils [and] coughing up handfuls of blood," and other grisly maladies. Yet these reports—which I verify in my independent historical research are absolutely true—are surrounded by a discourse of uncertainty and incredulity:

> "Even though huge amounts of territory were affected and large num-
> bers of people were exposed, it remains a major secret to this day."
> "So secret it may not be true," Matt said. (419)

The fiction sets up a readerly scenario in which ascertaining the relationship, within each text, between narrative strategy and the truth status of historical referent helps to clarify its implications for reading history and national identity. The texts manifest through historical fiction contemporary theoretical debates about the complex relationship between narrativity and historical referent and about narrating the nation. I hope to show how the texts clarify, elaborate, and in some cases offer correctives to certain elements of these debates.

Clearly, my project depends upon what Foucault first called "countermemory": a local, culturally specific memory that designates the residual, resistant strains that withstand the dominant versions of historical continuity ("Nietzsche" 93). Each novel in this study combines factual and experiential truths to inscribe facets of events that are integral to the nation's past and yet missing from its orthodox historical accounts—what *Free Enterprise* calls the "official version" of history. Toni Morrison expounds a practice of counterhistory that is evocative of the collective project of these historical novels. Her method of historical research and writing, she says, is "literary archaeology": "On the basis of some information and a little bit of guesswork," she digs in the historical archive and relies upon "the remains—in addition to recollection, to yield a kind of truth" ("Site" 112). As DeLillo explains it, historical fiction tenders "a version of the past that escapes the coils of established history and biography, and that finds a language...that can be a counterhistory" ("Power of History" 60). Though DeLillo's use of the term is certainly germane here, I derive my use of counterhistory from Foucault's related notions of countermemory and "effective history." Foucault defines countermemory as that which effective history constructs. Effective history "fragments what was thought unified" by introducing countermemories that are "discontinuities," or historical fragments, into its narrative ("Nietzsche" 88). *Counterhistory* denotes Foucauldian effective history, but it moreover underscores the practice of social antagonism by which it is produced. The extent and nature of the research that supports each authors' historical narrative differ, from Morrison's imaginative cultivation of an intensely psychological and mythological story from a kernel of historical fact to Cliff's and Mukherjee's vastly erudite investigation of numerous primary sources that support their characterization of their historical subjects. Counterhistory is thus both counterperspective and a counterpractice of historical and cultural excavation and reinterpretation: the narrative of an aggregate of countermemories that results, for my project, in a resistant, deeply heterogeneous comparative American literature.

II   TRUTH AND POWER IN A POSTMODERN WORLD

How does historical fiction function in a culture of "historical deafness"—"in an age," Fredric Jameson says, "that has forgotten how to think historically in the first place"? (ix–xi). Moreover, what is the place of texts that make historical truth claims at a time in which, philosopher Richard Rorty reports, "it is getting more and more difficult to find 'a real live metaphysical prig' who believes in such outmoded ideas as 'reality' and 'truth'"? (quoted in Himmelfarb 164). The narratives the subsequent chapters analyze not only repre-sent a politics of truth that runs counter to the postmodern trend of forgetfulness[7] but also wrestle with the poststructuralist epistemolo-gies that gird Rorty's opinion about reality and truth. The pages that follow navigate the debatable terrain of the poststructuralist chal-lenge to history, drawing on various critics and philosophers of his-tory, from Marxists to traditional historians, clarifying along the way relationship of poststructuralism to postmodernism as it relates to my project—for the literary-historical truth claims of these novels bear implicitly on the core issues of this critical dialogue about histori-cal truth.[8] As my analysis is grounded in Foucault's conception of a genealogy that constitutes a new politics of truth, I show how the poststructuralist eschewal of truth marks a critical departure from the work of Foucault. In this sense, Foucault's theorization of the late twentieth century as a moment of "insurrection of subjugated knowl-edges" lays the groundwork for my study of the cultural work of this body of contemporary historical fiction, which makes truth claims from perspectives of social marginality (*Power* 81–85, 133).

Robert Berkhofer sums up the poststructuralist challenge to his-tory: because the past "is absent by definition," the "only referent" for "history" is "the intertextuality that results from . . . other 'histories.'" Thus poststructuralist critics "fail to see much, if anything in the distinction drawn between fact and fiction, for factual construction is construction according to the working 'fictions' of normal history practice, which, in turn, are the premises of both historical realism and realistic mimesis" (148–49). Put another way, how can we say anything true about the past when the sources on which we base his-torical truth claims are themselves subject not only to the fallibility of what textualized remains survive the past but also to that of the historian who weaves a narrative about them? Under such premises, Berkhofer continues, "rather than show the reader how the (re)pre-sentation is structured to *look like* total factuality, the normal histo-rian . . . make[s] it appear *as though* the structure of factuality itself has determined the organizational structure of his or her account." The historian organizes the narrative "as the natural order of things, which is the illusion of realism" (149). Roland Barthes, in the 1960s, and Hayden White, in the 1970s and 1980s, underscored such historical realism *as illusion* by stressing the literary character of historical texts and the fictional elements they contained.[9] Barthes denied the distinction between history and literature and with it that between fact and fiction, which has generally been accepted in Western thought since Aristotle formulated it in his *Poetics*. White noted "the reluctance to consider historical narratives as what they most manifestly are: verbal fictions" (*Tropics* 82). Similarly, Jacques Derrida and Paul de Man argued that language constructs reality rather than referring to it. Derrida's well-known aphorism states, "There is nothing outside of the text" (158). Thus Terry Eagleton registers the problems that poststructuralism poses: "The work of Derrida and others has cast grave doubt upon the classical notions of truth, reality, meaning, and knowledge, all of which could be exposed as resting on a naively representational theory of language" (143).

Given that many of the critics whom I evoke are associated with postmodernism rather than, or in addition to, poststructuralism, let me briefly define the relationship of the two. I refer to postmodernity as a cultural condition prevailing in advanced capitalist societies characterized by a superabundance of disconnected images and styles—most notably in television, advertising, commercial design, and pop video. As Jean Baudrillard and others note, postmodernity is said to be a culture of fragmentary sensations, eclectic nostalgia, disposable simulacra, and promiscuous superficiality, in which the traditionally valued qualities of depth, coherence, meaning, originality, and authenticity are evacuated or dissolved amid the random swirl of empty signals.[10] Poststructuralism, as Bryan Palmer succinctly puts it, "is the ideology of a particular historical epoch now associated with postmodernity" where ideology is "the construction of false consciousness, the obscuring of the primacy of social practice" (106).[11] Poststructuralism, then, is the hegemonic theory of this epoch; it is "very precisely a postmodernist phenomenon" in Jameson's analysis (12). This is why, as I will show, a scholar such as the historian Gertrude Himmelfarb, although explicitly writing against "postmodernism," in fact criticizes poststructuralist theorists.

Poststructuralism is the false consciousness of this era because, as Palmer (among others) argues, the "rather uncritical adoption of what has come to be known as critical theory has resulted in the wholesale jettisoning of historical materialist assumptions and understandings [such as "truth, reality, meaning, and knowledge"] to the detriment of historical sensitivities and the denigration of the actual experiences of historically situated men, women, and children" (104). Jameson asserts of poststructuralism that it would be "inconsistent to defend the truth of its theoretical insights in a situation in which the very concept of 'truth' itself is part of the metaphysical baggage which poststructuralism seeks to abandon" (12). Christopher Norris similarly charges that a contemporary "narrow conception of 'critical theory,' one that derives almost entirely from French poststructuralism criticism...encourage[s] a leveling consensus-view of language, truth, and reason which deprives theory of its critical force by arguing that all such claims come down to a species of rhetorical imposition." This is the unfortunate outcome of the fact that "American deconstruction has been largely transformed from a philosophical activity into a branch of literary criticism," which, moreover, in the name of "inter-disciplinary contacts" has "colonise[d] other disciplines." "The result," Norris warns, may be "a wholesale undoing of histories of thought which have laboured long and hard to separate truth from the various currencies of true-seeming fictions" (91–93).[12]

In her well-known 1992 essay, "Telling It as You Like It: Postmodernist History and the Flight from Fact," Himmelfarb details some of the forms of self-criticism to which Norris alludes that the discipline of "'modernist' history, familiarly known as 'traditional' history," has developed. Like poststructuralist theorists, Himmelfarb acknowledges that "the remains of the past are incomplete and themselves part of the present," but she cites evidence that "historians, ancient and modern, have always known what postmodernism professes to have just discovered." She quotes germane articles from the first issue of *American Historical Review* (1894) and subsequent addresses to the American Historical Association from 1931, 1934, 1965, and 1975 to attest, "As long as historians have reflected upon their craft, they have known that past cannot be recaptured in its totality," yet it is both possible and vital to "communicate some truth about the past" (158–59). Yet given that postmodernist history, in Himmelfarb's view, denies "the reality of the past apart from what the historian chooses to make of it, and thus of any objective truth about the past," it finds modernist/traditional history uncritical and tenuous. To "demystify" this history, she bemoans, "postmodernism has to expose not only its ideology—the hegemonic, patriarchal interests served by this history—but also its methodology, the scholarly apparatus that gives it a specious credibility" (161). In sum, Himmelfarb refutes "postmodernist" history on the grounds that historians know that history is "vulnerable" and yet maintain the "search for truth" as "a practical, guiding rule of historical scholarship" (159–163). The commitment to "write true history" must not be abandoned (173).

Because the search for truth as a guiding rule of historical scholarship is a premise that underlies the works my book analyzes—Morrison's insistence that her "single gravest responsibility [is] not to lie" aptly paraphrases similar convictions stated by the other authors I consider here—I am sympathetic to this aspect of Himmelfarb's argument. However, the rest of Morrison's credo—that "the crucial distinction for me is not between fact and fiction but the distinction between fiction and truth. Because fact can exist without human intelligence, but truth cannot" ("Site" 111, 113)—is similarly apt for each of the historical novels *Amnesia and Redress* studies; and it underscores this fiction's collective departure from the historical philosophy Himmelfarb spells out. Historical fiction employs creativity to posit a certain kind of truth about history—not merely a fact that can be traced in the historical record but a truth that a critically imaginative interpretation of the archive yields.

Amnesia and Redress both arises from and writes against a postmodernism whose "ultimate aim," according to Himmelfarb, "is to liberate us all from coercive ideas of reality and truth" (161). This she attributes directly to the work of Foucault, who, along with White and Derrida, forms the trio of primary culprits who have "postmodernized" history (160). Perhaps because Foucault insists on the relationship of truth to power, which is at the heart of the double-edged crisis of historical ideology and methodology, critics have misappropriated him in this way. In fact, however, Foucault argued explicitly for the importance of both reality and truth. In a 1976 lecture, he observed that "in the course of most recent times" we have encountered "a thematic to the effect that it is not theory but life that matters, not knowledge, but reality"; and "arising out of this thematic," we are "witness" to "an *insurrection of subjugated knowledges.*" "By subjugated knowledges I mean," he continues, "the historical contents that have been buried and disguised in a functionalist coherence or formal systemisation." Consequently, "an effective criticism" of past events is "the immediate emergence of historical contents" that "criticism—which obviously draws upon scholarship—has been able to reveal" (*Power* 81–82). By linking the importance of "life" and "reality" to historical contents that are not merely "absent" as Berkhofer says but "buried and disguised," Foucault points to an archival past that, although it is in no way totally accessible, does "emerge" through the work of a criticism that mines absences and silences as omissions and as sources for history writing. A Foucauldian "effective history" is "a painstaking rediscovery of struggles together with the rude memory of their conflicts" (*Power* 83). Foucault's emphasis on the "re-appearance" of buried historical contents chafes against White's assertion that historical narratives "are more *invented* than *found*." Of course, Foucault dedicated his life to finding means of historical research and interpretation alternative to the traditional historical practice that is White's target. At the same time, with his assertion that criticism can "rediscover" "the ruptural effects of conflict and struggle" that various forces of institutionalized power "mask," Foucault establishes effective history as a process of finding rather than inventing.

For the purposes of this project, one of the most salient features of the poststructuralist critique of history is its emphasis that one such force of systemized power is traditional history—coextensive with nation-building—itself. Foucault's suggestion that genealogical researches unearth contents of the past that have been hidden or disqualified by dominant practices of history writing is integral to this critique—which, nonetheless, is not novel to the postmodern era. One modernist, Walter Benjamin, quoting Gustave Flaubert, puts it this way:

> "*Peu de gens devineront combien il a fallu être triste pour ressusciter Carthage.*" ("Few will be able to guess how sad one had to be in order to resuscitate Carthage.") The nature of this sadness stands out more clearly if one asks with whom the adherents of historicism actually empathize. The answer is inevitable: with the victor....There is no document of civilization which is not at the same time a document of barbarism. And just as such a document is not free of barbarism, barbarism taints also the manner in which it was transmitted from one owner to another. (256, Benjamin's italics)[13]

What Benjamin expresses in his inimitable, poetic style Foucault states directly: "Truth isn't outside of power." Foucault's point in "Truth and Power" that "each society has its regime of truth, its 'general politics' of truth: that is, the types of discourse which it accepts and makes function as true;...the means by which each [true and false statements] is sanctioned; the techniques and procedures accorded value in the acquisition of truth..." (*Power* 131), intimates the potential pitfalls to Himmelfarb's glib defense of the "discipline of checks and controls," which substantiate the "canon of evidence" (160). Foucault and Benjamin's common argument is that subjugated knowledges elude traditional historical methodology; and, without "resuscitating" them, traditional history serves history's victors— or, in Himmelfarb's words, "hegemonic, privileged, and patriarchal interests" (161). In sum, although (as Foucault points out) "we cannot exercise power except through the production of truth," the job of the intellectual is to "utilis[e] his knowledge, his competence and his relation to truth in the field of political struggles" to "detac[h] the power of truth from the forms of hegemony, social, economic and cultural, within which it operates at the present time" (*Power* 93, 128). Detaching truth from the power strictures within which it operates is not tantamount to dismissing truth altogether. In fact, it is a critical process of "constituting a new politics of truth"—of finding, that is, other means to uncover and tell truths that traditional history overlooks, neglects, or ignores (193). "The political question, to sum up, is not error, illusion, alienated consciousness or ideology; it is truth itself" (133). My point is not to make Foucault an empiricist but simply to suggest that in reading him carefully, I find that he constructs a place for truth that bears importantly on the kind of work attempted by the historical fiction I study.

Foucault terms the strategy for establishing a politics of truth a "genealogy": "the union of erudite knowledge and local memories which allows us to establish a historical knowledge of struggles and to make use of knowledge tactically today." Based on a "reactivation of local knowledges," Foucault's genealogy evokes Bhabha's emphasis, in writing the Western nation "as a form of living the locality of culture," and Morrison's approach to her own historical projects as "literary archeology." For Foucault further explains, "If we were to characterize it in two terms, then 'archaeology' would be the appropriate methodology of this analysis of local discursivities, and 'genealogy' would be the tactics whereby, on the basis of the descriptions of these local discursivities, the subjected knowledges which were thus released would be brought into play" (*Power* 85). Indeed, all three theories are mutually reinforcing approaches to learning, in Bhabha's words, "from those who have suffered the sentence of history." A Foucauldian genealogy that records the history of the development of humanity as a system of interpretations offers a model of history akin to the type of history that, I elaborate in chapter 3, Morrison's *Paradise* ultimately argues for. Indeed, careful examination of the works under consideration reveals that all the texts themselves take what might be called a Foucauldian approach to history. Through their creative archaeological and genealogical strategies, the historical novels at hand realize a dynamic between historical contents and narrative that produces a politics of truth.

Telling Truth, Telling History

If Himmelfarb misleadingly ascribes to Foucault and others a position that admits no possibility of communicating truth, she nevertheless acutely assesses the tension inherent to a "postmodernist" approach to the Holocaust. "Committed as they are to a theory" that sees history "as inevitably 'fictive,' it is only by an 'inordinately circuitous and abstract' mode of reasoning (as White describes it in a related context) that they can elude the most relativistic consequences of their theory—if not a denial of the fact of the Holocaust, then a denial of any objective truth about it" (164). A perusal of these Holocaust debates substantiates Himmelfarb's point. Elizabeth Ermarth's 1991 book, *Sequel to History*, begins with her "explicit" and implicit arguments: "the term 'event,' like 'text' or 'self' or 'historical' retains the essentialism that postmodernism challenges"; "the distinction between what is invented and what is real is one [that] we can no longer afford" (3). She then gives one reason for this extraordinary statement: "As Claude Simon, the 1985 Nobel-Prize winner has said, art and literature meet human needs as basic as hunger and thirst" (3). Perhaps testimonies like those of Anne Frank's father, who credits his shared recollection of classical symphonies with a fellow prisoner as one of the means by which he was able to survive a Nazi concentration camp, gives credence to such a claim. Nonetheless, I find that with this example, Ermarth shifts from tendentious postmodernism to platitudinous humanism. Indeed, it is recent discussions of the Holocaust as a historical event—such as the 2006 "International Conference to Review the Global Vision of the Holocaust"—that bring into sharp focus implications of statements like Ermarth's. In a similar vein, White, in "Historical Emplotment and the Problem of Truth," writes that "the conflict between 'competing narratives' has less to do with the facts of the matter in question than with the different story-meanings with which the facts can be endowed by emplotment" (*Figural Realism* 29). Thus Saul Friedlander's evaluation regarding White's position echoes Himmelfarb's: "There is no 'objective' outside criterion to establish that one particular interpretation [of the Holocaust] is more true than another" (6).

Indeed, it is one thing to point out that historical narrative—as narrative—always involves fictional elements, such as emplotment and metaphor, and another thing to infer from this observation that history and fiction are indistinguishable. Although White resists the complete eradication of this distinction, the logic of his theory invites it. The contradictions of considering historical narratives "verbal fictions" become plain in this debate about the Holocaust. White admits that from a moral perspective it is unacceptable to deny the reality of the Holocaust, yet it is impossible in a historical *narrative* to establish objectively that it happened. Because "figuration cannot be avoided in discourse," a narrative of "the Nazi epoch and of events such as the Final Solution...presented as a figurative representation of real events [means that] the question of its truthfulness would fall under the principles governing our assessment of the truth of fictions" (*Figural Realism* 17). What are these principles? White says, "As for the notion of a true story, this is virtually a contradiction in terms. All stories are fictions" (30). Several critiques of White's position opt for an epistemological approach, such as Perry Anderson's: "Certain absolute limits are set by the evidence. Denial of the existence of either—the regime or its crimes—is plainly ruled out (in Friedlander 8)" Other pleas for historical objectivity and truth are informed as much by ethical positions as by analytic categories. Of the controversy launched in France by "revisionists" about the existence of gas chambers in the Nazi camps, French historian Pierre Vidal-Naquet writes, "I was convinced that there was an ongoing discourse on gas chambers," that "everything should necessarily go through to a discourse; but beyond this, or before this, there was something irreducible which, for better or worse, I would still call reality. Without this reality, how could we make a difference between fiction and history?" (in Friedlander 8). Yet this is the difference that poststructuralists—from Barthes to Ermarth and, to a qualified degree, White—repudiate.

Indeed, the counterinsistence on maintaining, as Norris puts it, "a due sense of the difference between fact and fiction, historical truth and various kinds of state-sponsored myth that currently pass for truth" (95)[14] has added urgency in light of revisionist denials of the existence of the Holocaust, as well as the collective forgetting or ignorance of a myriad of historical events. Among these are aspects of American slavery; twentieth-century genocides of Armenians, Russians, and Cambodians; and the "ethnic cleansings" of the 1990s in the former Yugoslavia and Rwanda.[15] Indeed, the last of these was forgotten—that is, mostly ignored—by the US government and mainstream US media before it was remembered, overshadowed as it was (in the West's attention) by the events in Yugoslavia. With television "news" treatments that reduce problematic, conflictual, and multifaceted sets of events into 30-second consumable bytes, the media-culture in which we live promotes an amnesiac ignorance—that is, a simultaneous ignorance and forgetting.[16] Baudrillard effectively analyzes this contemporary collective inability to apprehend "a succession of non-meaningless facts," what he calls "the disappearance of history" (*Illusion* 2). Although I do not accept his postmodern proposition that dismisses history altogether, I find incisive his account of a contemporary loss of the historical real.[17] In a statement that evokes the

2000 U.S. presidential election—the television networks' fallacious designation of Florida's electoral votes hours before polls closed in the part of the state that lies within a later time zone, their succeeding recant and then second premature call of the presidency itself, and, following, the ensuing travesty of chaotic recounts characterized by the infamous, repeatedly disseminated images of "sunlight tests" and magnifying glass examinations of ballots for dimpled or pregnant chads—Baudrillard declares, "We shall never again know what history was before its exacerbation into the technical perfection of news: we shall never again know what anything was before disappearing into the fulfillment of its model" (6). Whereas Baudrillard concludes that "history itself, has always, deep down, been an immense simulation" (7), Jameson argues that the devolution of history into simulacra has produced "a society bereft of all historicity" (18) and finds that Jacques Lacan's account of schizophrenia offers a suggestive analogy for such cultural logic. As a society, we (like the schizophrenic) are "reduced to an experience of pure material signifiers, or, in other words, a series of pure and unrelated presents in time" (27).

Such a contemporary situation compels what Baudrillard terms "telling history," a task he alleges is impossible. However, the establishment of war crimes and human rights tribunals and, following the collapse of apartheid, of the South African TRC—as well as dozens of truth commissions established around the globe in the 1990s—indicates the cultural need to "establish a public record of truth," the stated purpose of the TRC (Harlow). A disturbing result of the 1992–1995 Bosnian-Serbian War attests to the human and ethical dimensions of this need. Countless Bosnian women testified that they survived systematic rape by the Serbian army through their conviction that if they did not survive, the ruthless truth of these war crimes would die with them. Yet, after the war, the indifference and disbelief with which their stories were received impelled scores of these female witness-victims to commit suicide (Žižek). This tragic and graphic account verifies Norman Geras's thesis about abdicating historical truth in favor of White's so-called "story-meanings": "If there is no truth, there is no injustice.... The victims and protestors of any putative injustice are deprived of their last and often best weapon, that of telling what really happened. They can only tell their story, which is something else. Morally and politically, therefore, anything goes" (110).

Although, like critics of White's position, I take the ethical necessity of truth as a premise for my investigation, I analyze the truth claims of historical fiction on epistemological and narrative bases. As

Norris argues of the "criteria or truth-conditions" that are standardly applied to historical discourse, "There is, to say the least, something premature and suspect about any treatment of historical texts that fastens exclusively on their narrative or tropological aspects while ignoring these other constitutive dimensions" (96–97). I believe that my methodology of analyzing both the truth status of the historical referents each novel deploys and the diverse strategies each employs to convey its truth claims is one way to avoid the problems that Norris and others rightly point to in poststructural criticism. The particular fiction I examine offers a unique opportunity to work through these concerns about empirical validation in relationship to alternative interpretive practices. At the crux both of the poststructuralist critique of history and of my project, then, is this relationship between historical referent and narrative strategy. Although, as White clarifies, modern literary theory suggests "we must reject, revise, or augment the older mimetic and model theories of historical discourse,"

> It does not suggest that everything is language, speech, discourse, or text, only that linguistic referentiality and representation are much more complicated matters than the older, literalist notions of language made out.... It is absurd to suppose that, because a historical discourse is cast in the mode of a narrative, it must be mythical [or] fictional.... If myth, literary fiction, and traditional historiography utilize the narrative mode of discourse, this is because they are all forms of language use. This in itself tells us nothing about their truthfulness.... Anyway, does anyone seriously believe that myth and literary fiction do *not* refer to the real world, tell truths about it, and provide useful knowledge of it? (*Figural Realism* 2–22)

White's point that historical discourse is not necessarily fictional— that fiction, to put it loosely, is not the opposite of truth—grates somewhat against his insistence that "historical discourse is ultimately a second-order fiction, a fiction of a fiction, or a fiction of fiction-making" (9). This fact notwithstanding, White raises issues of *narrativity* that pertain to the significance of this polemic for the contemporary truth-telling historical novel that *Amnesia and Redress* addresses. Although poststructuralist theory has destabilized history to the point of crisis,[18] it has also opened up a space for the truth claims of contemporary historical fiction—and it reflects the need for the kind of "effective histories" such fiction advances. Indeed, White's comments suggest that because history and fiction utilize the same mode of discourse—that is, narrative—historical language resides in fictive discourse (and vice versa). Thus, through narrative innovations proscribed by traditional history writing and marked by self-consciousness of the constructive elements of history, the historical fiction at hand not only interrogates the premises of realistic mimesis but provides a conceptual and artistic foil to it. It evinces a cognizance of the problems with history that poststructuralist critiques target yet negotiates the problems of traditional historiography through unique and resourceful narrations that stake a claim to a politics of truth about the past. For example, whereas traditional historical methodology, as Himmelfarb notes, endorses a "canon of evidence" that produces in turn "logical, orderly" historical narratives, postmodernism has deconstructed as "arbitrary" several conventions upon which narrativity, historical and otherwise, depends—"chronology, causality, and collectivity" (161). In *Postmodernist Fiction*, McHale elucidates a cross-fertilization between such postmodernist theoretical approaches and postmodernist fiction, detailing "creative anachronism," "spatial displacement of words," "*trompe-l'œil*," "metalepsis," and other narrative techniques that call attention to narrative construction. The absence of such postmodern strategies in the type of historical novel with which *Amnesia and Redress* is concerned is one reason why it cannot usefully be labeled "postmodern." However, it does disrupt conventional chronology in various ways (from telling history by moving backward in time to creating multidimensional times in which the past, present, and future interpenetrate); posit alternative relations of causality (such as the black women allied with John Brown's raid on Harper's Ferry); and—by depicting peoples who represent the point of fracture between America as a homogeneous, consensual community and the forces that arise out of contentious, unequal interests and identities within the population—it challenges notions of what constitutes collectivity. Yet such narrative innovations do not merely call attention to or undermine the conventions of historical writing but introduce historical referents in ways that reform a retrospective view of the national past.

This new form of the historical novel both engages and implicitly critiques poststructuralist theories of history, challenging traditional history on two related fronts. The first is the process and form of history making—the writing of history that determines what counts as history in the collective imagination—which it foregrounds as exclusionary, subjective, teleological, and characterized by omissions. The second is the (resulting) content of what is understood as "American history." The form of history produces its content, in traditional histories as in the counterhistories that contemporary truth-telling fiction introduces. These novels reminds us—through their form and their content—that narrative, as White puts it, is "a discursive mode whose content *is* its form" (*Figural Realism* 21).

The arguments of White and others certainly mean that truth claims—in historical as in literary narrative—must be made with attention to the complexity that representation of the referent always involves. That is, the epistemologies underlying truth claims in narrative should, as Susan Stanford Friedman says in a related context, "aim for a negotiation between objectivism and subjectivism, between the search for the Real and a recognition that all access to the Real is mediated through discourse" (235). Dominick LaCapra—another intellectual historian who, like White, has launched in recent decades an influential sustained critique of positivist historiography—insists that his critique does not entail abandoning the empirical: "Extreme documentary objectivism and relativistic subjectivism do not constitute genuine alternatives. They are mutually supportive parts of the same larger complex." LaCapra argues for a "dialogic and mutually provocative" relation between the empirical and the rhetorical as equally necessary parts of history writing (137).

Indeed, the empirical-rhetorical dialogic relation is another vocabulary for the relationship between history and narrative that informs my method of analysis. Each text these chapters consider utilizes its historical referents in ways that constitute different engagements of *mythic history*. Mythic history is that narrative of national identity that partially represents experience and gains particular currency in the popular imagination. Formulated as much from myth as from historical occurrences, mythic history both produces and reflects collective historical imagination.[19] The means by and extent to which each text reinvents mythic histories of America produce what I distinguish as revisionary and redemptive versions of history. All these texts scavenge among the ruins of history to reconstruct a story of the past that exists in fragments, proceeding according to the Benjaminian "truth: [that] nothing that has ever happened should be regarded as lost for history" (254). Reading this theoretical claim against the practice of contemporary historical fiction reveals narratives that, as I will show, revise or redeem the histories of their subjects.

CHAPTER 2

"The Downfall of the Empire and the Emergence of Detergents": Underhistory in Don DeLillo's Historical Novels

More than perhaps any contemporary writer, Don DeLillo has been keenly attuned to national mythic history from the onset of his career—as the title of his first novel, *Americana*, suggests. DeLillo's three Cold War–era novels particularly—*Americana* (1971), *Libra* (1988), and *Underworld* (1997)—mine documentary materials from World War II to the Kennedy assassination and the Cold War only to deconstruct the myth-narratives that have pervaded these land-mark events. DeLillo, then, is among the foremost authors of this new "truth-telling" historical novel. *Americana*, the vital precursor to *Libra* and especially to *Underworld*, is the definitive harbinger of DeLillo's four-decade oeuvre that writes both within and against postmodernism. In these texts, DeLillo ultimately moves beyond the ironized perspective of history that is the distinguishing feature of "historiographic metafiction"; his postmodern narrative techniques (from irony to looping novelistic structures and dense intertextuality) inscribe a critical distance from history only to force a raw encounter with it. His work simultaneously invokes mythic history and unearths the buried contents of the past that fracture it to portray heterodox accounts of national identity. As such, DeLillo exploits the tension between innocence and violence—the literally malignant legacy of the Cold War—to reveal the way in which official culture is amnesiac by definition.

I take my chapter title from *Underworld* because it captures the language of American mythology by exposing the collusion between American imperialism and consumer society, a tenet of DeLillo's

cultural critique that was well under way by *Americana*. The collusion is ubiquitous: it arises out of teenager Cotter Martin's "world
history book. They made history by the minute in those days. Every
sentence there's another war or tremendous downfall. Memorize
the dates. The downfall of the empire and the emergence of deter-
gents" (141). *Americana* protagonist David Bell's allusions to this
complicity presage *Underworld*'s profound excavation of American
history. In this sense, the 1997 novel is a striking portrait of what
it means to live with the contemporary legacy of a past that DeLillo
began to explore in the 1971 novel. There is a pattern and structure
to DeLillo's first and eleventh novels by which they turn back to an
origin that is polluted, engaging in a looping pattern that unearths
an adulterated underhistory. Eponymously and in scope and content,
then, *Americana* and *Underworld* suggest DeLillo's stated intention
to tackle "the whole picture, the whole culture" ("The Art of Fiction"
279). Although these novels span the 1950s to the 1990s, connecting
the consumer culture of the 1950s to various Cold War flash points,
Libra, with its clear-minded account of the Bay of Pigs and antago-
nisms between John F. Kennedy and Fidel Castro and between the
United States and the Soviet Union, focuses on the underlying political and economic tensions of the Cold War era. Taken together and
viewed through the retroactive lens of *Americana*, these historical
novels thrust an American consumerism and related mythologies of
American innocence and the American dream against brutal histories
of the nation—disclosing history as that which the marketing mechanisms of the capitalist state cannot, finally, consume.

"THE POWER OF THE IMAGE": MYTHMAKING AS AMNESIA IN *AMERICANA*

DeLillo has said, "It's no accident that my first novel was called
Americana. This was a private declaration of independence, a statement of my intention to use the whole picture, the whole culture.
America was and is the immigrant's dream, and as the son of two
immigrants I was attracted by the sense of possibility that had drawn
my grandparents and parents" ("The Art of Fiction" 279). But from
Americana on, DeLillo's novels reveal that the American dream "of
possibility" does not exist independently of the violence endemic
to American nationhood. To unravel this knot, DeLillo personifies
America in a protagonist who defines himself by fascination with the
image and his ensuing self-conception as innocent: unadulterated,
that is, by history.[1] David Bell cites his experience as a film major in

college when he was first "seized by the power of the image...that flicker[s] across America's screens, the fantasies that enthrall America's imagination" (31). Many critics have discussed the role of film and representation in DeLillo's later novels; but John Frow's observation that *Running Dog* (DeLillo's sixth novel) is "'about' representation" (145) can be as productively applied to *Americana*. For David, the "mediated constructions of the world themselves become substantial," the basis on which he charts his life (*Americana* 164).

Moreover, as two primal stories issuing from David's childhood show, the montage of images with which David grew up bred a mythology of innocence. A third-generation successful New York advertising executive, David shares a tale passed on from his grandfather to his father and told to him "dozens of times." On a train, David's grandfather comes up with an advertising campaign: "McHenry—the Star-Spangled Pajamas," which "made McHenry rich and my father famous. That's how they wrote ads in the old days, kid—sloshed to the eyeballs on the Union Pacific Railroad...that story...has a fine innocence to it...the campaign itself. The star-spangled pajamas. It has a lovely innocence to it. You could afford to be innocent in the old days" (197). In the story, David's grandfather becomes a kind of ironic modern-day hero—not for military bravery or daring but for recycling nationalist images from the Revolutionary battle at Fort McHenry to save a fellow American from bankruptcy. By projecting the commercials his agency has produced onto a basement screen for his children's entertainment, Clinton Bell likewise creates a kind of postmodern family tradition—a gathering not around the dining table but around watching TV commercials. "All the impulses of the media," David says, "were fed into the circuitry of my dreams." David's childhood, which he recalls with an jaded nostalgia yielded

> the dream of the good life, innocent enough, simple enough on the surface, beginning for me as soon as I could read and continuing through the era of the early astronauts, the red carpet welcome on the aircraft carrier as the band played on....as a boy, and even later, quite a bit later, I believed all of it, the institutional messages, the psalms and placards, the pictures, the words....For...the true sons of the dream, there was only complexity. The dream made no allowance for the truth beneath the symbols, for the interlinear notes, the presence of something black...at the mirror rim of one's awareness. (130)

The heroic narrative of the American dream can be sustained as long as history—the complex interlinear notes—disappears into the realm of simulation. *Americana* progresses, however, to divulge historical experiences that splinter the montage and confront David with dis-contents of "the dream"; eventually he disabuses himself from the American myth of innocence.

The "truth beneath the symbols" moves from the "mirror rim" of David's focus to its forefront, returning him—and the reader—from the realm of simulation to history. Both against and within the post-modern grain, *Americana* is thus a desperate search—brimming with awareness of its futility—for genuine selfhood on David's part and by extension for the lost innocence of American selfhood.[2] Paradoxically, he attempts to solve "the only problem I had [of] living in the third person" by making a film of his life in the midst of a road trip across America (58). In the process, he loses his ironic edge and becomes morosely self-critical, unflinchingly honest about both his own past and that of the nation.

Herein wartime nightmares tell ugly truths about Cold War his-tory, fragmenting mythic conceptions of America. The actor whom David casts as his father narrates the Bataan Death March, which David's father made as a POW of the Japanese during World War II. It is an account of grotesque inhumanity that shocks a soldier "who considered...his country the only invincible power on earth" (293): the Japanese behead 400 Filipino officers—a slaughter that takes two hours—and tell the American soldiers to defecate in a ditch, "but it was full of dead bodies and the smell of the dead and dying kept most of us away. Men with dysentery couldn't control themselves and had to defecate where they stood. Others just fell down and died" (295). Throughout, David's "father" punctuates the recapitulation with visions of home, America. Before the Japanese load the POWs on trains, he recounts, "We all looked forward to the trains, some dim and still functioning part of our minds thinking of god knows what childhood times we had spent on trains. . . . everything is vast and wild and mysterious because you're ten years old and America is as wide as all the world and twice as invincible" (296–97). The childhood associ-ation of trains echoes the McHenry pajamas campaign, concocted on the Union Pacific, but these trains transport them to Balanga, where

> they forced us to bury the dead. . . . I was throwing dirt onto the body of a Filipino when he suddenly moved. . . . Dozens of dead men around him covered already with maggots, completely covered so that the ground, the earth, seemed to be moving, rotting bodies everywhere and the whole saddle trench about to erupt. . . . I pointed to him, trying to rise, and then the guard...pointed his bayonet at the shovel on the ground and then at the boy in the ditch. (298)

In fact, this passage echoes (verbatim in places) the first written survivor's account of the horrific Bataan Death March, recorded in *The Dyess Story: The Eye-Witness Account of the Death March from Bataan and the Narrative of Experiences in Japanese Prison Camps and of Eventual Escape* (1944).[3] Earlier in 1944, the *Chicago Sun* had originally published Bataan survivor Lt. Col. William E. Dyess's story as a serialized narrative. Since the war's end, popular and scholastic histories of World War II have largely ignored the infamous march; to date, Bataan has merited scarcely a mention in high school and college history textbooks. Yet over a half-century after the war, in what columnists and reviewers as well as academics have called the "age of memoir" in which we currently live, Bison Books has reprinted the Dyess story—under the notable new title *Bataan Death March: A Survivor's Account*.[4] Strikingly, the 2002 Bison edition is among nearly a dozen Bataan Death March survivor accounts printed by various presses between 2001 and 2007. These discrete memoirs include James Bolloch's *A Soldier's Story*, originally published by Carlton Press in 1993. When Pelican Publishing republished the book a decade later, it too changed the title to *Bataan Death March: A Soldier's Story* (2003). Bison's and Pelican's decisions to front the phrase "Bataan Death March" appears to capitalize on a surge of interest in Bataan as indicated by contemporaneous publications of dramatic accounts, which compete with Dyess's and Bolloch's but which also foster public attention to this little-known aspect of World War II in the Philippines—as one such book subtitles it, *"The* Forgotten *Epic Story of World War II…"* (emphasis added).[5]

This departure from a historical focus on European and US battlegrounds—such as Normandy and Pearl Harbor—represents the public expression of vernacular memory that, as Bodnar details, has increasingly contested official memory in the last two decades. Although both of these celebrated battles were further enshrined in American public imagination by the big-screen Oscar-winning films *Saving Private Ryan* (1998, famously directed by Steven Spielberg) and *Pearl Harbor* (2001, directed by Michael Bay), the recent issue and reissue of so many individual Bataan survivor accounts suggests a concern for and receptivity to soldier experiences of World War II that are not heroic in the traditional sense of war.[6] Unlike Normandy and Pearl Harbor, Bataan is conspicuous neither for its strategic importance nor for its grand scale. Although Joe Rosenthal's famous 1945 photograph, *Raising the Flag on Iwo Jima*, and Norman Mailer's top-ranked *The Naked and the Dead* (1948) generate recognition of Iwo Jima specifically and of the war in the South Pacific generally, official history's neglect of the Pacific theater, especially Bataan, reflects the US–Europe First military policy that dominated the war.[7] The United States' lack of prioritizing and preparation in the region resulted in the United States losing the Philippines and in the unnecessary fall of Bataan—the inhumane deaths of thousands of soldiers that were due not to a lack of ability or courage heralded in wartime but in significant part to a dearth of food, medical supplies, and weapons that led to their becoming victims of the Bataan Death March, one of the worst atrocities of World War II.[8] Like the recent disclosure of the Japanese Imperial Army's massive use of "comfort women"—and, with tacit approval from US occupation authorities, US servicemen's use of a similar system Japan set up for American GIs—the Bataan Death March reflects poorly on Japan's military of that era but also on that of the United States.[9]

The recent publication and pervasive interest in Bataan, like that in the comfort women, is part of the current climate of truth telling that this book addresses. *Americana*, of course, is the only novel published prior to the decade that witnessed the issue of the rest of the novels in this study, the 1990s. I begin with it not only to show that a politics of truth was a defining element of DeLillo's cultural critique at the outset of his career but also to emphasize DeLillo's insistent use of the historical archive to force a confrontation between the citizen experiences such materials reveal and national mythologies. Through exploring cultural crises—which constitute, according to the historian Richard Slotkin, "the mother of myth/ideological invention" (*Gunfighter* 636)—DeLillo has always been engaged in a critical project of demystification. In this sense, DeLillo is a key player in a post-Vietnam American environment ripe for myth revision. His 1971 novel can be thought of in relation to, for example, Clint Eastwood's recent groundbreaking films, *Flags of Our Fathers* and *Letters from Iwo Jima* (2006). Reflecting the current climate fatigued by war, *Flags* and *Letters* deconstruct the World War II heroic genre. So too does *Americana*, reflecting the contemporaneous disillusion ensuing from Vietnam, demystifying World War II by focusing it through the disturbing Bataan Death March. When one considers that it has taken half a century for an artist to make films such as *Flags* and *Letters*—to critical but not popular acclaim[10]—DeLillo's truth telling about World War II and Vietnam (while the latter was still raging) is avant-garde.

Writing more than three decades prior to this newfound interest in Bataan, DeLillo situates his account of World War II, evidently adapted from Dyess's, in the same section of the novel as its only

direct engagement of Vietnam, throwing this remote and yet contemporaneous war into sharp relief. Indeed, although DeLillo wrote
Americana over the course of four years in which the distant Vietnam
War came to a heated head at home (1966–1970), the book's setting
against Vietnam as a remote backdrop depicts an American preference
for entertainment and distraction over history. "The war was on television every night," David says in the first pages of the novel, "but we
all went to the movies" (5). The novel's singular account of Vietnam,
succeeded by that of the Bataan Death March, occurs during a pause
in the road trip to shoot the film; set in the Midwest, these related
segments are geographically and otherwise distinct from the rest of
the narrative. One of David's childhood friends, a recently returned
Vietnam vet, tries in vain to escape nightmares of his tour: "I can
feel it in my skull. The old violence…inside my head the action is
constant.…Davy, you don't know what it's like to lay down some 20
mike-mike on a village. See it fall apart. Come down low and strafe
a hootch or two. Your cans of nape. Your 500-pounders. Your rock-
ets" (251–52). This recollection of Vietnam juxtaposed with Bataan
concludes with the Bataan survivor confessing "total self-hatred," but
the "self" to which he refers here is the self-as-indissolubly-American:
"We didn't hate the ginks. They hadn't gotten us into this. We had,
or our generals had, or our country which treasured the sacrifice of
its sons, making slogans out of their death and selling war bonds
with it or soap for all we knew" (297). His comments recall, again,
the McHenry pajamas campaign and David's childhood indoctrina-
tion in the image and promised "dream of the good life." Bell is the
prototype of the DeLillo protagonist who lives in a cultural context
shaped by various crises, which cannot be fully explained by invoking
the received precepts embodied in American media-generated myth.

Although DeLillo's characters inhabit this familiarly postmodern
environment, they are atypically unable to maintain an ironic distance
from a history that haunts and weighs heavily on them. *Americana*'s
Bataan and Vietnam memories illustrate the tension between the
mythic meaning of America—"invincible," "vast," "wild," "mysterious," "innocent," and "beautiful"—and American experiences of
alienation and horror that erupt throughout DeLillo's texts, produc-
ing cognitive dissonance. For it is clear in *Americana* as throughout DeLillo's oeuvre that, as a character in *Great Jones Street* points
out, "history is never clean" (74). Just as later DeLillo protagonists
find that, in John McClure's words, "the secret agencies dedicated
ostensibly to the protection of sacred cultural values are actually no
more than subsystems of a vast criminal enterprise that encompasses

capitalist corporations, and corrupt governments," David concludes, "There were many visions in the land, all fragments of the exploded dream, and some of the darkest of these visions were those processed in triplicate by our generals and industrialists—the manganese empires, the super-sophisticated gunnery, the consortiums and privileges." Just as "history" refers both to the events of the past and to the representation of those events through narrative, the images that constitute a public mythology are inseparable from the institutional mechanisms that produce, enshrine, and facilitate consumption of those images. David continues, "To achieve an existence almost totally symbolic is less simple than mining the buried metals of other countries or sending the pilots of your squadron to hang their bombs over some illiterate village.... Better living though chemistry. The Sears, Roebuck catalog. Aunt Jemima" (129–30). The symbolic "dream of the good life," in which the "Sears, Roebuck catalog" and "Aunt Jemima" stand for "better living," effects a kind of amnesia. *Americana* thus launches a crucial interrelationship between image and myth that becomes a set piece in DeLillo's work at least through the 1999 *Valparaiso*: it is the circulation of mass-media-generated images that functions as amnesiac mythmaking in America.

Yet a historical real that ultimately surfaces to fill in the experience of "Americana" belies such cultural amnesia. The penultimate moments of the novel firmly establish the indivisibility of David's personal past with the nation's; both corrupt histories collide and any vestige of ironic distance from history collapses. Upon wrapping his autobiographical film, David discovers an insistent longing, a powerful urge to escape his own life, to drop out of the trip for which he was the organizing force and to continue to go west alone, into his own wilderness, "to smash my likeness, prism of all my images, and become finally a man who lives by his own power and smell" (236). He makes this solitary journey in the novel's final section, in a violent and dissolute trip westward, initiated by hitchhiking away from his companions.

David's "attempt to find pattern and motive, to make of something wild a squeamish thesis on the essence of the nation's soul" (349) culminates with a bodily reverberation of "the shattering randomness of the [Kennedy assassination]" with all of its "ambiguity and chaos" ("The Art of Fiction" 299, and "An Outsider in This Society" 287). David's "second journey, that great seeking leap into the depths of America," takes him to the American desert in the speeding Cadillac of a renegade Texan who engages David in a lewd exploit of drunken debauchery that is degraded even from the perspective of the modern spiritual wasteland of T. S. Eliot's J. Alfred Prufrock, the mythical modernist figure to whom David likens himself in this final section of the novel.[11] Despite the fact that Sullivan (David's traveling companion and one-time lover) has recently said that David is "innocent as a field mouse," in this last segment of the book, David's delusion of innocence totally unravels, as does, by extension, the ideal of America as innocent. DeLillo has said that the idea for *Americana* first hit him when, in Maine, he glimpsed "a street…and a sense of beautiful old houses and rows of elms and maples and a stillness and a wistfulness—the street seemed to carry its own longing"; and he believes that in writing the novel he "maintained the idea of that quiet street…as lost innocence" ("The Art of Fiction" 279). David's desert experience—a literal and metaphorical antithetic of DeLillo's quiet Maine street—can be seen as the nadir of this American loss. David escapes an orgy of perverse sexuality and rents a car with which he drives the route of JFK's limousine through Dealey Plaza, horn blaring the entire way. David's final drive becomes a palimpsest upon the event that, according to DeLillo, "changed [our culture] in important ways," by threatening "our grip on reality" ("The Art of Fiction" 299). David's quest ends in a place that signifies uncertainty and violence, in American history and even more so within DeLillo's fiction. Accordingly, rather than becoming illuminated as to the meaning of the nation's soul, or of his own, David is beset by confusion and chaos.

Written nearly two decades before DeLillo's rise to literary and popular acclaim—and his entrenchment in the postmodern canon—-*Americana* imbricates quintessential American mythologies with intractable matter of the nation's past, making it an indispensable forerunner to DeLillo's subsequent historical novels especially. In the pages that follow, I emphasize this approach to the Cold War era in *Libra* and *Underworld*. DeLillo's rich engagement with empirical history results in a distinct historical novel form, one that manifests a provocative dynamic between narrativity and historical referent to articulate a politics of truth. Like *Americana*, both *Libra* and *Underworld* present storylines appropriated directly from archival sources that are neither documented nor even alluded to within the pages of the texts. Each is a counterhistory that is both a counterperspective and counterpractice of historical and cultural excavation and reinterpretation. Working in a way that is incipient in *Americana*, DeLillo produces in *Libra* and *Underworld* postmodern narratives (in structure, technique, and environment) that are yet rejoinders to an ironic and distant postmodern sense of history. Asserting countermemories to defining national events, these two later novels, like *Americana*, revise the contours of national identity. As Frank Lentricchia has noted, *Libra* is clearly written from a post-Watergate and post-Iran-Contra perspective in which criticism of the American government and public awareness of its lies, along with the plenitude of conspiracy theories ensuing from the assassination itself, makes DeLillo's politically caustic event perfectly plausible to the contemporary reader. But I am more interested in the way in which, for DeLillo, this lens results in an exploration of the Kennedy assassination that is as much about the 1950s America that bred Lee Harvey Oswald as it is about the various historical Cold War forces—from the CIA to the Bay of Pigs and the Mafia—that together converged with Oswald in the Kennedy assassination. Similarly, *Underworld*'s narrative proper begins in the multinational-capitalist perspective of the late 1990s and gradually winds, knowingly, back to the 1950s with (like *Americana*) an irony that eventually dissipates under the (literally) toxic remains of Cold War history.

LIBRA: THE ELUSIVE DREAM
AND ITS DISCONTENTS

Although *Americana* reveals DeLillo's raw engagement of documentary materials, it is not until *Libra* (a decade and a half and eight novels later) that DeLillo grapples with "an historic event in a large scale way," taking up the Kennedy assassination, which his first novel echoed and prefigured, by purposeful documentary research. Because he wanted "a clear historical center" (as opposed to "a novelistic intention"), DeLillo conducted no interviews, viewed crude film footage of the event, traveled to the many places Lee Harvey Oswald lived—and, mostly, delved deeply into the 26-volume Warren Commission Report. Together its 15 volumes of written and recorded testimony (vital to DeLillo's finding the voice and historical characters for his novel) and 11 volumes of exhibits "propel[led] the story," says DeLillo. "I found the research invigorating. I depended on it. I needed it" ("An Outsider" 44, 62). And yet the evidence—"a masterwork of trivia ranging from Jack Ruby's mother's dental records to photographs of knotted string"—for all its bulk, is conclusive only in its uncertainty. "There is confusion over the autopsy, over the autopsy reports—which were eventually burned. There is confusion over the fact that the President's brain disappeared from the National Archives. There are dozens of anomalies" ("Seven Seconds" 45).

Given this ambiguity and the ensuing proliferation of theories about the assassination, the obvious amnesiac element to

JFK's murder is *what really happened*. *Libra* does not answer that nineteenth-century historical question; in the author's words, "the book is an exploration of what variations we might take on an actual event rather than an argument that this is what really happened." At the same time, DeLillo felt he "had to do justice to historical likelihood"; a refreshing element of *Libra*'s truth telling is its incisive consideration of "the most obvious possibility: that the assassination was the work of anti-Castro elements." The anomalous facts that frustrate any definitive history of the assassination allow the novelist to construct a politics of truth about it. "The novel which is within history can also operate outside it," as DeLillo puts it. "The novelist can try to leap across the barrier of fact" to find "a redemptive truth waiting on the other side." In this sense, "fiction rescues history from its confusions" ("An Outsider" 58, 64). At the same time, however, *Libra* complicates its "theory of the assassination"[12] with a metafictional narrative that highlights the constructive elements of history—and its limitations. Chapters set in the late 1980s, contemporaneous with *Libra*'s publication—interwoven throughout the primary chapters devoted alternately to Oswald and the CIA and anti-Castro plotters—introduce the reader to the retired CIA analyst Nicholas Branch, who has been hired to write "the secret history" of the assassination. We meet Branch "in the fifteenth year of his labor," when the anonymous "Curator" begins to send him esoteric and macabre material—"autopsy photos of Oswald...the results of ballistic tests carried out on human skulls and goat carcasses, on blocks of gelatin mixed with horsemeat" (*Libra* 300)—that exacerbates Branch's struggle to select and archive the plethora of details from the past into a narrative. As John Johnston notes, Branch "explicitly represents the failures of a strictly empirically-governed account" of the event. However, "by acknowledging the inherent failure of the [Warren Commission] exhibits and heterogenous collections of data to coalesce into an intelligible pattern, Branch functions to seal of the rest of the novel from its contaminations by an unintelligible chaos by allowing *Libra* to stand 'apart' and complete" (324). Indeed, isolating Nicholas Branch's retrospective sets apart the irony and enormous paranoia that ensued from the assassination, resulting in a keen and nuanced sense of the event.

But what more profound amnesia obtains from the Kennedy assassination can be gleaned from the powerful collective memory of the event—the answer to the inevitable question that every adult citizen of the era knows: Where were you when John Kennedy was shot? The official public narrative, captured and replayed in the Zapruder film[13] as well as in the news footage rerun interminably on televisions November 22, 1963, and the days after, grounds millions of individual certain responses to that question. As DeLillo says, "Nothing in *Libra* can begin to approach the level of disquiet and dread characterized by the assassination itself" ("An Outsider" 74); but the reason for this, in part, is that against the Camelot myth and collective sense of shock, disbelief, vulnerability, and sorrow, *Libra* carefully constructs Lee Harvey Oswald's story and thereby tells something more precious than a compelling, research-driven assassination theory. *Libra* discloses an acute truth about the history of that era—a typically forgotten slice of American life. "What was valuable to me most specifically," DeLillo says of the Warren Report,

> was the testimony of dozens and dozens of people who talk not only about their connection to the assassination itself but about their jobs, their marriages, their children. This testimony provided an extraordinary window on life in the fifties and sixties and, beyond that, gave me a sense of people's speech patterns, whether they were private detectives from New Orleans or railroad workers from Fort Worth. I'm sure that without those twenty-six volumes I would have written a very different novel and probably a much less interesting one. ("An Outsider" 62)

The seldom-glimpsed "window on life in the fifties and sixties" *Libra* reveals is an insight to the feeling of being unable to grasp the promise of consumer fulfillment in America and the loneliness, desperation, and sometimes violence that perpetually being on the outside breeds. Marina, for example, Oswald's Russian wife and a recent émigré to the United States, is dazzled by this world of consumer promise; her gaping in department store windows in downtown Fort Worth shows "her desire to become more fully a part of this paradise she'd been hearing about all her life"—and gnaws at Lee's "ambivalent feelings about being a husband who provides for his family and at the same time being a leftist who finds an element of distaste" in the American culture of consumption (*Libra* 227, "An Outsider" 61).

Libra's focus of the Kennedy assassination through Oswald—whose fated role in the plot begins with his nonidyllic 1950s childhood—underscores the tension between the American dream and violence first probed by *Americana*. A member of the underclass, fatherless, unskilled, and learning disabled, Lee is troubled by the contradictions between the American dream and lived reality: "Everyone wants to love America. But how can an honest man forget what he sees in the daily give-and-take that's like a million little wars?" (*Libra*

113). Beginning in his childhood, Lee lives on the fringes of what he perceives as "the forces of history" and yet believes that "the struggle is to merge your life with the greater tide of history." He imagines that "an old scratchy film" playing on his television "carried his dreams....Lee felt he was in the middle of his own movie" (87, 370). He is like David Bell both in his longing to enter human history and in his hyper self-consciousness. Lee seizes the building assassination plot as his opportunity to merge.

Lee's conflicted ambitions reflect the tenuous fabric of the American dream. He alternately immerses himself in Marxist ideology and memorizes his brother's Marine Corps manual; enlists in the Marines and shoots himself in the arm to get out of active duty; emigrates to and applies for citizenship in the Soviet Union, tries to enter Cuba to live out his Marxist ideal, and attempts to gain employment with the US government as a spy. After shooting Kennedy, Lee is at first afraid that he is "a dupe of history"; he later realizes that he has "found his life's work...Everybody knew who he was now" (435). That Lee sees himself both as a victim of history and its agent is symptomatic of his own schizophrenic desires that inspired the novel's title and perspective. Though his astrological sign is *Libra*, the scales, Lee is the "negative Libran who is, let's say, somewhat unsteady and impulsive. Easily, easily influenced. Poised to make the dangerous leap" (315). Lee's frustrated grasp of, alternately, Marxist and American ideals, makes him prone to violence. In DeLillo's version of the assassination, Lee becomes a "patsy." An expert marksman, a Cuban revolutionary from the Bay of Pigs who welcomes a passionate revenge, exercises the primary responsibility for killing Kennedy; poised in a parking lot, he shoots the president from the front. Oswald becomes the fall guy in the history he so desperately wishes to influence.

Although the assassination of JFK figures in the national memory bank as an emblematic tragedy of the American twentieth century, DeLillo does not emphasize this loss. Instead, drawing on the Warren Report's wealth of "factual information [about] Oswald and his wife and his mother, and Jack Ruby," DeLillo privileges Oswald's internal world (Connolly in dePietro 26). DeLillo reconstructs a psychology of Oswald and faithfully renders "the twisted syntax of Marguerite Oswald and others" from its hundreds of pages of recorded testimony (ibid.). It is this resurrection of the life, language, and aura of the event and era that ultimately forecloses the irony that elsewhere informs the novel and brings the reader close to an otherwise distant and chaotic history. For although the ironic character of Nicholas Branch—who mirrors, parodies, and emphasizes the work of DeLillo's interpreting the assassination—aligns *Libra* with historiographic metafiction, Branch's voice has neither the greatest authority in the novel nor its deepest resonance. "Branch" eponymously suggests not only the immense bureaucracy of his employer—the CIA, an institution in which data seems to multiply and mystify rather than coalesce into meaningful information—but also, by extension, the futility of his task.

DeLillo's engagement with empirical history, in contrast to Branch's brute archive, provides several different lenses through which to decipher the Cold War and serves to turn the chaos of the era into something not only fathomable but ultimately moving. DeLillo restores palpability to the cultural and personal context of Oswald that the sheer abundance of data and innumerable theories and speculations about the assassination occlude. Oswald's Historic Diary and medical records, for example, which DeLillo recovers directly from the Warren Report, illuminate the psychology of the "other" of the American era of peace, domestic happiness, and prosperity. From Oswald's dyslexia and lack of grammar skills to his frustration in wanting a better life for himself, his Russian wife, and his young children, to his finding a sense of self and home in both Japan and the Soviet Union and his longing to live in Cuba, DeLillo presents a not-unsympathetic Oswald who feels America and its government have let him down. Encountering Oswald in his 1950s boyhood and young adulthood in the Bronx, abroad, and eventually Texas provides a background to the early 1960s and the culture of fear and political unrest of those years. In establishing this cultural context, DeLillo deconstructs the mythology of the lone gunman against society by reconstructing what Lyotard calls the "petit narrative" of a gunman at the nexus of several historical and social forces. In DeLillo's hands, Oswald moves to the center of history and ceases to be the ex-centric protagonist of historiographic metafiction.

UNDERWORLD: "THE TRUTH BENEATH THE SYMBOLS"

DeLillo is no stranger, then, to the dialectic of cultural memory and forgetting; although it occupied him as early as *Americana*, it is vital not only to his excavation of the underhistory of Cold War America in *Libra* as well as *Underworld*, but to later novels' metahistorical project of revealing the workings of mythic history. In his essay coincident with *Underworld*'s publication, "The Power of History," DeLillo's explains his "entering the narrative." An initial forgetting precipitated his pursuit of the "story concerning the 40th anniversary of a famous ballgame played in New York in 1951," which he read in his morning paper. "The minute I finished reading," he writes, "I forgot it all.... The newspaper with its crowded pages and unfolding global reach permits us to be ruthless in our forgetting" (60). Thus it was weeks later that the event returned for the writer, such that in the basement of a local library he discovered the mated headlines of the *New York Times* from October 4, 1951. DeLillo's foray into the archives despite "the ruthless forgetting" inherent in the contemporary environment is symptomatic of *Underworld's* unsheathing "the events and documents of the past [with] a clarity and intactness," to borrow DeLillo's words, amid its simultaneous display of the culture's drive to "disremember the past" (7).

As with the standard literary-critical appropriation of DeLillo's oeuvre for postmodernism, the almost-universal critical claim of *Underworld* for "historiographic metafiction"—what Linda Hutcheon famously defined as the key feature of postmodernism—obscures the novel's articulation of a politics of truth. Incisively arguing that *Underworld* produces a critical historiography, Molly Wallace quotes Hutcheon to underscore the novel's "alternative representation" of the past; it "comment[s]...on the production of history as commodity" and "foregrounds the postmodern epistemological questioning of the nature of historical knowledge" (380). Along the same lines, Kathleen Fitzpatrick categorizes *Underworld* as historiographic metafiction in that it "interacts with" historical traces in the present and "comments on the natures of both history and narrative" (151). As with *Americana* and *Libra*, I hope to show that DeLillo more than "comments on," "foregrounds," or, in Hutcheon's own words, "problematizes the nature and status of our information about the past" (5). Both Wallace's and Fitzpatrick's critical analyses of commodified histories and "reified histories" focus on *Underworld's* deconstruction of Cold War history and of the traditional story of self-making, respectively. These aspects of *Underworld's* probe of mythic history are central concerns, which rightly have been much studied.

Yet little critical attention has been devoted to the ultimate vile legacy of the Cold War that *Underworld* excavates straight from documentary details of the atomic testing era: a poisoned earth and poisoned citizens. DeLillo does not merely call ironic attention to conventional representations of history. As in *Americana* and *Libra*, he exhumes evidence of government-sanctioned violence to revise mythic history—an intentional and particular use of material history that remains virtually unacknowledged. DeLillo not only ties, as

Fitzpatrick puts it, "the Cold War's logic of destruction to the refuse and decay of American culture" but also causally connects that logic to the utterly real decay of human health and the environment. And DeLillo revises another articulation of the myth of American innocence, the myth of the West as virgin land—the persistent notion that American life and character is shaped by western migration. That geographical movement west is also a temporal movement away from history is manifest in the idea that the westward course of empire—from England across the ocean to America, and then across America to the Pacific—corresponds to progress for civilization. Central to this trope is the Western "myth of the garden": the West as a natural, regenerative, agrarian utopia.[14]

The cognitive dissonance between mythic history and actual history in DeLillo often corresponds to westward migration: his protagonists in *Americana, End Zone, Running Dog, Libra*, and *Underworld* all move "westward…to escape the hard-luck past with its gray streets," paradoxically engaging in oedipal journeys of self-discovery (*Underworld* 90). Their passages, which originate in New York and cease in Texas, Arizona, California—always the American desert—underscore the persistent hope that westward migration can raze the past. *Americana* and *Underworld* most clearly depict this enduring myth alongside its repeated unraveling. *Americana*'s David Bell asserts, "Fragmentation, the settling of a myth into its component parts, had come to the West quite early" (145). In *Underworld* as well, DeLillo personifies America's westward expansion in a protagonist who is microcosmic of America as a whole. *Underworld*'s Nick Shay, like David, is unable to find "the beginning of time"; he can return only to his personal past, just as America can return only to hers (*Americana* 197). Nick, his brother, his mother, and his ex-lover all go west. Separately, they leave New York for better jobs and new lives in Arizona and New Mexico. The Shay brothers work in waste management and nuclear weapons, respectively, and represent what *Underworld* calls "the fusion of two streams of history, weapons and waste" (751), which converge in the American West. The toxic pollution of their industrial practices, however, belies the myth of the West as a life-nourishing garden. As Nick's tainted past haunts him, so the national past infects its present. In DeLillo's hands, the myth of rebirth in the American West is shattered by the spectral and material demons of history, foremost of which is the human cost of empire building.

Underworld's narrative proper begins in the desert, where two former lovers, Nick Shay and Klara Sax, encounter one another for the first time in 40 years following their separate departures from the Bronx. Nick was raised as a poor city kid with a mostly absent father. Nick's teenage years were spent on the streets with his friends, occasionally working temporary manual labor jobs. At 17, he has an affair with the older, married Klara Sax. This same year, he shoots an acquaintance, a heroin addict, in a sort of accidental murder, which initiates his leaving the city. After his arrest, he is sent to a Jesuit center near the Canadian border—a place for "poor city kids who showed promise...those who were bright but unstable" (539)—and there educated and straightened out.

Now, at 57, Nick is an executive in a Phoenix-based firm that handles waste management; he convinces himself that the teeming ghosts of his past are far behind him. He "drinks soy milk and run[s] the metric mile" on streets that he calls "westward dreams, the kind of place my father could have taken us half a century earlier, lightward and westward" (89). Nick's sanguine view of westward movement speaks to a tradition inherent in the American psyche; the western frontier, according to the historian Richard Slotkin, "symbolize[s] a national past because its major themes—emigration in the quest for new and better things—had close cognates in the experiences of mobility and displacement that belonged both to foreign immigrants and to internal migrants in an industrializing and urbanizing nation" (*Gunfighter* 638). In this sense, Nick, the son of Italian and Irish immigrant parents and an internal migrant himself, is evocative of America. In the tradition of his ancestors, Nick repeatedly describes his move west as a flight both from his past and the national past: "The only ghosts I let in are local ones...New York ghosts in every case....the ghosts are walking the halls. But not these halls and not this house. They're all back there in those railroad rooms at the narrow end of the night" (82, 810). He further claims, "And I like the way history did not run loose here. They segregated visible history. They caged it, funded and bronzed it, they enshrined it carefully in museums and plazas and memorial parks" (86). The eastern city of wandering ghosts in small rooms is distant from the West—a place of open, public, safely entombed history. Such "visible history," however, suggests an invisible history, or what a character in *Great Jones Street* calls "latent history": "events that definitely took place but remai[n] unseen and unremarked on...Real events that go unrecorded [which] are often more important than recorded events" (74). This East-West delineation of (in)visible history feeds the mythology of the West as virgin land, free from the history that both individual and nation wish to bury—what is called elsewhere in the novel "underhistory."

The prologue of the novel, set at the 1951 playoff game between the Giants and the Dodgers in New York, inaugurates *Underworld*'s central discrimination between visible, public history and its latent, covert counterpart. The story alternates between the broadcast commentary of the game, delivered by sportscaster Russ Hodges, and "the narrative that lives in the spaces of the official play-by-play," foreshadowing the "interlinear notes" within *Underworld* (27). The headline of the next day's *New York Times* records the official history of October 3, 1951: "The Shot Heard 'Round the World" refers to both the Bobby Thomson homer that won the Giants the pennant and the detonation of the Soviet A-bomb. Yet this visible, mythic history belies the social underhistory of America's national pastime and the secret political history of the Cold War, which DeLillo's rendition of the game spotlights. In the prologue, latent history is narratively embryonic. A struggle in the stands for the homerun ball between a black teenager and a middle-aged white man continues in the New York streets outside the stadium and climaxes in a chase and standoff fraught with racial tension. The Soviets explode an atomic bomb at a secret site inside their own borders. However, the ensuing chapters depict racial and class tension surfacing in the 1950s and in the latter decades of the century, and the novel articulates the lethal consequences of the Cold War in increasingly trenchant ways.

The text focalizes the latent history of October 3, 1951, significantly through J. Edgar Hoover (director of the FBI), whose sinister perspective on the moment is a quiet counterpart to Russ Hodges' hoarse and triumphant broadcast. During the game, an FBI agent surreptitiously conveys news of the Soviet Union's successful nuclear test to spectator Hoover. He imagines "the lonely tower standing on the Kazakh Test Site....What secret history are they writing?...This is what he knows, that the genius of the bomb is...in the occasion it creates for new secrets. For every atmospheric blast...a hundred plots go underground, to spawn and skein" (51). As *Underworld* develops, the reader becomes privy to some of the secrets and underground plots that make up latent history—from the baleful designs of weapons manufacturers who work at secret sites "somewhere under the gypsum hills of southern New Mexico" (401) to the radioactive waste laid by both American and Soviet bombs that travels "downwind," wreaking havoc in the bodies and lives of ordinary citizens.

Through exploiting the historical connection among consumerism, munitions, and war, *Underworld* insists that the latent history of Bell's so-called "dream of the good life" is the waste material of culture—in all senses of the word *waste*. "Waste is an interesting word," says the narrator, "that you can trace through Old English and Old Norse back to the Latin, finding such derivatives as empty, void, vanish and devastate" (120). Incrementally, *Underworld* elaborates the devolution of both consumption and weapons to waste. The fans at the baseball game drop paper everywhere: "The contagion of paper—it is giddy" (38). One fan tears pages out of his copy of *Life* magazine, which

> keep falling. Baby food, instant coffee, encyclopedias and cars, waffle irons and shampoos and blended whiskeys....the resplendent products, how the dazzle of a Packard car is repeated in the feature story about the art treasures of the Prado....Rubens and Titian and Playtex and Motorola....In a country that's in a hurry to make the future, the names attached to the products are an enduring reassurance. Johnson and Johnson and Quaker State and RCA Victor and Burlington Mills and Bristol-Myers and General Motors. (39)

With its emphasis of proliferating American consumer products, this seminal passage connotes the geopolitical reality of the game's 1951 setting, in which the Marshall Plan has simultaneously secured a European market for US exports and forestalled communism in Western Europe by its massive contribution to industrial and military expenditures there. Yet DeLillo portrays the result—a boom domestic economy under a nuclear umbrella—as literal waste: the falling paper. Later chapters set in the 1990s reveal the future of the "resplendent products": a refuse heap that in ensuing decades exhausts the world's landfills, is processed in recycling centers, and is laden upon a mysterious ship that travels from port to port, seeking to deposit its toxic cargo.

Underworld's narrative structure implies its truth-telling project. Following the 1951 prologue, the story spirals backward from 1992 to 1951 and concludes with an epilogue, "Das Kapital," that returns to 1990s. One reads *Underworld*'s 1950s chapters, then, through the retrospective lens that introduces and concludes the novel. This view makes this early scene a portentous one that foretells two long-standing, profound implications of "waste" in terms of "vanish and devastate." The flip side of the optimistic bounty of the 1950s becomes in the 1980s and 1990s a garbage problem of enormous—and toxic—proportions. At the end of the twentieth century, "vacated military bases are converted to landfill use" and there is "a bunker system under a mountain in Nevada that will or will not accommodate thousands of steel canisters of radioactive waste for ten thousand years" (804). At this contemporary moment, waste—which recalls the vivid profusion of paper and disposable products in the prologue scene—occupies our physical underworld, pervading the planet and endangering its inhabitants. Moreover, some of the same companies that promise better living through chemistry effect mass death through chemistry. A later scene in the novel depicts the future of "the names attached to the products": "Dow Day" in Madison, Wisconsin—October 18, 1967—is "a protest against Dow Chemical, whose recruiters were active on campus and whose products included a new and improved form of napalm with a polystyrene additive that made jellied matter cling more firmly to human flesh" (599). That is, rather than vanishing, Cold War waste devastates both land and citizens. The fans' waste is further connected to the bomb both by the fact that their celebration precisely coincides with its detonation in the USSR and by the singular transformation of the falling waste into the bomb: a magazine page that has lit upon Hoover's shoulder turns out to be a reproduction of the Peter Brueghel painting *The Triumph of Death*. Staring at this "landscape of visionary havoc and ruin.... Terror universal...the raven perched on the white nag's rump, black and white forever, and he thinks of...the bomb" (41, 50). Thus ensues the narrative's mutating deathscape: from the Brueghel painting to Hoover's own imagination of the Soviet bomb site, to the "downwinders" in the American desert, to the corporeal reality the epilogue reveals, wherein the connection between weapons and waste becomes gruesomely palpable.

The "happy garbage" the fans drop—"pocket litter, personal waste, a thing that carries a shadow identity"—insinuates a latent history that becomes more visible in advanced decades as DeLillo continues to link waste with weapons of mass destruction (45). Hundreds of pages later, Matt Shay, Nick's younger brother, and his colleagues (called "bombheads") reveal the name of the western desert underground where they do "weapons work but of the soft-core type": "The Pocket." Like the "pocket litter," the Pocket and its inhabitants are defined by "shadow identity": Matt "wanted to do weapons" because he had wanted "the identity, the sense of honing his silhouette, knowing himself better—a secret installation in the desert" (402). He can be known only as a silhouette, an outline that circumscribes a dark, occluded mass. Here Matt conflates his identity with the Pocket: both are the "secret installation in the desert." The Pocket—named after "the pocket gopher that lives in tunnels it frantically digs under the furrowed dunes" (402)—conceals weapons in the desert, as Nick's firm, Waste Containment, buries waste in desert landfills, "engineered crater[s] five hundred feet deep" (285). The purpose of both types of desert installations—and the meaning of "waste management"—is to keep the latent history of the Cold War period and its boom economy underground: the West is the literal receptacle of its detritus.

DeLillo excavates chilling historical truths about the atomic testing era, however, which show how that latent history becomes manifest in the citizens who live downwind of the test sites just outside the Pocket—who "have a name, incidentally, that totally defines their existence...Downwinders." Like the workers at the Nevada Test Site during the atomic testing era of aboveground shots and the atomic veterans who participated in nuclear atmospheric testing, downwinders were exposed to fallout—waste, that is—from the test bombs. Downwinder accounts throughout *Underworld* overlap with oral histories from photojournalist Carole Gallagher's documentary book, *American Ground Zero: The Secret Nuclear War* (published in 1993), from which DeLillo apparently crafted the details of the "secret" history of the downwinders. A former New York photographer, Gallagher spent seven years interviewing and photographing radiation survivors in the southwestern United States, including dairy farmers, ranchers, professors, Native Americans, housewives, soldiers, artists, and shepherds. What this diverse population has in common are leukemias, brain tumors, birth defects, diabetes, sterility, miscarriages, thyroid cancers, the death of children, medical bills, and funerals. *Underworld*'s Eric Deming, Matt Shay's colleague at the Pocket, correctly adds to the list "multiple myelomas, kidney failures," "great red boils [and] coughing up handfuls of blood"; their afflicted bodies constitute, in part, the no-longer-invisible waste from the test bombs (405–19). As Gallagher elaborates, "The more than 760 announced nuclear explosions always were detonated when the wind [was] blowing toward Utah." In one "'top secret' AEC [Atomic Energy Commission] memo," she discovers, "the people living downwind...were described as a 'low-use segment of the population'" (xxxii, xxiii). Similarly, Deming narrates, "They let the fallout drift to Utah, where kids are getting born with their bladders backwards"; and Bonnie Daniels, a Test Site worker, describes her son: "His bladder is backwards" (quoted in Gallagher 47). Of a fictional atomic veteran, Deming says, "You wake up one day a few years later, all your inner organs are fused. It's one big jellied lump" (*Underworld* 405–10). Gallagher interviewee Grace Swarzbaugh relates the account of her husband, who "worked at the Nevada Site right from the day it opened for business": exploratory surgery found that "his whole insides...just came together, just looked like a big bowl of solid Jello. There was nothing they could do for him" (quoted in Gallagher 43). In 1994, the year after Gallagher's book was published, the US government declassified AEC documents from 1951 to 1962 that further corroborate the testimony Gallagher records. Three years after that, in 1997, the story was reported in the mainstream press, by which time *Underworld* was in press.[15]

In implicit contrast to the Western segregation of "visible history" that Nick Shay celebrates—from tourist destinations to gleaming recycling plants—the devastated downwinders are part of the latent history of the Cold War. Gallagher's book, renowned among scholars of atomic testing era, testifies to the appalling truth of what Deming calls "the latest secret" about the AEC, "an old thing just now surfacing...something that's more or less out in the open but at the same time...Secret. Untalked about. Hushed up" (*Underworld* 405). The US government, he adds, "knew the tests weren't safe but they went ahead anyway. They marched troops to zero point after the detonations. They sent manned aircraft through radiation clouds....They did this deliberately, without telling people what the risks were. They exposed troops to the atomic flash and some of them were given protective eye filters and some were not" (417). Indeed, as Gallagher documents, the AEC repeatedly told downwinders and test site workers that "there is no danger" (quoted in Gallagher xxi), although "the government admitted finally that they had known of the dangers of radiation since the early forties. They knew it caused cancers, they knew it could cause birth defects, but they felt it was worth the sacrifice of a few men for the good of the country" (Pat Broudy, widow of an atomic veteran, quoted in Gallagher 91). Yet the Compensation Act, finally introduced to Congress in the 1980s, never passed; and it "provided enormous loopholes and escapes from liability" (Gallagher xxvii). In *Underworld*, Eric, Matt, and their bombhead colleagues must remain complicit in this same breed of denial if they are to continue to design nuclear weapons. Matt "wanted to call his brother many times...let him know that the kid was doing important work but that it troubled him now and then...maybe he would give the kid advice about the moral and ethical aspects of this kind of work....Matt didn't make the call" (416). The post–Cold War outlook *Underworld* represents is echoed in Gallagher's conclusion: "Deadened by fifty years of nuclearism, we may have mutated into a nation of 'good Germans' unwilling to see" (xxxiii).

These aspects of *Underworld* have been misinterpreted by Tony Tanner as "playing at dread, thereby devaluing it," emblematic of the novel's "paranoia" (138). Accusing DeLillo of "atrocity tourism," Tanner argued that "a direct report from Beirut by Robert Fisk of the London *Independent* has far more impact" than the "bad news" that DeLillo "heap[s] up" (135); this, finally, misses the pith altogether. DeLillo is not nearly as interested in affecting his reader with atrocities—which are already exhaustively and graphically documented by the "news" and historians—as he is in probing the mindsets that perpetuate the atrocities and tacitly accept their existence.

For in the interior monologues and dialogue of the bombheads, DeLillo portrays not merely the "secrets" about the bomb but the effect of those secrets on knowing citizens. As Deming presses upon Matt Shay,

> "Even though huge amounts of territory were affected and large numbers of people were exposed, it remains a major secret to this day."
> "So secret it may not be true," Matt said.
> "Do you believe it's true?"
> "I believe mistakes were made...Do you believe it?"...
> "It's awfully, I don't know."
> "Of course. It's very hard to believe. That's why I don't believe it"...
> "I think oddly of my mom, who was a super sensible lady and used to wear rubber gloves to do the dinner dishes back in the placid days when we were bombing our own people." (418–19)

Waste, then, in *Underworld* is not simply the suppressed content of visible history; but *waste management* is a model for the containment of latent historical material and the processes by which mythic history—in this case, a certain Orwellian mentality—is created and sustained.

It is only at the novel's very end—after dismantling the traces that mythic history has left in the present, laying bare the statist perspective and complicit players in commodified histories (weapons and waste manufacturers) and deconstructing their narratives—does *Underworld* bring the reader into direct contact with human results of the fallout from "five hundred nuclear explosions at the test site" during the Cold War in Kazakhstan; rather than irony, the tone simply is sober. "There is a long low room of display cases filled with fetuses....There is the two-headed specimen. There is the single head that is twice the size of the body. There is the normal head that is located in the wrong place, perched on the right shoulder...there is the cyclops. The eye centered, the ears below the chin, the mouth completely missing. Brain also missing" (799). Here DeLillo "finds," as he puts it, a very particular "language that can be a counterhistory" to "forgetting." In a May

2007 public interview with DeLillo, the *New York Times Magazine* interviewer Gerald Marzorati called such language *"visual"*—DeLillo's singular manner of describing images—the way something actually *looks*, whether it be a film, painting, sculpture, or human bodies ravaged by nuclear fallout. A clinic for downwinders of the former Soviet Union succeeds the fetus display cases; here is

> the boy with skin where his eyes ought to be, a bolus of spongy flesh, oddly like a mushroom cap, springing from each brow…the bald-headed children…the man with the growth beneath his chin, a thing with a life of its own, embryonic and pulsing…the dwarf girl…the woman with features intact but only half a face somehow.…The clinic has disfigurations, leukemias, thyroid cancers, immune systems that do not function. (800)

What has been lost in the last half-century, DeLillo suggests, is the ignorance of the truth beneath the symbols: the ignorance that allowed us to invest optimistically in the American dream, to consume resplendent products that produced happy garbage, and to feel that Americans possessed "a purpose, a destination" without consequences. The latent history of the Cold War period at midcentury was only "unconscious fear" (171). In the 1990s that history comes home to roost in the form of toxic garbage and devastated human bodies. As Marian Shay, Nick's wife, muses, "the difference" between the 1950s and the 1990s is "less in lost things than in knowledge become suspicious and alert.… She had a garden hose but did not drink from it and did not allow her kids to drink from it" (165).

Reading *Underworld*'s downwinder accounts against Marian Shay's rumination intimates DeLillo's revision of the myth of the American West as a garden and as "virgin land." Central to the nineteenth-century mythology of the West was the idea that beyond the eastern cities "lay the West, a realm where nature loomed larger than civilization" (Smith 48). In his meditations upon the West, Walt Whitman "dwelt with ecstasy" upon the Western life that included a "clean and sweet blood…litheness, majestic faces, clear eyes, and perfect physique there" (Whitman 183). This vision sharply contrasts the depiction both of the ailing downwinders living in DeLillo's late-twentieth-century American West and that of Arizona "nature" by Marian Shay: water that is unpotable.[16]

In fact, DeLillo inverts this mythological perspective of the American West altogether. All descriptions of nature in the novel, and certainly of the natural West, depict the waste material of American civilization—that is, of a realm where civilization looms larger than nature. For Marian's birthday, Nick gives her a balloon ride over the desert. But the "first light, a foil shimmer at the desert's edge," the "open earth, bone brown and deep in shadow" that delights Marian, is not the pith of the gift. "Ain't seen nothing yet," Nick tells her. The climax of the desert balloon ride is gliding over Klara Sax's painted bombers; now a famous artist, Klara has made them an installation, "saving them from the cutter's torch" by painting them in gallons of brightly colored paint. Nick says they are "a heart-shaking thing to see," "a power in the earth" that he depicts as the ruins of American civilization. He wonders if the bombers—which comprise, in part, the refuse of the Cold War—are "visible from space like the land art of some lost Andean people" (77, 123–26).

In another scene, Nick's colleague at Waste Containment Brian Glassic similarly envisions waste as the great ruins of our civilization. He contemplates a landfill: "It was science fiction and prehistory, garbage arriving twenty-four hours a day...he imagined he was watching the construction of the Great Pyramid at Giza—only this was twenty-five times bigger, with tanker trucks spraying perfumed water on the approach roads" (184). Nick and Brian's observations directly invert the American realm in which nature looms larger than civilization and indicate that, to borrow reviewer Steffen Hantke's words, "nature has long ceased to compete with this material manifestation of human history" (2). At the vision of the landfill, Brian is stung with "enlightenment" about the meaning of his job in waste management, realizing he deals in "people's habits and impulses...certainly their excesses and indulgences" (184). To manage waste is in fact to treat latent history because waste is the overflow of America, that which exposes us at our core.[17]

At the century's (and the novel's) end, nature is merely a garnish to civilization: Nick drives with his granddaughter "past the Indian tribe streets" into the desert to visit "the sage gray truss of the waste facility and the planes in their landing patterns," to which "the showy desert plants" are decoration, "spilling over the pastel walls above the parking area" (805). Similar to Brian, Nick feels that a sacredness envelops the waste. His granddaughter, Sunny, "loves this place and so do the other kids who come with their parents or teachers to stand on the catwalk and visit the exhibits. Brightness streams from skylights down to the floor of the shed, falling on the tall machines with a numinous glow. Maybe we feel a reverence for waste, for the redemptive qualities of the things we use and discard" (809). Whitman (along with his colonialist predecessors, his generation, and future generations) foresaw "immense spiritual results, future years, inland, spread there each side of the Anahuacs" (183). Such repercussions from westward migration ensue, in DeLillo's vision of America at the end of the millennium, from waste. "Waste is a religious thing," Nick asserts. "We entomb contaminated waste with a sense of reverence and dread. It is necessary to respect what we discard" (88).

That *Underworld*'s western residents pay homage to the desert recycling facility suggests that the mythology of western regeneration is extant and yet is undermined by the "dark underside of human consumer consciousness" (*White Noise* 259). In *Underworld*, civilization is not given an opportunity for rebirth through virgin land. Rather, civilization is recycled through technology. DeLillo's revision of the myth of the American West is a consummate illustration of a notion his 1984 novel *White Noise* advances, that "technology is lust removed from nature" (285). In the postmodern world, humankind's desire for renewal can no longer be placed in nature, which civilization has contaminated and all but annihilated. Instead, lust for redemption can be displaced onto technology.[18] Yet *Underworld*'s portraits of waste as sacred, of recycling garbage as renewing to the spirit, and of the notion that we can use nuclear weapons to destroy the most dangerous waste that exists are counterpoised to the voluminous amounts of toxic waste ubiquitous throughout. The potentially redemptive aspects of waste function as a dire hope against hope that the deadly waste our century has produced will not, in fact, consume our bodies and our habitable planet.

Like the western desert he inhabits, gorged with the virulent and interminable refuse of American history, Nick is neither free nor segregated from his past. At the novel's end, he confesses, "I long for the days of disorder. I want them back, the days when I was alive on the earth, rippling in the quick of my skin, heedless and real. This is what I long for, the breach of peace, the days of disarray when I walked real streets" (810). If, as his friends assert, Nick Shay "has fallen from grace" (95), it is only because he has pursued the American myth of better living through westward migration. Like all romantic myths in DeLillo, it cannot be sustained because it is based in a profane origin. Life doesn't get better in the West; it just gets recycled. Furthermore, as Nick and Sunny's drive "past the Indian tribe streets" insinuates, just as the land was not "virgin" in the nineteenth century but peopled for ages with Native Americans who suffered brutal consequences of manifest destiny, it was not innocent during the 1950s but the site of waste-making bombs. Nick's fall from grace lies not in his moving west but in the doomed hope that this flight could unleash him from his past. Likewise, the dangerous past of the Cold War remains, in the form of waste—"waste is the secret history, the underhistory, the way archeologists dig out the history of early cultures, every sort of bone heap and broken tool, literally from under the ground" (791). Waste is both the content and processing of latent history. These two meanings of waste are singularly embodied in Nick, who maintains his personal life by containing his past and maintains his professional life by containing—burying, recycling, destroying—the poisonous past of the nation. The novel's archeological excavation of the underworld of American history and culture, as well as of Nick's self, reveals the persistence and indissolubility of these national and individual histories.

DeLillo's attention in *Underworld* to the downwinders and the environment—the collateral damage of the Cold War—and the related secret political history of the Cold War era constitutes both his most sustained engagement of empirical history and his most trenchant critique of official history to date. Each of DeLillo's Cold War–era novels tenders, in his own words, "a version of the past that escapes the coils of established history and biography" ("The Power of History" 60); and DeLillo's counterhistorical sensibilities, inchoate in *Americana* and developed in *Libra*, fully ripen in *Underworld*. Fitzpatrick also argues that *Underworld* "dismantles the genre of historiographic metafiction"; "working to excavate and deconstruct the traces a reified history has left in the present," it "point[s] out that many of those narratives are lies" (159). One can only deconstruct a lie, however, by countering it with truth: that is how, as Fitzpatrick puts it, DeLillo "unmakes" "the mythic structures of the Cold War itself—the epic battle between good and evil" (152). What collapses this binary is the truth *Underworld* reveals of "downwinders" in the United States and the former USSR—the similar desert testing grounds and strategies of "bombing our own people." DeLillo unravels mythic history by telling the truth.

CHAPTER 3

The Other Side of *Paradise*: Toni Morrison's (Un)Making of Mythic History

In his unmaking mythic history by telling the truth, DeLillo has more in common with contemporary colleague Toni Morrison than with Thomas Pynchon, for example, whose two most recent historical novels—*Mason and Dixon* (1997) and *Against the Day* (2006)— are quintessential historiographic metafiction. Morrison's historical novels, not unlike DeLillo's, all began with historical anecdotes she discovered while editing *The Black Book* (1974)—an archival collection of African American history. Although, like DeLillo, Morrison is often labeled "postmodern," she insistently engages empirical history, writing novels that are a rejoinder to a postmodern sense of history. *Paradise* (1998), Morrison's seventh novel and her first since becoming the first African American woman to win the Nobel Prize in Literature (1993), was greeted with the most mixed reviews of the author's three-decade career. Reviewers criticized the unconvincing logic of its "war between men and women," its "rigid and legalistic" male-female dichotomy that results in "a contrived, formulaic book." A journal review concludes, "Morrison's new novel falls prey to... one of paradise's shortcomings as a concept": "It's too schematic....Virtue and vice seem to have been rigorously sorted along the convenient divide of gender; all the women are good, all the men bad."[1] Such comments, however, overlook the novel's self-consciousness of its own dynamic: the gender dichotomy is only one part of a larger series of oppositions that the novel stages and then explodes for its central project of interrogating the processes by which popular national histories are made and sustained.[2] Indeed, through its schematic account of gender and racial oppositions and its strategies of self-referential inversions and displacements, *Paradise* denotes

the unsettling paradox of a nation born as the first modern democracy that excluded whole populations from its citizenry based upon
precisely such "rigid and legalistic" constructions of identity. More
recently, Katrine Dalsgård has incisively identified this incongruity as
Morrison's deconstruction of America's original ideal of exceptionalism, which, *Paradise* shows, "is inevitably entwined with a violent
marginalization of its non-exceptionalist other" (237). Yet Morrison
is also deeply interested in the means by which certain versions of
history—including but not limited to the exceptionalist paradigm—
become master narratives. Thus *Paradise* deconstructs certain founding American narratives in the service of an overarching design that
probes the workings of narrating the nation.

Critics have universally recognized Morrison for redressing the
limited perspectives of mainstream US history by reclaiming the
narratives of African American history, often from a female point
of view. To take only the most famous example, *Beloved* draws on
the little-known story of an escaped female slave and her relationship
to motherhood, family, and community during the antebellum and
post–Civil War period. Yet I argue that *Paradise* extends this earlier
genre of the historical revision, creating a springboard for the novel's metahistorical argument about traditional national history and
the politics of truth it involves—an argument, that is, that probes
the ways in which truth is linked to systems of power that produce
and sustain it. The title of Morrison's most recent novel evokes various tropes for the United States that mainstream literary history has
produced: the American Adam—an embodied state of innocence,
free from the burden of history; Virgin Land—an uninhabited and
unspoiled wilderness; the Garden—a natural, regenerative, agrarian
utopia. The title is the novel's first hint that, unlike Morrison's previous historical works, this text explores not only a particular historical
moment but also a particular national ideal—and the way in which
national history itself becomes inscribed in our collective imagination
as mythic history. *Paradise* scrutinizes the tropes of national mythic
history, working to reveal not only its sins of omission and exclusion but also its narrative processes. *Paradise* combines factual and
experiential truths from African American history to construct an
insistent countermemory to national American mythologies in order
to investigate the relationship of truth both to history (the complex
of actual events as well as that which becomes the sanctioned version of the past) and to myth (those stories we tell ourselves about
what has happened). Specifically, *Paradise* explores the ways in which
truths are constituted, maintained, and subjugated in the process of

mythologizing history, a process Morrison suggests is endemic to national community.

PARADISE INVERTED: THE GENEALOGIST'S COUNTERNARRATIVE

Morrison creates in *Paradise* a microcosm of America in the uto-pian all-black community of Ruby, Oklahoma. As with *Beloved* and *Jazz*—the two other novels in her trilogy of excessive love—Mor-rison's conception of the novel developed from kernels rooted in nineteenth-century African American history that center on slaves or descendants of slaves fleeing the rampant, violent racism of the South.[3] *Beloved*'s Sethe flees her Kentucky slave owner in 1855; and in what becomes a backdrop for *Paradise*, Morrison writes in *Jazz*, "The wave of black people running from want and violence crested in the 1870s; the '80s; the '90s but was a steady stream in 1906 when Joe and Violet joined it" (33). The historical timeline of *Paradise*, though not the narrative, begins in the "crest" of that flight. By situating the flight this time as a specifically north*west-ern* exodus, Morrison inscribes African Americans in the US mythic history of westward migration. "So far from being the bucolic Utopia of Rodgers and Hammerstein," writes Christopher Hitchens, "[Oklahoma] was the land of heartbreak for the free black citizens who voyaged there, post-Reconstruction, to set up 26 all-black towns" (144). Founded by descendants of Southern blacks who were effectively re-enslaved during the post-Reconstruction era through the sharecropping system and adamant white determination to block them from economic and political enfranchisement by legal and ille-gal means, Ruby is a paradise for its inhabitants that is also estab-lished on the principle of exclusivity. The founding families of Ruby are distinguished by their impeccable dark skin, which is evidence that they have not been corrupted by "racial tampering." The grand-fathers of Ruby's citizens—always referred to by the community as the "Old Fathers"—fled the white terrorism of the South, only to be rejected by a prosperous settlement of light-skinned blacks, appropri-ately called "Fairly." This rebuff, known as the "Disallowing" by the townspeople, is the historical moment that provides the impetus for migrating westward to found the township of Haven and, later, for moving "farther westward" to found Ruby (194). As the novel pro-gresses, Morrison explores several issues central to African American history of the late nineteenth and twentieth centuries, from the Booker T. Washington–W. E. B. DuBois rift to the rifts occasioned by the Black Power movement of the 1960s and civil rights activism to the Vietnam War's decimation of young black men.[4]

Morrison uses this past, however, as the backdrop to her more urgent subject in *Paradise*: the relationship of history and myth to the practices of exclusion that have characterized notions of America *as* paradise, as well as explorations of paradise *within* America. As if taking a cue from Richard Wright, who wrote, "The Negro is America's metaphor,"[5] *Paradise* considers the way in which a fantasy of black nationhood, arising from a mythology and history that correspond to the evolution of the United States, devolves into a dystopia. Morrison thus interprets a metaphor for America with which its colonizers characterized it for centuries: "paradise." If (as Homi Bhabha claims) "the entitlement of the nation is its metaphor," in *Paradise*, Morrison questions the terms of America's entitlement. The post-Reconstruction flight of ex-slaves northwestward from which *Paradise* begins reflects Bhabha's conceptual framework of the modern nation that emerges from mass migrations and "fills the void left in the uprooting of communities and kin." This "'middle passage' of contemporary culture, as with slavery itself, is a process of displacement and disjunction." Increasingly then, "'national' cultures are being produced from the perspective of disenfranchised minorities," resulting in contemporary "counter-narratives of the nation that continually evoke and erase its totalizing boundaries—both actual and conceptual" (*Location* 139–49, 5–6). Through precisely such an evocative and deconstructive counternarrative, *Paradise* investigates the ways in which the nation becomes home to its people through their investment in the nation's founding metaphor.

As in her critical monograph *Playing in the Dark* (1990), Morrison is keenly attuned to the contested conceptual territory of America, and she uses African American history to critique it. Thus the black skin of Ruby's citizens, termed "8-rock" for "a deep deep level in the coal mines," inverts the historical landmark of Plymouth Rock; Ruby's Old Fathers are avatars of none other than the founding fathers of the United States. These terms function as only two in a series of inverted echoes of the traditional history of America that *Paradise* dramatizes. The biblical language that Morrison re-creates for her story further evokes Puritan America. Like the early English immigrants, the 8-rocks create a harbor from persecution that is maintained by geographic and cultural isolation and, when needed, violence against violence, committed by men who "bowed to no one [and] knelt only to their Maker." "Unique and isolated," "free and protected," Ruby is "justifiably pleased with itself" (99, 8). Although the 8-rocks seek to build a haven that will allow them to pursue their ideals in freedom, it is a freedom maintained by enforcing their own disallowings. In an inversion of the United States' one-drop rule, the town obeys an unspoken "blood rule" that forbids its members to marry light-skinned people and an even more insidious practice of maintaining an ideal of female purity that both reproduces the hegemonic nineteenth-century US "Cult of True Womanhood" and critiques it through the violent annihilation of a community of dispossessed women who inhabit "the Convent," a neighboring dilapidated mansion. That the mansion was formerly a Catholic school for Native American girls explains the nomenclature, but more importantly it functions as another echo of the nation's suppressed history: the removals and forced assimilations of Native Americans. Previously in residence at the Convent were Native American girls who "whisper[ed] to each other in a language the sisters had forbidden them to use" and who "softly s[ang] forbidden Algonquian lullabies" (229, 237). The founding fathers of Ruby reproduce the logic of discrimination endemic to the nation's history by intercalating their own repressed fears and inability to live up to the austere moral code of their haven into their perception of occurrences in town and at the Convent. Armed with invented dark myths about the Convent women, they effectively execute a lynching in which the perpetrators, not the victims, are all black men. Turning traditional accounts of US history on their head, the novel introduces its larger interrogation of national history making and its broader exploration of the possibilities for telling historical truth.

Paradise (un)makes two seminal (African) American mythic histories: spiritual regeneration in the American West and an idealized femininity.[6] These two mythologies intersect in the origin of Ruby, founded "two hundred and forty miles west" of the "dreamtown" of Haven—itself "way west of the unassigned lands." In 1952, "when all their dreams outstretched the men who made them," the sons of Old Fathers establish Ruby expressly to rebirth the lost original "idea" of Haven, to which they have been devoted all their lives (10, 6). Ruby is defined explicitly by a conservative and domestic vision of womanhood, continually evoked by its name, given to it after a recently deceased sister and mother (6, 14). *Paradise* simultaneously betrays the genuine investment of African Americans in US mythic histories of the West and of femininity and deconstructs them as master narratives. For vital to the national community enacted by *Paradise* is a dialectic between memory and forgetting, which Bhabha identifies as essential to nationhood. "It is the will to nationhood that unifies historical memory and secures present-day consent." This will "is itself the site of a strange forgetting of the history of the nation's past: the violence involved in establishing the nation's writ. It is this forgetting…that constitutes the *beginning* of the nation's narrative." The discourse of national community, that is, requires a forgetting—or omitting—"the perplexed histories of the living people, their cultures of survival and resistance" (149, 159–61). Through baring the violence, isolation, and contradictions involved in maintaining a paradisiacal community, *Paradise* refigures these *sites* of "strange forgetting" as *cites* (that is, citations of) of countermemories. Its insistent narrative recuperation of fragmented, subjugated voices stresses a slippage between written and oral stories and between memory and forgetting—what Bhabha calls "the 'obligation to forget,' or forgetting to remember" (160).

By illustrating the subjectivity, distortions, and abuses of power to which oral history is vulnerable, Morrison applies to oral history the precise critical examination to which written history has been particularly subject in recent decades. In this sense, *Paradise* opens the door for a reassessment of contemporary American historical novels, suggesting the limits of any critical position that overly celebrates the capacities of the oral. The novel posits history and myth as diachronic realms and employs storytelling to problematize memory and (particularly oral) narrative as legitimate acts of cultural recovery. In *Paradise*, these function in the service of the will to nationhood and hence as a site of forgetting. Morrison continually highlights the subjective aspect of memory that relies upon omission of some details to preserve others. By representing forgetting as memory's dark shadow, Morrison exposes a tension between oral and written histories and between memory and forgetting. At the same time, Morrison's treatment of the relationship between history and myth reveals both oral and written histories to be subsumed as part of American mythic history. *Paradise* thus warns of the limits of history—positivistic history as well as personal, subjective history—to convey truth. Morrison's credo—that "the crucial distinction for me is not between fact and fiction but the distinction between fiction and truth. Because fact can exist without human intelligence, but truth cannot"—is more fundamental to *Paradise* than to any of her other novels ("Site" 113). For the definitive space she carves out for truth in this novel is one in which truth is ascertained—for the reader as well as for some of the novel's characters—through wrestling with the discontinuities and competing interpretations with which the novel teems.

The methods of a lone genealogist among the citizens of Ruby serve as a model for reading *Paradise* and as a metaphor for the novel's sense of historiography: "Any footnotes, crevices or questions to be put took keen imagination and the persistence of a mind uncomfortable with oral histories. Pat had wanted proof in documents where possible to match the stories, and where proof was not available she interpreted—freely but, she thought, insightfully because she alone had the required emotional distance" (188). Patricia wrests a counternarrative to the town's mythic history through her excavation of written as well as oral narratives and her perspicacious interpretation of both. The difficulties she faces in historicizing Ruby epitomize Morrison's vision of a historiography that must deal with certain oppositions that continually break down: between oral and written narratives; between history and myth; and, most poignant for Patricia, the untenable oppositions between black and white and between subject and object. These dialectics are evocative of the "doubleness" that, Bhabha emphasizes, is fundamental to the "production of the nation as narration....The concept of 'the people' emerges," that is, "as a double narrative movement" wherein "the people are the historical 'objects' of a nationalist pedagogy" based on a "constituted historical origin *in the past*" and also "the 'subjects' of a [performative] signification that must erase any prior or originary presence of the nation-people to demonstrate the prodigious, living principles of the people as contemporaneity." Patricia's struggle in writing the genealogy of Ruby may be understood in relation to the "conceptual ambivalence of modern society [that] becomes the site of *writing the nation*" (5–6, 145–46).

If *Paradise* is Morrison's counternarrative of America, Patricia's genealogy is the counternarrative of Ruby. The "emotional distance" Pat claims she possesses is because she is the issue of her 8-rock father and his "wife of sunlight skin, of racial tampering" (197). The town's sole surviving light-skinned resident, Pat is a target of Ruby disapprobation and treated largely as an outsider. This subjectivity drives her to examine the town's stories as objects. However, given that the practices of racial exclusion central to the town's history apply to her, she is also the object of that history—a personal experience that provides her the insight necessary to penetrate the town's snarled narratives. On the one hand, the novel's endorsement of Patricia's genealogy as a truthful account of Ruby suggests the necessity of being outside the pedagogical history one writes; on the other hand, it is specifically Patricia's authorship—or her own performative history—by which the novel emphasizes the impossibility of being outside of that history. The dilemmas Pat faces in writing her genealogy as well as in her own person manifest the split between the discourses of pedagogy and performative and represent the metahistory that the novel underscores. In fact, the novel asserts a chain of counterhistories—at the core of which is Pat's carefully inscribed genealogy—that complicates all the oppositions that critics of the novel have incorrectly identified as rigidly dualistic.

Ultimately, Morrison's novel both exposes historical discourse as inherently gendered and racialized and argues for an alternative version of US history from a disenfranchised point of view that might supplement official accounts. In other words, the novel affirms knowledge as perspective and truth as meaning that can be made through a rigorous process beginning with what Morrison has called "literary archaeology": "You journey to a site to see what remains were left behind and to reconstruct the world that these remains imply" ("Site" 112). Arguing implicitly for this type of counterhistoriography, *Paradise* renders an alternative account of the past as a way of making truth meaningful outside of the dominant narrative of mythic history, inherently complicit with prevailing structures of power. Yet if Morrison's novel advocates for a kind of Foucauldian genealogy, or "effective history," her narrative also exposes the limitations of any analysis that does not take gender and race into consideration. For the novel's argument for a counterhistory finds its manifestation precisely in a female African American genealogist whose scribbled accounts consistently expose the omissions and gaps in those histories that conflate distinct political and cultural phenomena into a universal language of power.

Indeed, Patricia's iteration of Ruby can be understand as a kind of analogue to Morrison's own historical work in *Paradise*, in which she *cites* the lived experiences of African Americans in the post-Reconstruction South and West against certain *sites* of forgetting intrinsic to US mythic history. Respectively, the first and second parts of this chapter seek to illuminate two cites/sites of memory, forgetting, and nationhood with which the novel is centrally concerned: exclusions to "paradise" based on race and gender, and African American westward migration. The counterhistory that Morrison excavates and narrates in *Paradise* is, however, merely the demonstration within which her novel embeds a theory of historical truth telling that becomes clear by a juxtaposition of an accumulation of scenes. Accordingly, each of the chapter's three sections focuses around a cluster of related textual moments; and the concluding section elaborates the politics of truth claimed by the novel particularly through Patricia's genealogy.

I   MEMORY AND FORGETTING, NATIONHOOD AND HISTORICAL MEANING

Ruby's citizens record an autonomous history through imaginative workings of memory and story in order to achieve their goal of constituting a separate political sphere defined by its own unwritten laws and mythic history. The foremost of the Old Fathers, Big Papa and Big Daddy, are the grandfather and father, respectively, of what turns out to be the two leading patriarchs of Ruby, twin brothers Steward and Deacon Morgan—so named, we surmise, to be the guardians of Haven (their birthplace) and of the memory upon which it was built. "The twins were born in 1924 and heard for twenty years what the previous forty had been like. They listened to, imagined and remembered every single thing because each detail was a jolt of pleasure, erotic as a dream, out-thrilling and more purposeful than even the war they had fought in." That, "between them," the Morgans remember "everything that ever happened—things they witnessed and things they have not"—foreshadows the intimate relationship of memory, imagination, and forgetting, which Morrison emphasizes throughout (16, 13).

Two separate but overlapping memories surrounding the reasons for the exodus of Haven contradict one another, intimating the limits of memory and of the oral history that memory generates. Memory is related as both subjective—shaped and forged partly by imagination—and an unreliable indicator of historical truth. The war interrupts the twins' experience of Haven, and their return to the town does not satiate the longing that their prewar memories of it breed. "The twins stared at their dwindling postwar future and it was not hard to persuade other home boys to repeat what the Old Fathers had done in 1890." So to escape the "sheer destructive power" of "snakes, the Depression, the tax man and the railroad...fifteen families moved out of Haven...deeper into Oklahoma, as far as they could climb from the grovel contaminating the town their grandfathers had made" (16–17). This vague disintegration of Haven and ensuing desertion appears to be clarified by the nature of Ruby, the town the 15 families found. It is entirely self-sufficient and completely isolated (as was Haven initially) and therefore not subject to the fluctuations of the national economy or to the "tax man."

However, given that a later recollection by Deacon (also known as Deek) reveals "the crash [of 1929] had not touched" Haven, that in fact "in 1932 it was still thriving," and given that the twins abandon Haven in 1949—during postwar boom years—the relationship of the

Depression to the desertion is tenuous at best (108). The Morgan twins' explanation for the desertion (like the tale of the earlier Disallowing) is one of several explications in the novel for which the particulars are sketchy and even contradicted in later memories and narratives. The reader is left to infer probable causes and details of several principal moments in Ruby's history not only by adjudicating various memories and focusing on certain details while disregarding others but also by weighing each narrator's character against his or her stories. A better explanation, then, for the desertion is gleaned from the "contaminating grovel" the twins escape, which comes from the railroad that threatens Haven's isolation and hence its racial and sexual purity, allowing for the corruption of the twins' memorialized vision of Haven. These memories are ones they imaginatively cultivate, repeatedly return to, and vigilantly protect.

Deek's "most powerful" memory, "one of his earliest," constitutes the primal scene of the novel; hence I quote it here at length. It eventually crystallizes an understanding of the Haven desertion, the Convent massacre, and the patriarchs' conception of womanhood—central to understanding Morrison's argument about the gendered and racialized nature of narrating (and mythologizing) history. During the Depression, in 1932, Big Daddy takes the twins on a "Grand Tour" to see how the other "Colored towns" have fared. Most have failed, but one particular light-skinned town immediately recalls the flourishing community of Fairly—site of the Disallowing—for which they had been "too poor, too bedraggled-looking to enter, let alone reside in" (14). Like Fairly, this town has thrived:

> In one of the prosperous [towns] he and Steward watched nineteen Negro ladies arrange themselves on the steps of the town hall. They wore summer dresses of material the lightness, the delicacy of which neither of them had ever seen....Laughing and teasing, they preened for a photographer....Slender feet turned and tipped in thin leather shoes. Their skin, creamy and luminous in the afternoon sun, took away his breath....Without a word [the twins] agreed to fall off the railing. While they wrestled on the ground, ruining their pants and shirts, the Negro ladies turned around to see. Deek and Steward got the smiles they wanted.
>   ...Even now the verbena scent was clear; even now the summer dresses, the creamy, sunlit skin excited him. If he and Steward had not thrown themselves off the railing they would have burst into tears. (109–10)

This episode provides the Morgan twins with an idealized vision of womanhood for which they will actively seek to create a haven in

Ruby, the town they will found together as adults. This experience catalyzes the twins' collective will to nationhood and unifies their historical memory. The Morgans are acutely aware of the fact that any white town or city is an unsafe place for black citizens and for black women in particular. Again and again, throughout the ensuing years, the twins return to the laughing ease and lack of self-consciousness of "the nineteen summertime ladies" that they agree to provide for the women they perceive as their own.

If this scene constitutes the beginning of Ruby's narrative, however, it also becomes a site of forgetting. Inherent to the twins' ideal of femininity is the memory of the women as aesthetic objects: that the ladies are posing for photographs is perhaps the most significant aspect of this scene. For their "laughing, "teasing," and "preening" foregrounds not only the external interest of the photographer, which competes with the interest of the Morgan boys, but also the ladies' own sexual agency, both of which suggest a kind of adultery between the ladies and photographer. The sexual energy of the scene thus elides the vision and rules of female chastity that the brothers enforce in Ruby and simultaneously contains the seeds of the 8-rock fear of miscegenation that can only occur when Ruby citizens couple outside the coal-black bloodlines innate to Morgan males. These mulatto women would have no place in Ruby, a town whose abiding logic Patricia astutely describes: "The generations had to be not only racially untampered but free of adultery too....in that case...everything that worries them must come from women" (217). Through this scene, the Morgans construct not only female identity but their own sense of masculinity as well: they are protectors of a certain kind of woman and assailants to anyone—man or woman—who undermines their conception of a femininity that is simultaneously fragile and threatening. In keeping with the ambiguities of race essential to *Paradise*'s project, the adjective "creamy" to describe the ladies' skin could refer to texture and/or color. However, Morrison's repetition of the word in this context insinuates "peaches-and-cream" complexions, suggesting the likelihood that the women are the issue of both black and white genealogies. Moreover, because the story is set against the historical background of American plantation slavery under which masters regularly raped their female slaves—a violation that (*Paradise* makes clear) commonly recurs after the demise of slavery in the rape of black women by white men—the ladies' "creamy" skin invokes this history. The very creamy skin that "excites" Deek is a result, that is, of the violence inherent in establishing the nation; and the Morgans' consequential founding the "nation" of Ruby on the basis of this primal scene requires a forgetting of its concomitant history. Creamy skin is an outcome of the miscegenation intrinsic to slavery—which is not only forbidden in the "haven" that this memory engenders but also inevitable. Moreover, as we will see, the transgression of the "blood rule" by Ruby men is seminal to the violence that taints Ruby from the onset of the novel, which begins with the racially coded massacre: "They shoot the white girl first" (3).

The evocative language of this scene further underscores the subjectivity and imagination—that is, the element of forgetting—that inflects memory throughout. The passage concludes, "Deek's image of the nineteen summertime ladies was unlike the photographer's. His remembrance was pastel colored and eternal." Morrison's metaphor suggests Deek's memory is filtered through a lens of chastity and innocence and that his view of women is biased by the emotion that accompanied the scene then as well as that with which he repeatedly invests the memory as he recalls it. Although the affluent beauty of the women arouses the prepubescent boys to an ecstatic state—they are spared tearful eruption by the energy they expend that ruins their pants, and they are relieved by the ladies' reciprocal affection—time passed heightens the power of the image and newly imbues it with that "jolt of pleasure, erotic as a dream." This is the sacrosanct Morgan memory that is imperiled, not once but twice in the novel, and both times the Morgan brothers respond with unmixed zeal to protect their vision.

Thus this scene, which occurs much later in the novel than the Haven desertion—yet chronologically decades prior to it—is one of several narrative places wherein historical meaning is revealed to be contingent upon perspective. The accumulation of such scenes in *Paradise* clarifies my notion of Ruby as a microcosmic "nation," defined by Bhabha as "a contested conceptual territory [in] which national life is redeemed and iterated as a reproductive process" (*Location* 145). *Paradise* reproduces national culture out of the contents of the past specifically by revising the given past (the mythic history of Ruby and, by implication, the United States) through its narratives of memory and forgetting. Morrison employs the distant past—this cherished memory from the Morgans' childhood—to reveal the near past and present: the founding of Ruby, its blood rule, and the violation and violence it begets. In the penultimate chapter, Steward decides, "The women in the Convent were for him a flaunting parody of the nineteen Negro ladies of his and his brother's youthful memory and perfect understanding.... He could not abide...this new and obscene breed of female...for sullying his personal history" (279). Steward's

interpretation of the Convent women's "degradation" of Ruby is pat-
terned on his interpretation of the "contamination" of Haven, and it
similarly provokes drastic action. Scenes such as the Haven desertion
and Convent massacre reverberate in the context of other scenes, such
as the primal scene, allowing meaning to be made through a complex
weaving of shifting interpretations.[7] Although this narrative technique is characteristic of Morrison's other novels, Morrison employs
it in *Paradise* for the express purpose of underscoring the power and
process of memory whereby current needs shape the recollection of
past experiences and allow a people to justify discrete actions in the
present based upon this subjective use of memory—to emphasize,
that is, the mechanisms of the will to nationhood and of the suste-
nance of national community.

II   THE DIACHRONY OF HISTORY AND MYTH

Although the perpetrators of the Convent massacre trace the "evidence" that incites their attack to "rumors that had been whispered
for almost a year" (11), this event that literally frames the novel is
rooted in the stories of the Disallowing and of the ensuing founding of Haven—tales that, as they have been circulating since before
any Ruby or Convent residents were born—constitute the people as
historical objects of Ruby's national pedagogy. The specific narration
of these memories in the present and the way the stories function in
Ruby life illuminate not only the motivation of the killers but more
importantly the complex evolution of oral history into myth that fos-
ters the totalizing will to nationhood. The citizens of Ruby collectively maintain the story of the Disallowing as an intrinsically biblical
one to the extent that this historical event, which predates all of their
lives, becomes not merely communal history but a narrative of mythological proportions—that is, a mythic history. Morrison has said that
she wanted to re-create a language that was true to the setting of her
story, wherein African American belief in God and familiarity with
the Bible would be ubiquitous and deep seated (Morrison in Bryan
1). Nonetheless, her biblical allusions are hardly "gratuitous," as one
reviewer complains (Kakutani 3), for as the Ruby residents interpret
and cast their history with biblical tropes, they generate their own
cultural mythology, steeped in ancient, sacred narratives.

Just as vital for Morrison's implicit analogy between Ruby and
early America is the fact that Ruby's stories, flush with both Old and
New Testament allusions, make a knowledge of the Bible essential
for the reader of the novel as for the fictional generations who share

the tale: this aspect of the Ruby community inevitably recalls the function of the Bible in Puritan American culture. *Paradise* moreover belies the seeming disparity of communities of Puritans and modern African Americans, for (as Dalsgård's recent article patiently elaborates) each envisioned a "City on a Hill" as the basis for national community and returned to the biblical text as a way of garnering authority. One watches this process at work when Steward relates the most detailed version of the Disallowing at Fairly: the families "on foot and completely lost" reverberates the Israelites' wandering the desert, and "the shame of seeing one's own pregnant wife or sister or daughter refused shelter" invokes the rejection of the holy family at the inn. Steward additionally shores up his authority by introducing his fathers' story as essentially his own. He remembers "every detail of the story his father and grandfather told," and despite the fact that he and his wife are infertile and childless, he "ha[s] no trouble imagining the shame for himself" (95). The ensuing components of Steward's version of founding Haven cast Zechariah (Big Papa) as Moses leading his people to the Promised Land, yet they also inflect the story with references to the Gospels. Leaving Fairly, the families wander westward for three days, after which Zechariah leads his son Rector to a spot deep within "the piney wood," where both kneel and wait all night. "My Father," Big Papa says. "Zechariah here." This short narrative alone is replete with biblical allusions. Zechariah echoes Old Testament figures Abraham, Moses, Samuel, and Isaiah, each of whom respond to the Lord calling their names with the declaration, "Here I am" (Genesis 22:1, Exodus 3:4, 1 Samuel 3:4, Isaiah 6:8). Zechariah leading his son to the pine garden where he initiates an all-night prayer vigil echoes Jesus leading his disciples to the Garden of Gethsemane at night, where He kneels and desperately prays, calling out, "My Father ...." And, like Jesus's disciples, Zechariah's son succumbs to sleep during the night. Rector wakes in time, however, to witness God's reply: "Footsteps—loud like a giant's tread...They saw him at the same time. A small man, seemlike, too small for the sound of his steps." Lame from a gunshot wound in his foot, Zechariah has had to be carried part of the way until now. Yet, when Rector, at his father's command, returns with the whole of the sojourners whom he has gathered, "they f[ind] him...standing straighter than the pines, his sticks tossed away." Thus begins the families' "purposeful" journey, led by Zechariah led by God—whom none but he "and sometimes a child" can see—which concludes with their finding the "extravagant space" where they build Haven (96–99). The progression of the story patterns God's first revealing Himself to

Moses alone and then leading Moses and the Israelites by a cloud that moved across the wilderness and settled on the promised land, and Zechariah's miraculous healing echoes Christ's healing the lame.

Yet while Morrison explores the creation of mythic history through the conflation of sacred narrative with personal history, she also broadens the specifically US mythic history of westward migration. *Paradise* shows that the myth of the American West as a "haven" where one can begin anew is a shared myth, upon which both dominant and marginalized cultures have depended; simultaneously the novel denotes the exclusion of African Americans from the US history of westward expansion. Morrison herself notes that *Ghost Towns of Oklahoma*, for example, "scarcely mentions any of the black ones" (quoted in Hitchens 144). She thus locates the origin of her fictional townships in the post-Reconstruction migration of former slaves to the sparsely settled territory of Oklahoma and concurrently layers this cultural history onto the biblical mythic history of Haven and Ruby. In the previous excerpt, God appears to the Moses figure, Zechariah, just before dawn, as a "man walking away from the palest part of the sky"—leading the lost people, that is, due west. As Zechariah stares after the vision, "his back [is] to the rising sun"; he is poised to leave the East behind and migrate west for life anew.

In other words, Morrison's portrait of the mythic history of Ruby inserts a Judeo-Christian countertext into the official history of US westward migration, from which African Americans have been excluded. Her detail of the importance of both Christianity and westward migration to African Americans is yet another deconstruction of the opposition between white and black America that the novel has staged. In this sense, the novel offers a reminder that Christianity was foundational not only to nineteenth-century African American community and culture but to the nineteenth-century abolitionist movement that, in its fruition, facilitated the very westward migration on which Morrison focuses. Morrison therefore employs a foundational religious text to interrogate the prevailing national text, in much the same way that abolitionists employed the Christian tenets on which the United States was founded to interrogate the institution of slavery. Her portrait of the African American experience of the West as a haven from persecution both extends that national mythic history and invests it with a character independent of the national tradition.

Marrying myth to their personal history, Ruby's citizens similarly perpetuate a mythic history that carries a tremendous weight and moral authority, as evidenced by the dire consequences suffered by those who transgress its moral code. As with the primal scene that reverberates in Stewards's interpretation of the contamination of Haven and of the degradation of Ruby by Convent women, the original Disallowing—ironically—is used to justify contemporary disallowings. The repetition of the tale in the present, and its manifestation in these disallowings, serves to keep the past relevant and to maintain a patriarchal authority rooted in the past—to secure, that is, present-day consent. Thus the town uses the annual staging of the school Christmas play as the principal vehicle for communal memory of the Disallowing. The priority of the Disallowing to the biblical story is reflected in the play's history as well as its content: "The school program, featuring the Nativity and involving the whole town, was older [than the church programs], having started before the churches were even built" (185). The play explicitly conflates the Disallowing with the holy family's rejection at the inn. When the innkeepers reject a group of families seeking "room," the families' response first echoes Joseph's—"But our wives our pregnant!"— and then abandons all pretense of faithfulness to the Nativity: "Our children are going to die of thirst!" This pattern of subordinating the Christmas story to the Disallowing script characterizes the play. "Away in a manger, no crib for His head. Slowly from the wings a boy enters," who reenacts God's appearance to Zechariah as the "small man" who led the families to Haven. The description of the play's action continues seamlessly, "The little Lord Jesus lay down his sweet head." Naturally, Ruby's mimicry of the Christmas story is readable only to the initiated. Reverend Richard Misner, Ruby's newest citizen, watches the children's movements "with growing interest. He had assumed it was in order to please as many children as possible that there were four innkeepers, seven Marys and Josephs. But perhaps there were other reasons. Seven holy families?" He misreads the "big-hat boy" as one of the Magi: "And why only one Wise Man? And why is he putting the gifts back into his satchel?" (210–11). Misner's reasonable misinterpretation of the Christmas play underscores the Disallowing, rather than the Nativity, as the town's most hallowed text.

Whereas the primal scene occupies the private memory and imagination of the Morgan twins, the Disallowing is the paramount catalyst of the public will to nationhood. As the very raison d'être for the nation-people of Haven/Ruby, it engenders the primary dialectic of memory and a recurrent forgetting that characterizes its citizenry. Misner's questions—put to a guarded Pat—expose the deleterious function of the memory of the Disallowing in the present. Although Pat, as the children's schoolteacher, helps the children decorate and costume themselves for the play and she "had seen the play all her life[,] ... she had never been chosen for any part other than the choir." Along with Pat herself, the reader is led to infer that this is because her father "was the first to violate the blood rule" (195). Her genealogy later unearths this as the true reason for the disdain with which her neighbors have treated her family her whole life. It is the same reason for her mother's and little sister's untimely deaths: nobody offered medical assistance during the complicated and ultimately doubly fatal delivery. It is the reason, thus, for her and her daughter's profound loneliness in their own town. Through Misner's inquiry, Pat notices that the nine original founding families traditionally represented in the play have been "cut" to seven. The play manifests Ruby's active perpetuation of their mythic history of 8-rock purity: the missing (we might say "forgotten") families represent the town's internal disallowings of lineages whose members have sought light-skinned partners.

Because the play reflects the interaction between the pedagogy of the Disallowing and its performance in the present—the contemporary subjects who enact disallowings—it depicts the way in which the people of Ruby are "an ambivalent *movement* between" these two discourses fundamental to the production of the nation as narration (as Bhabha argues of modern nation-people generally, 149). Moreover, Ruby's enforced contemporary disallowings reverberate not only the original Disallowing but also the larger, national exclusion that sent the Old Fathers west in the first place. In this way, the mechanisms of nationhood endemic to Ruby echo and illustrate those of the United States. These mechanisms—the will to nationhood and its pursuant dialectic of memory and forgetting and the people as alternating objects of their nationalist pedagogy and perplexed subjects who fulfill or resist that narrative—reveal how mythic history is created and upheld as the sustaining force of national community.

Viewed (as the novel's circular narrative inevitably demands) as a prequel to the ensuing massacre, Ruby's mythic history of the Disallowing makes clear the violence involved in narrating the nation, for the patriarchs again promote a mythic history marked by a blood-stained forgetting. Because Misner is out of town when the massacre occurs, "it took four days for him to learn what had happened. Pat gave him two versions of the official story"—both of which render the men innocent of anything but initiating a civil warning visit to the Convent that accidentally gets out of hand. Yet Pat withholds from Misner her own (correct) interpretation, written urgently in the pages of her genealogy, "that nine 8-rocks murdered five harmless women: (a) because the women were impure (not 8-rock); (b) because the women were unholy (fornicators at the least, abortionists at most); c) because they *could*" (297). The 8-rocks will not undermine the authority of their mythic history by admitting either their vicious disallowing of the Convent women or their disallowing of Patricia's "cracker-looking" mother and Menus's "pretty sandy-haired [fiancée] from Virginia" because to do so would discredit the very narrative on which their (nationalist) authority is based: their moral and practical renunciation of the original Disallowing (196). Interwoven threads of memory and violent forgetting, that is, constitute the very fabric of the nation's narration.

III   COUNTERHISTORIES AND A POLITICS OF TRUTH

The chapters of *Paradise* collectively assert a series of female-authored counterhistories that correct the patriarchs' mythic history. Although the narrative centers on the Ruby township, ruled by men, the novel relates its true story primarily through women whose individual names entitle each chapter: these include each of the Convent women, Patricia, and Lone (Ruby's resident midwife). Men's voices do enter the narratives—as in the excerpts earlier in which they convey the town's heritage and guiding principles—but the women's stories that impart each respective chapter account consistently reveal the men's perspectives to be skewed. Billie Delia's observation of town dynamics, that "the stallions were fighting about who controlled the mares and their foals," evokes the text's reliance upon a formal rhetorical strategy of inversion, whereby the margins reveal the center—and the power that excludes female agency—whereas the township itself relies upon a quixotic and univocal account of experience (150). This formal and thematic narrative relationship highlights the schism in Ruby's community between 8-rock power and those disenfranchised by it.

Women's statements—fragmented throughout the novel—thus form a succession of explanations that render Ruby's sites of strange forgetting as cites of countermemories, the most dramatic of which emerge as the patriarchs plot their Convent assault, basing it on "outrages that [take] shape as evidence." Patricia's own narrative discloses her identity as what the plotters profess is a mother "knocked down the stairs by her cold-eyed daughter" (11). Yet it is Pat who "run[s] up the stairs with a 1950s GE electric iron...clutched in her fingers to slam against her daughter's head," and her daughter who runs for

her life. Not only do the facts of the event reverse the plotters' version, but Pat's violent fit is also misdirected vengeance at the 8-rock
disdain of her "lightish" child. Confronting her own internal racism,
"Pat realize[s] that ever since Billie Delia was an infant, she thought
of her as a liability.... The Royal Ease in her hand...was there to
smash the young girl that had lived in the minds of the 8-rocks, not
the girl her daughter ever was" (196–204). The outrage—Patricia's,
Billie Delia's, and the 8-rocks'—that the particular disallowing of
the Best family has provoked is in fact the effect of 8-rock racism that
haunts the town. Also woven into this narrative is a likely explanation
for the next outrage, "four damaged infants born in one family":
Patricia's genealogy represents a complex history of incestuous Ruby
marriages that were entered into because many 8-rock men, unlike
her own father, "shunned temptation or any thought of looking outside the families" (197).[8] Although the list of outrages seems, in the
men's rendition, to refer to events integral to the Convent, every one
of them is rooted in their way of narrating their nation: their successful mythologizing of the Disallowing has created a totalizing, master
narrative that engenders the chronic disallowings plaguing the integ-
rity of the Ruby nation.

   Thus both structurally (through the chapter titles and related stories) and practically (through assertions like Billie Delia's), women's
enunciations disrupt what the novel terms Ruby's "official story"—
its "heroic version of history" (Dalsgård 239)—revealing the turbu-
lent inconsistencies of its moral code. The dissident opinions of the
rejected and alienated individuals among Ruby's community constitute an aspect of the town that is never revealed in its official narratives
but rather show Ruby as it is silently experienced and imagined by its
own pariahs and mute loners. These thoughtful, hushed, estranged
citizens—mostly women but also some men—are part of "what
nobody talked about" (83). Yet their silence—and in some cases,
their lies—is complicit with the patriarchal nationalist discourse and
as such belies the simplistic gender divide between "good women"
and "bad men" alleged by the novel's early critics. *Paradise*'s women
reveal "the scraps, patches and rags of daily life" that, in the production of narrating the nation, Bhabha explains, "must be repeatedly
turned into the signs of a coherent national culture, while the very act
of the narrative performance interpellates a growing circle of national
subjects" (145). The novel's intricate narrative discloses the split that
occurs whereby the women's narrative performances erase the originary presence of Ruby's nationalist pedagogy, and the "people are the
articulation of a doubling of the national address" (149).

At the crux of these female counternarratives is Patricia's chapter. Because it revolves primarily around her writing furiously her private genealogy of the community, it lends a Chinese-box structure to the novel that points to Morrison's metahistorical concerns in the novel. The genealogy

> used to be a history project but was nothing of the sort now. It began as a gift to the citizens of Ruby—a collection of family trees; the genealogies of each of the fifteen families. . . . When the trees were completed, [Pat] had begun to supplement the branches of who begat whom with notes . . . gleaned from her students' autobiographical composition . . . from talking to people, asking to see Bibles and examining church records . . . letters and marriage certificates. (187)

The caustic and penetrating interpretative notes Pat inscribes are a desperate attempt to defy the rigidity of 8-rock history and myth represented in the genealogical trees with which she began her project and to dismiss the privilege long placed on the purity of bloodlines. Yet the novel's insistence on the intertwined relationship between oral and written histories brings scrutiny to both forms of accessing historical truth. Like the oral histories in the novel, Pat's genealogy is subjective and shares some of the same gaps where information to fill them is simply unavailable to its author.

Ultimately, however, the novel stakes out nothing less than a politics of truth that rests centrally on Pat's genealogy. Pat's alternative histories serve as clues for the reader to constitute, in fact, a true story embedded in, between, and outside of Ruby's official story in the same way that the African American history narrated by *Paradise* (like other Morrison novels) makes truth meaningful outside of dominant, traditional US histories. The novel is vitally concerned with the distinctive truth claims of the various historical referents its narrative deploys—in reference to Haven/Ruby history as well as to US history. Notwithstanding the novel's complications of oral and written histories, there are several key differences between Pat's narrative of Ruby history and the other citizens' narratives, which, considered together, suggest the novel's support of Pat's genealogy as a valid repository of historical truth. The genealogy does not share with the oral histories (which function as official history in Ruby) the willful omission of known facts, suggested by the determined silence of Ruby citizens in response to Pat's requests for information. Moreover, the citizens, unconscious of the conceptual distinction and fundamental connection of event and interpretation, use their stories to "support" the "official story": the tale of the Disallowing authorizes further disallowings in Ruby based upon race and gender; and the tale of the Convent massacre exculpates the killers and affirms 8-rock identity and rule.

Pat's genealogy, on the other hand, disturbs the immobility of 8-rock racial and moral purity. It introduces discontinuities that expose the ironic history of Ruby, countering the grand history received and maintained as inviolable fact by the town's collective narrative. In admitting that her version of the Convent assault differs from the "official story" she reports to Misner, Pat exposes her perspective as that which threatens to unmask the truth deliberately suppressed by the attackers in their application of racial power. Fully aware of the indissoluble relationship of a historical event to the discourse surrounding it, Pat recognizes her record of history as a system of interpretations, reflecting a level of self-awareness considered crucial by most contemporary historians. Pat's genealogy is distinct, however, not only because she acknowledges her perspective but because her perspective is unique among the town's residents: it is both politically efficacious and intellectually justified. She reveals her preoccupation with Ruby events in her "supplementary notes" without "pretense to objective comment," which lay bare 8-rock injustice. Coming up against the task of her own project has "her biting her thumbnail in frustration," as if to suggest that her genealogy is inherently linked to her body and to the violence of history upon her body.[9] Indeed, Pat's own body—her skin and that of her daughter, which she tried, literally and metaphorically, to destroy—is the corporeal proof of her father's marriage as violation of the law. Her body is thus indelibly imprinted by the history of violation of the blood rule, and her genealogy registers this fact. Her shrewd analysis of the Convent massacre is underpinned by her keen experiential knowledge that truth is produced by 8-rock systems of power—a knowledge to which, in Ruby, Patricia virtually alone is privy.

The novel asserts its politics of truth most persuasively, however, through its sinuous narrative, for it demands a process of sorting through the various versions of Ruby's past and present that ultimately supports the truth claims and even the speculations Pat makes in her genealogy. Lone, for example, becomes "unhinged by the way the [massacre] story was being retold: how people were changing it to make themselves look good.... every one of the assaulting men had a different tale and their families and friends (who had been nowhere near the Convent) supported them, enhancing, recasting, inventing misinformation" (297). As the sole witness to the nine men's plotting just prior to their trip out to the Convent, who furthermore arrived at the Convent just after the first shots were fired, Lone provides a trustworthy account of the event; and it concurs with Patricia's interpretation. The novel's entangled narrative, then—its fragmented, multiple-voiced, and competing stories—does not yield, as Dalsgård and other readers have suggested, an entirely "open-ended fabric" (238). Pat encounters several insistent absences in her history that she correctly infers are deliberate omissions by the townspeople she attempts to interview. Pat promises "she alone would figure out why a line was drawn through Ethan Blackhorse's name in the Blackhorse Bible and what the heavy ink blot hid next to Zechariah's name in the Morgan Bible....older women...hinted the most while saying the least. 'Oh, I think those brothers had a disagreement of some kind'" (188). Pat never does fill this crevice, but her attention to it allows the reader, over 100 pages later, to piece together the puzzle. In an odd outpouring of mixed narratives of confession to Misner, Deacon tells a story of a long-ago incident in which white men "encouraged" the Blackhorse twins—then known as "Coffee and Tea"—to dance as they brandished their pistols. Tea "accommodated the whites, even though he was a grown man, older than they were"; "Coffee took a bullet in his foot instead" (which explains Zechariah's lame foot). Deacon concludes, "Coffee couldn't take it. Not because he was ashamed of his twin, but because the shame was in himself....So he went off and never spoke to his brother again" (303). This story does not readily recall the Blackhorse and Morgan Bibles' secret given that Deek refers only to "Coffee" and "Tea"—names that insinuate another layer to the shame "in himself." Coffee is a shade darker than tea, suggesting that Tea's skin color may reflect "racial tampering" among the 8-rock ancestors—ubiquitous, after all, in the slave system into which they are born and which did not allow them to maintain the blood rule that becomes inviolable to their descendants. Perhaps Tea's "accomodat[ing] the whites" reminds Coffee of the white ancestry in his blood—whiteness that becomes synonymous with the terror, oppression, and rejection that drives the 8-rocks out of the South, then from Fairly to found Haven and, finally, Ruby.

This story serves many functions. It is one of several examples of fragmented narratives that, added to Pat's "stories about these fragments," intimate that a certain historical truth resides in her genealogy. Other residents' silence about the fraternal conflict has the mythological effect not only of smoothing over a familial rejection (an action that is contrary to the principle of absolute brotherhood on which Zechariah founded Haven) but of refusing to acknowledge, as the genealogist must, that there is always impurity in the tracing of origins, dissension and disparity at the sites of historical beginnings. Pat's genealogy thus fragments the mythical unified ancestry of the Old Fathers and discredits the myth of community fidelity. Loyalty to family and neighbor in Haven, as in Ruby, is ultimately expendable when an individual does not conform to the patriarchs' model of what constitutes black identity.[10] The event worth noting in Patricia's genealogy is not the founding of Haven by Zechariah—that narrative is transmitted repeatedly through the "town's official story"—but rather the absence of his brother at that event, brought to light by her observation of the erasure of his name in the family Bible. A genealogical event is not, as in traditional history, a reign of power such as that of the 8-rocks but rather a moment when power is most nakedly experienced or exposed. Patricia's emphasis on the microphysics of power in her town suggests the novel's affirmation of this type of counterhistory.

An astute genealogist, Patricia sees absence and silence as sources. Although Morrison has said the character with whom she most identifies is Misner because he is "closest to my own sensibility about moral problems," I submit that her identity as a writer is most closely aligned with Patricia (quoted in Jaffrey 1). Pat's description of her process of researching and writing the genealogy reverberates Morrison's depiction of her writing process as literary archaeology: both begin with interpretation of autobiographies[11] and excavating the available historical remains. The family Bibles, church records, letters, and marriage certificates that Pat mines are traditional sources for historians of black history.[12] The personal, experiential speculations with which Patricia inflects all of her "notes" echo Morrison's reliance on her memory and others' recollections. Yet the absences that remain despite Patricia's tenacious investigations demand, as they do for Morrison, "imagination," or what Pat terms her insightful interpretation. In *Paradise*, both Patricia and the reader are made to walk in Morrison's footsteps, and it is largely through Patricia's own literary archaeology that the reader can creatively probe Ruby history.

Yet Patricia's chapter closes dramatically with her burning the genealogy, rendering it ultimately unread by anyone but its author. How effective, then, can her history be? This enigmatic act is in fact the key to the novel's sense of historiography, its most articulate pronunciation of the limits of oral and written histories and, at the same time, of the potential of counterhistory. Confessing that she has snubbed Misner as an outsider, Patricia regrets her replication of 8-rock behavior: "When he asks questions, they close him out of anything but the obvious, the superficial. And I of all people know exactly what it feels like" (216). The confrontation with Misner exposes her knowing silence as complicity in the perpetuation of racial and sexual exclusion practices that are repulsive to her. On the heels of this encounter, Patricia tosses her trenchant genealogy into the fire, washes her hands, and asserts that she "fe[els] clean" (217). Her burning the revealing genealogy—the result of her patient and incisive analysis—yields to the confusion and mystery that has resulted from the simultaneous maintaining and breaching the unspoken blood rule. It relinquishes the verifiable past (her genealogy is the most accurate and thorough record of Ruby) as a source of history and identity, paving the way for the unbridled hazardous mythmaking that her silence and the absence of the genealogy only serve to sustain. This sequence of scenes around the destruction of the genealogy suggests that the layers of knowledge of 8-rock practices represented in Pat's genealogy as well as in her own person and family are too weighty a burden for her to bear—particularly because rather than finding ways to use her knowledge and perceptions to try to ameliorate conditions in Ruby (as does Misner), her investigations and unrestrained writings only exacerbate her frustration and sense of alienation.

More importantly, though, the poignant destruction of Patricia's genealogy echoes the status of untold counterhistorical narratives. The novel underscores this historiographical comment by its plot point wherein Ruby's "stock of stories"—the citizens' communal practice of mythologizing history—discredit (in Ruby) the female narratives asserted by the novel (for its reader) as true. Most notably, the multiple spurious and discrepant tales the citizens circulate to explain the Convent massacre prevent its reliable narrators (Lone, Patricia) from informing that account of the massacre the town officially adopts. Similarly, Misner's prediction about the historical record of the civil rights movement of the 1960s functions as a synecdoche for such counterhistories:

> What could not be gainsaid, but would remain invisible in the newspapers and the books he bought for his students were the ordinary folk. The janitor who turned off the switch so the police couldn't see; the grandmother who kept all the babies so the mothers could march; the backwoods women with fresh towels in one hand and a shotgun in the other; the little children who carried batteries and food to secret meetings; the ministers who kept whole churchfuls of hunted protestors calm till help came; the old who gathered up the broken bodies of the young; the young who spread their arms wide to protect the old from

batons they could not possibly survive; parents who wiped the spit and tears from their children's faces and said, "Never mind, honey"...years from now, those people will be dead or forgotten, their small stories part of no grand record or even its footnotes. (212)

Nonetheless, *Paradise* consistently contends that the oral histories that might supplement the grand record from which such microhistories are absent are subject to other willful omissions, distortions, and denials of their subjective interpretations. Oral and written histories—particularly those of historically marginalized peoples who have largely depended upon oral histories—are intimately related. In *Paradise*'s interrogation of national history making, the "small stories" along with the "grand record" are recast as and subsumed by mythic history, which can distort but also illuminate the true stories reflected in Misner's meditation, Patricia's discoveries, and Morrison's writing, which seeks to "find and expose a truth" about the interior lives of African Americans. Pat's genealogy—and the fruitful if arduous process of interpreting her genealogy alongside the novel's multitudinous narratives—suggests that historical truth need not be "dead or forgotten," and it moreover illustrates the careful, critical process of construing that truth and wresting it from power.

CHAPTER 4

A Politics of Truth and the Transnational Comm(unity) of Abolitionists: Michelle Cliff's *Free Enterprise*

If *Paradise* illustrates the politics of truth endemic to national history making, Michelle Cliff's *Free Enterprise* (1993) exemplifies an aspect of fictional truth telling germane to the recent key paradigm shift in the field of American studies toward a new Americas studies. Recognizing the overlapping histories of colonialism within which the cultures of the Americas have been shaped, this hemispheric perspective questions modes of history that are delimited by the modern nation-state. *Free Enterprise* rewrites nationally delineated narratives of US history that intersect in the Civil War and black resistance to slavery throughout the Americas, with particular attention to women's roles therein. The novel is set both during and after the Civil War, yet it recontextualizes the war not as a nationalist narrative that consolidated the United States but as a transnational slave revolt against imperialism in which black women, capital, and the discourse of "free enterprise" played a crucial role. The novel enacts this grand tale by telling the remarkable story of Mary Ellen Pleasant, the successful San Francisco businesswoman and passionate freedom fighter who allegedly financed John Brown's raid on Harpers Ferry. *Free Enterprise* transforms the virtually unknown Pleasant into a New World abolitionist who played a major role in a landmark event (Harpers Ferry) that led to the Civil War. It asserts a persistent, historically based difference that yet stakes claim to a national—though not a nationalist—identity. Cliff recasts the Civil War as a major battle in a transnational war on slavery, constructing a compelling counternarrative to nineteenth-century US history. This chapter elaborates the politics of truth that informs Cliff's transnational community of abolitionists—her rendering an alternative history, that is, as a way of telling the truth outside of traditional nationalist narratives.

Free Enterprise's focus on a transnational community of abolitionists and its remembrance of a complex black female abolitionist history—differentiated from and yet a component of US Civil War history—disrupts the essentialist identity of abolitionists and liberators of US slavery as (primarily) white activist citizens and Union soldiers. Specifically, it develops the relatively obscure and enigmatic historical figure of Mary Ellen Pleasant. Pleasant was a black entrepreneur, civil- and human-rights activist, and abolitionist who made her primary home and extraordinary fortune in San Francisco through her luxuriant boardinghouses and her savvy investments in mining and real estate between the 1850s and 1880s. Among her many abolitionist ventures, the one at the center of Cliff's novel, and the one of which the historical Pleasant was most proud, is her collusion with John Brown.[1] An unapologetic and successful capitalist, Pleasant dedicated her talent for personal profit within the system of "free enterprise" to abolition in a number of ways, including funding Brown's raid on Harpers Ferry. "She gave him thirty thousand dollars in gold to buy fifteen thousand rifles, which he did," Cliff explains. Moreover, gesturing to the Chatham convention at which Brown, together with a majority of blacks including Pleasant, signed a constitution that established a black state within the United States, Cliff asserts, "There was a really complicated revolutionary movement prior to the Civil War. What has come down to us is this notion of John Brown, this flaming, crazy, white man who was patriarchal and patronizing—and that's not the historical case at all" ("Art of History" 65).[2] That liberation of the slaves was to be achieved by the slaves themselves, through this armed rebellion, rather than by US government decree (which came four years later), is central to *Free Enterprise*.

Russell Banks's best seller *Cloudsplitter* (1998) also takes up this tenet of Harpers Ferry. Asserting likewise that "the Civil War was a concussive trauma that erased all memory of what life had been like before it," *Cloudsplitter* attempts to "revise once and for all the received truth about John Brown and his sons and followers" (29). Through the fictionalized voice of Owen Brown (one of John Brown's sons who, in fact, fought alongside him in many abolitionist struggles from boyhood on), the novel details the "continuous consideration of context" that alone can tell "the whole truth" of John Brown. At the same time it seeks to "reverse...our century's received opinion" that Brown was a "madman," *Cloudsplitter* broadly contextualizes Brown's devotion to what Pleasant calls "the Cause": "The three-hundred-year-long War Between the Races, from before the Revolution up to and including Harpers Ferry, was fought mainly as the War Against Slavery. Then, briefly, in '61, it became the War Between the States," explains Owen. "The truth is, for us, the so-called Civil War was merely an aftermath. Or rather, it was part of a continuum. Just another protracted battle" (7).[3]

But if *Cloudsplitter*, like *Free Enterprise*, seeks to recover this "minority view," it does so in the form of a traditional historical novel that links its untold events causally along a linear historical timeline beginning in Owen's boyhood. Rather than deconstructing Western historiography, Banks retains a faith in the historical process and its ability to reflect "truth." Owen relates his story through all the conventions of realism intrinsic not only to the classical form of the historical novel but also to traditional history. Telling its story chronologically to climax at the dramatic raid on Harpers Ferry, the novel neither abandons nor critiques the historical process. More closely resembling a Ken Burns documentary in its form and content, *Cloudsplitter* offers as its main contribution to the representation of the antebellum period, as Owen says, "to fill out the historical record with my eyewitness account…to tell Father's untold story" (7, 29). In Banks's words, which echo the "historical authenticity" central to Lukács's "classical form of the historical novel," Owen Brown is "the truth-telling representative figure of his age" ("In Response to James McPherson's Reading of *Cloudsplitter*" 77). Whereas Banks, writing through Owen, seeks to correct the "lies" of the historical record of John Brown and Harpers Ferry, Cliff (writing through Pleasant) seeks to expand and complicate the known history of John Brown by exposing Pleasant as his accomplice. In "writing through," in her words, "an American protagonist—Mary Ellen Pleasant, who's been written out of the history books," Cliff identifies herself with Pleasant as "a black American woman who was not seen as an American by mainstream America" ("An Interview with Michelle Cliff" 615).

Moreover, unlike *Cloudsplitter*, *Free Enterprise* extends the history of the struggle against slavery not only temporally but spatially as well. Cliff's imagination of a transnational community of abolitionists across spatial and temporal distances anticipates what Paul Giles—a decade after the publication of *Free Enterprise*—describes as the "spatial turn in United States literary studies," inherent to the transnationalist perspective on American literature he and other leading Americanists urge (64).[4]

In her discussions of the novel, Cliff strategically moves between the terms "United States" and "America/n." Her profile suggests the transnational focus of American studies realized in the years subsequent to her writing *Free Enterprise*. Using "America" to mean "United States" belies that the rest of the Americas—Canada, Central and South America, the Caribbean—have histories and cultures independent of the United States, as do territories within its own borders; yet using the term "America" in a transnational context also broadens it, indicating that its traditional referent—the United States—shares overlapping histories and cultures with the rest of the Americas. As it has from its inception, American studies continues to examine US culture; yet one facet of its recent transnationalization is the consideration of the relationship of the rest of the Americas (in particular) to the United States. A transnational approach to US literary studies calls attention to processes of displacement and dispersion within and between the Americas; to the circulation of people and capital, languages, and ideas; and to the new cultural geographies these mobilizations engender.

Yet through its historical focus on the transatlantic slave trade and transnational alliances against "the Trade" and other forms of colonialism around the globe, *Free Enterprise* underscores the fact that America has been implicated by a global economy from its genesis—and it is the conditions of the United States' emergence as a nation-state that demands its consideration in a global context. I employ the term "transnational" throughout this chapter to evoke the transatlantic circulation of slave labor and related capital central to the United States' emergence as a neocolonial state and the corresponding movement—of both slave traders and their cargo as well as of abolitionists—between multiple continents and countries figured by free enterprise. When I use "America/n" then, I use it in this multifaceted sense of a transnational United States. In this sense, *Free Enterprise* recalls another novel that transforms a little-known historical character—another black woman at the margins of US history—into a full-fledged narrator of her own vibrant tale, Maryse Condé's *I, Tituba, Black Witch of Salem* (1992).

The publication history of Condé's novel itself reflects the circulation of people, capital, languages, and ideas that informs the transnational context in which US literary studies increasingly must be understood. Originally published in France as *Moi, Tituba, Sorcière… Noire de Salem* (1986), Condé's novel has been claimed for the literature of Guadeloupe—Condé's native home where she lived before moving to Paris for college (and more recently, to London and then the United

States). Condé, then, appropriates a figure embedded in the margins of US history for francophone Caribbean literature. At the same time, although her plot centers on the fictional Tituba's trials and transformation by her forced migration to mainland America, Tituba's placement in the Caribbean context transforms US literary history. For Condé first and foremost brings Tituba's West Indian origins—about which the sparse historical record on Tituba merely speculates—into sharp focus. She locates Tituba in her native Barbados for nearly half of the novel, situating her there at the onset as she colorfully imagines her childhood, her upbringing by native African parents, family, culture, and ancestry. Following Tituba's part in the Salem witch trials, Condé returns her to Barbados where she lives the remainder of her life as a healer of slaves, eventually dying as a martyr for the abolitionist cause. Unlike *Free Enterprise*, Tituba's narration is not spatial but chronological and causal—like *Cloudsplitter*'s but with the notable difference of its ironic treatment of the extant historical record, rife with omission and bias. Nonetheless, by emphasizing Tituba's enslavement as that which leads both to her role of scapegoat in the Salem witch trials and to her return to Barbados, Condé effectively recontextualizes the Salem witch trials in terms of the voracious triangular slave trade among Africa, the Caribbean, and the United States.[5]

Although *I Tituba* shares with *Free Enterprise* a pressing, long historical story of the Africa–Americas trade in human flesh and the violent struggle to vanquish it, it exemplifies postmodern historiographic metafiction in its use of anachronism[6] and ironic juxtaposition of history and fiction. "*Tituba* is just the opposite of the historical novel," states Condé. "I was not interested at all in what her real life could have been. . . . I am not involved in any scholarly research." Condé puts Tituba's deposition testimony—"the only historical part of the novel"—at her novel's center and marks it with a footnote that explains where to find the original document ("Interview with Ann Armstrong Scarboro" 201). At the same time, she uses the deposition to call attention to the glaring absence of Tituba's authentic voice—both in the deposition and from the rest of history: "I can look for my story among those of the witches of Salem," says Tituba, "but it isn't there" (149).[7] Ironically, the fully human, passionate, and fluent Tituba whom Condé invents effectively parodies the scant trace of the one-dimensional Tituba who survives in the historical record. In so doing, Condé foregrounds the relative inaccessibility of black women's history, highlighting it as problematically "outside" national history; she uses her novel to remind her readers that silence in the historical record is not equivalent to absence and to fill the gaps in the historical record with a vivid imaginative account of Tituba.

Although *Free Enterprise* is steeped in a theoretical self-consciousness not unlike that which permeates *Tituba*, it is also, in marked contrast, drenched in archival research of its subject, making it part of the emergent genre of historical fiction that succeeds the postmodern to articulate a politics of truth. Thus, though it is among a host of novels (and films) appearing in the last two decades[8] manifesting the hemispheric perspective that currently informs American studies, *Free Enterprise* is unique in that it situates its "New World" view in relation to its urgent project of truth telling. It is in this sense that *Free Enterprise*, though distinctive for its transnational perspective on abolitionist history and culture, represents and joins the company of historical novels with which this book is concerned. Cliff's explicit identification with Pleasant—the unrecognized black female accomplice to John Brown—manifests the tension that the contemporary truth-telling novel consistently takes up as its primary project. Like *Americana*, *Underworld*, and *Paradise*, the title of *Free Enterprise* is a metonym for the United States, which suggests its likewise revisionist project. Its articulation of national identity through an inscription of historical marginality reflects a particular idea of "America"—increasingly characteristic of contemporary collective historical imagination—that, as these chapters detail, has important implications for American cultural history and the historical novel as genre. *Underworld* and *Paradise*, however, present a distinctly unredemptive view of history, in which what Walter Benjamin calls "the storm of progress" ravages minority populations. This storm propels the "angel of history" "into the future, to which his back is turned, while the pile of debris" in the past, which he faces, "grows skyward" (257–58). By moving backward in time, DeLillo's and Morrison's narratives trace human and cultural devastation to revise fundamental episodes in American history; but the textual constructions survive the human and cultural victims of the storm. *Underworld* and *Paradise* thus enlarge our retrospective view of the historical periods they treat not by their stories of the victors, nor of hegemonic tales of the coincident historical events, but rather by probing those documents of barbarism that correspond to those periods and events. DeLillo's and Morrison's narrative strategies do not attempt rescuing critiques of the past; instead they expose communities and landscapes wasted by discrete projects of American nation building. Their novels uncover a politics of difference by telling the truth of heretofore-obscure populations in the American West. At the same time, they reveal how dominant cultural forces ultimately consume these marginalized peoples, assimilating them into a homo-geneous national identity.

In contrast, *Free Enterprise* (like *Holder of the World*, the subject of the next chapter), creates a redemptive narrative temporality in which the past is not opposed to the future but rather coexistent with it, as with the present. What results is fiction that realizes an antiteleological relationship between narrative and history, in which historically forgot-ten voices and stories are inscribed not as debris fixed in the past but as living cultural resources for the present and future. Remarkably, *Free Enterprise* symbolizes its conception of spatiality and the way in which the narrative attempts to redeem marginalized voices and stories from official history by a pictograph. A Mesopotamian cosmogram—a cross surrounded at its four points with four circles—recurs throughout the narrative, in dreams and etched on walls.[9] As I detail, the presence of the cosmogram throughout *Free Enterprise* suggests a transna-tional unity among abolitionists of the multiple nations, territories, and times in which the symbol appears. Respectively, the two parts of this chapter that follow elaborate the contested conceptual territory forged by *Free Enterprise* as inherently transnational and yet defini-tively inflected by traditional notions of "America." This conceptual territory is evocative of "that structural duplicity" of transnationalism, Giles asserts, through which "the national and the transnational can be seen as uncomfortably interwoven" (64).

I   A Transnational America

Free Enterprise's US setting and its explicitly "American" concerns (signaled immediately by the title) expand our sense of "America" to include a postcolonial perspective on US history, complicating the categories for which critics have appropriated Cliff from the begin-ning of her writing career. Cliff's early writing, between 1981 and 1987, focuses on a young woman's quest for the suppressed history of Jamaica and her processual commitment to an anticolonialist politics. *Free Enterprise*, her third novel, marks a significant shift in Cliff's orientation: set in the United States, it features characters whose migrations from Jamaica, Europe, South America, and the Pacific Islands figure prominently in the narrative. Cliff's most recent pub-lication, *The Store of a Million Items* (1998), is a collection of stories set in Jamaica, Europe, and the United States that also highlights transnational concerns. A survey of the wealth of scholarship on Cliff reveals a curious omission of her 1990s fiction, for critics consistently and almost exclusively address either one or both of her first two novels—*Abeng* (1984) and *No Telephone to Heaven* (1987)—or *The Land of Look Behind* (1985), a collection of poems and essays, and Cliff herself as a "Caribbean" and "postcolonial" writer.[10]

Yet my study of *Free Enterprise* as a counternarrative to US ante-bellum history is informed by recent work in postcolonial studies and in American studies that suggests we rethink the initial prem-ises on which American studies was founded to consider slavery and empire. Amy Kaplan's introductory essay in *Cultures of United States Imperialism* (1993), for instance, traces an instructive "coun-ter-narrative of migration to that of the Puritans...beginning with Jamestown" and "the forced migration of Africans on slave ships and the unarticulated expression of another historical trajectory" (7). America's a priori history in Jamestown betrays a triangle of Europe, America, and Africa in which American slavery and colonialism are mutually implicated. The American historical relationship of slavery to empire and to national identity illuminates the colonialist forms of subjugation woven into the American fabric from the colonial period to the Civil War and beyond. Kaplan notes that the defini-tion of the postcolonial implies "a temporal development (from 'colo-nial' to 'postcolonial') that relies heavily on the spatial coordinates of European empires, in the formal acquisition of territories and the subsequent history of decolonization and national independence," and she queries—but does not answer—"What would postcolonial culture mean in relation to US imperialism, both on its own territory and [in other parts of the world]?" (17).

Just as the formal independence of former European colonies (from India and Asia to Africa and the Caribbean) initiates the temporal development from "colonial" to "postcolonial," the formal emancipa-tion of US slaves in 1865 inaugurates the movement from colonial-ist forms of domination to an eventual postcolonial consciousness in recent criticism and in literature such as *Free Enterprise*.[11] Indeed, in a 1993 interview, Cliff underlines her new hemispheric writing that extends her attention to an anticolonialist politics, emphasizing that although *Free Enterprise* is set in the United States, "it's also set in the Caribbean. The whole novel is about resistance. It has a Jew from Surinam, a woman who becomes a Maroon, and freedom fighter, and [other] political activists....One is a Hawai'ian and one is from Tahiti...and Annie who is from Jamaica" ("Interview with Michelle Cliff" 595–98). The narrative, she says, is "trying to show the com-plex relations among peoples in the world" ("The Art of History" 57). Cliff's characterization, like the novel itself, places the United States in an international context; her transnational depiction of the narrative, however, veils its investment in belief systems endemic to the United States. For instance, Pleasant insists, "We built this blasted country from the ground up. We are part of its futures, its fortunes"—insinuating the novel's trenchant critique and revision of myths informed by the discourse of "free enterprise," which this chapter's concluding section details (*Free Enterprise* 151).

I wish to recast, then, the paradigm of American studies as sketched by Kaplan and reiterated a decade later in the 2003 *PMLA* Special Issue "America: The Idea, The Literature" by Paul Giles, Djelal Kadir, and Marietta Messmer. "American studies," Kaplan claims, "analyzes American society and culture in terms of internal differ-ence and conflicts, structured around the relations of race, gender, ethnicity, and class." Kaplan warns, "American nationality can still be taken for granted as a monolithic and self-contained whole, no matter how diverse and conflicted, if it remains implicitly defined by its internal and social relationships, *and not* in political struggles with other cultures and nations, struggles which make America's concep-tual and geographic borders fluid, contested, and historically chang-ing" (15, my emphasis). Similarly, Giles posits as "antithetical" the "[Annette] Kolodny method [that] defined America from the inside out, seeking to regenerate native culture through a series of ever-expanding identifications" and "reconceptualiz[ing] America from the outside in"—considering it in relation to "global displacements, situating it in a postnationalist context where the country would no longer be susceptible of being validated in experiential terms." Giles warns against an American studies that incorporates marginal fig-ures "into the ever-expanding circle of national subjects," what Kadir calls "homogenizing diversity" (62, 20). Likewise, Messmer asserts, "What is needed…are strategies of integration—not only within but also across national borders" (52).

In dialogue with such scholarship, I would add a causal relation-ship, at work in various contemporary truth-telling historical fictions and especially in *Free Enterprise*. Such fiction grounds its narrativ-ized internal relationships in a long historical sense of transnational struggles and an associated conception of fluid national borders. Such literary-historical portraits of the United States belie the mutual exclu-sivity and antithetical interrogation of American nationality as Kaplan and Giles respectively characterize it. *Free Enterprise* explores hybrid cultures of citizens living within US borders to emphasize that such citizens' identities and extended histories derive from nations extrin-sic to those borders. As such, the political alliances of its intercon-tinental participants stress the "race, gender, ethnicity, and class" issues central to slavery and the rise of empire in the United States as well as to European colonialism. The novel situates US abolitionism within a capacious transnationalism colonialism and racism that spans the whole era of modern European colonialism, from the fifteenth century forward, rearticulating what Carolyn Porter calls the "politics of location" in the Americas "in relation to a history that encompasses the entire post-Columbian period, including European colonialism" (506). Cliff puts into spatial relation colonialism, slavery, and modernity, highlighting not only the common structural relations between them but also the cultures of resistance within them. Her creation of such a transnational sphere evokes the critical work of Paul Gilroy, who, in *The Black Atlantic* (published the same year as *Free Enterprise*), also explores such interrelations by turning to the writings of nineteenth- and twentieth-century African American intellectuals and musicians. However, Cliff's long historical view of a global America, anchored in its complicity in narratives of liberation and enslavement, is informative for new scholarly initiatives in comparative American studies. Populated by persons in what Günter Lenz calls "interrelationships among various, often conflicting dimensions of difference" who both contest what it means to be American and share an investment in "America," *Free Enterprise* figures cultural identities (African, Caribbean, Jewish, Pacific Islander) that precede claims to the American nation and yet avow American particularity (362).

Free Enterprise's first section, "Annie Christmas," immediately transnationalizes the Civil War by introducing Pleasant's Jamaican comrade, Annie, and Annie's Surinamese friend Rachel. As a young woman, Annie left her island home to join the abolitionist fight in the United States. Annie is now an old woman, for the year is 1920, and the place is Annie's provisional home, a rundown house near the Carville leper colony on the Louisiana banks of the Mississippi River. At their first meeting 62 years ago, Pleasant gave Annie a "*nom de guerre* fit for a woman," that of a "legendary African-American woman, a sort of female John Henry": Annie Christmas (Letter to the author). According to Pleasant, Annie's legendary namesake was born in Africa and "worked" the Mississippi during the revolutionary years; when she died, she and her sons "drifted down the river and out into the Caribbean" (25). The sparse details of Pleasant's story imply that Christmas was an abolitionist, originally abducted from Africa, and perhaps, like Annie herself, escaped captivity in the Caribbean by fleeing to the United States to work underground. Annie's singular visitor from the leper colony, Rachel, has a similar history: she has crossed continents before arriving in Carville. A Surinam Jew, Rachel is descended from the *marranos* (Spanish for "swine"), late-medieval Spanish Jews who practiced in secret, having been forced to convert to Christianity. Moreover, she has lived among African slaves who escaped Dutch slavery by moving to the interior of Surinam, South America. Like Annie, Rachel has worked with "like-minded rebels, all focused on one thing, the cessation of the Trade" (182).

The overlapping histories of these three covert abolitionists—all women of color living and working in discrete periods at the geographic and political margins of national identity—foreground not only the transnational histories of US inhabitants but a historically deep inter-American resistance to slavery. A close reading of the first chapter shows that its portrait of Annie's home sets the stage for the novel's counternarrative of American slavery: the history of the Mississippi as the main waterway for the US slave trade is evocative of the story's integral relation to the Civil War; at the same time, the marginal locale of Annie's house suggests the story's relegation to the margins of US history. Annie's cabin is "secluded," a place where her friends say she would have "to be crazy to live," and "on the very edge—She and the house" (3). This setting also suggests the story's critical interrelation to other countries and cultures. Initially disorienting in its unindicated shifts between various times and places, Cliff's narrative organization in fact invites her readers to step back and connect this setting of the southern Mississippi and US slavery to the international slave trade and particularly to the triangular commerce among Africa, the Caribbean, and the United States. A portrait of Annie's Caribbean heritage—including the multifaceted history and character of Jamaican slavery—follows the description of her US home. A traditional African American bottle tree adorns Annie's yard; the bottles themselves reflect early-twentieth-century African American culture: "Aunt Sally's Witch Hazel. Mr. Bone's Liquid Blackener. Khus-Khus Original African Scent." Despite Annie's scrubbing the bottles with river water, they still hold

a babel of scents...She stroked the Khus-Khus bottle as you would stroke the magic lamp. She put her nostrils against it. With its essence some of her ghosts were raised, and she was at a house party, on a July night, the dark perfume rising from a wicker loveseat on a verandah in Runaway Bay, on an island to the south.

The Original African Scent took her upstairs, as enlacing itself in a coverlet pieced by a slave....

On that bed at that moment the entire history of the island could be captured. Arawak. Slavery. Cane. And herself, lying on that bed, having served the landowner well. (5)

Like Toni Morrison's "re-memoration" by which something—an image or sudden scent—places the subject in the past, and hence makes the past present for the reader, Cliff's narrative moves freely between past and present time and space and brings Annie's painful past, in sexual slavery, to bear on the current story.

This passage, the first such narrative shift in the novel and the only one explicitly indicated *as* a narrative shift ("With its essence some of her ghosts were raised, and she was at a house party..."), takes us to Annie's girlhood in Jamaica. Several pages of exposition on that setting ensue, bringing to light what Anna Brickhouse characterizes as "the zones of contact inhabited by various European colonial cultures, indigenous Americans, and African slaves throughout the New World" (409):

> They inhabited a confused universe, this Caribbean, with no center and no outward edge. Where almost everything was foreign. Language, people, landscape even. Tongues collided. Struggled for hegemony...French...English...Spanish...Latin...Hebrew and Chinese and Arabic, oriental and surreptitious, kept mostly to themselves, for reasons of safekeeping, of the language and the people and their varied strangeness—to the European gaze of course. The sand on the floor of the synagogue muffled the sounds of the services....Against these tongues Africans of every stripe collided. (6–9)[12]

What is the place of this transnational canvas in a novel that rewrites the US Civil War? The slave-pieced coverlet connotes centuries of oppression, from Christopher Columbus's voyages to Annie's own servitude, and reveals slavery and colonialism as the common thread among Annie's native Jamaica, Rachel's native South America, and the United States that they currently inhabit. "Arawak," the first people whom Annie's "entire history of the island" names, indigenous to the West Indies, were the first natives whom Columbus encountered. Because, as Columbus wrote in his log, they possessed "little knowledge of fighting," he easily captured some. "With fifty men," he continued, "one could keep the whole population in subjection and make them do whatever one wanted" (quoted in Cummins 241). The introduction of European diseases combined with Spain's policies of enslavement, resettlement, the separation of families, and the encomienda system resulted in the Arawak's drastic decline within a few decades after Spanish contact. Attacks by putatively ruthless Carib tribes accelerated the process. Annie's recollection thus evokes centuries-old layers of colonization, conflict, slavery, and destruction in the Americas.

Cane sugar, which Annie next mentions, was among the industries that rapidly expanded in Jamaica during the final decades of the seventeenth century, when Jamaica became an English colony. As in the North American colonies, the consequent demand for plantation labor led to large-scale importation of black slaves, and Jamaica soon became one of the principal slave-trading centers in the world. Annie's childhood is duly influenced by the legacy of the plantation system: her light-skinned family resides on an estate and seems to have lived in a sort of feudal relationship with their landlord—her mother tells Annie that her "many nights on the slave-pieced coverlet" is "a small price to pay to be secure" (10); to Mary Ellen's later question, "Slave or free?," Annie answers, "A bit of both" (24). The Hebrew, Chinese, and Arabic are the more recent and wary immigrants to the New World who, like the Jewish worshippers, resist the contemporary hegemony. The collision of African tongues "of every stripe" foregrounds the protracted history of the slave trade in the West Indies as well as in the American colonies and begets the common cause uniting all the novel's characters.

Annie's Caribbean vision is in fact a remembrance of all the Americas; as the commencement of the novel, it discloses the complex and entwined history of New World colonization, slavery, and counterhegemonic resistance. As the backdrop for an account of a civil war in a very young nation, it restores the heterogeneous cultural histories and international struggles over slavery that precede and inform the US Civil War, rendering it as a battle within a transnational, rather than a national, war. Before Annie's Jamaican reminiscence dissipates into the 1920 present of the American South, the narrative shifts to an 1858 abolitionist meeting at Tremont Temple, Boston, where Annie meets Mary Ellen. After Annie comments in the public meeting, Mary Ellen passes her her card with an invitation to supper written on the back, and Annie agrees. Yet the details of their meeting are withheld for a couple of chapters. First, the narrative visits another array of historical places and times.

Only after Cliff has developed these juxtapositions in an effort to imagine a transnational community of abolitionists across spatial as well as temporal distances does the chapter close—with the narrative's first, and equivocal, identification of the current date. The year is 1920.

So says the calendar on the wall which came to her courtesy of the Black Star Shipping Line. Above the numerals, days of the week, phases of the moon, is an artist's rendering of the S.S. *Phillis Wheatley*—imagine it.

With each month, the progress of the ship is imagined, from her baptism in a berth on the Harlem River, to her passage past the Ambrose Light, through the blackness of the Atlantic she plows, her prow slicing the water, glancing white caps, the name of the poet

> glazed with salt, over burial ground she goes, arriving like Cleopatra,
> triumphant, amid throngs carrying armsful of fantastic flowers, at the
> dock to greet her, sweeping her path with palms, offering her bas-
> kets of fruit, tottering in their height and fullness, in Accra—Africa
> achieved, finally, by a ship that never came to be. (14)

The space of the Atlantic Ocean and the time that the calendar marks
interpenetrate to form a chronotope (literally "time space"); the space
of the Atlantic becomes charged with both the movements of the
history of African Americans and a utopian vision of homecoming.[13]
Bearing the name of the first African American known to have mas-
tered the language and poetic conventions of her captors and to write
accomplished English poetry, the ship figuratively returns Wheatley
to her homeland and is synecdochical for the millions of Africans
forced into American slavery. With the inscription of this conceptual return in her novel, Cliff implicitly replies to her fellow Jamaican
Marcus Garvey, whose Black Star Line was to facilitate the literal
return of African Americans to Africa.

Free Enterprise invents a multidimensional narrative space that
makes possible this metanarrative "exchange" between Cliff and
Garvey, one of many conversations and components of connection
across differences—political, geographic, and temporal—that the
novel forges. The SS *Phillis Wheatley*'s movement—reversing the
Middle Passage inscribed in Wheatley's famous poem, "On Being
Brought From Africa to America," crossing over its burial ground
as the calendar moves forward in time—makes manifest the novel's
theory of history whereby the past, present, and future interpenetrate in the same narrative space. Yet the ship's berth on the Harlem
River—an internal city river that does not connect to the Atlantic
Ocean—suggests the historical failure and impossibility of a literal
reverse passage. Pleasant similarly rejects black American identification with Africa in favor of black American identification with the
Americas, when (at another point in the novel, ca. 1858) she anticipates Garvey and refutes a back-to-Africa movement: "Neither will
it do us any good, as some have suggested...to take a boat back
to Africa in search of home, as if a reverse passage can reverse history. The time has passed for all that. We are no longer African. We
are New World people" (150–51). The "Harlem River" berth also
connotes the Harlem Renaissance (contemporaneous with the calendar's date). This juxtaposition foregrounds the growth of racial
pride and awareness that characterized the 1920s by signifying both
the rise and fall of Garvey and the pan-African consciousness—not

limited by geography—which the cultural movement of the Harlem Renaissance both drew upon and imagined. Cliff's response, then, to Garvey's back-to-Africa movement, his antipathy to mixed-raced blacks, and his militant African nationalism is a plural celebration of African ancestry, history, and culture among African diasporic peoples located in multiple times and places. That the image of the ship's journey is imprinted above two forms of temporality—a Western, linear denotation of time ("numerals, days of the week") and a circular representation of time ("phases of the moon")—further underscores this alternative, redemptive temporality through which the novel narrates a myriad of countermemories.

Cliff's first chapter, a mere ten pages, traverses continents and juxtaposes times from different centuries and a utopian future with the present of an American leper colony, all in its performance of initiating the reader to a narrative space in which a long history of transnational abolitionism challenges the synchrony and homogeneity of US Civil War history. Part of the difficulty for resistance narratives is carving a space in what *Free Enterprise* calls "the official version presented to the people [that] has been printed, bound, and gagged, resides in schools, libraries, the majority unconscious... walks across tapestries, the television screen. Does not give aid and comfort to the enemy. Is the stuff of convocations, colloquia, is substantiated—like the Host—in dissertations" (16). The authority and pervasiveness of official history is daunting: Where and how can one assert counternarrative and how can one foster its survival? Put another way, "How does one encounter the past as an anteriority that continually introduces an otherness or alterity into the present?" (Bhabha, *Location* 157). To interrupt official history, *Free Enterprise* figures a multidimensional, redemptive temporality through what Bhabha has called a "time-lag."[14] Providing just enough information to orient the reader to her story—a reference to the Mississippi River and the American South (which are evocative of US slavery)—Cliff snatches her reader into the variegated past of international slavery and colonialism. Similarly, she appropriates a familiar sign of the progression of time—a calendar—only to inscribe it with an alternate concept of temporality that, in its plurality, unites the narrative times and places of the novel.

With this multidimensional narrative space, Cliff implicitly places Phyllis Wheatley, Mary Ellen Pleasant, and Marcus Garvey in dialogue with one another, not through postmodern anachronism[15] but rather through writing an imagined transnational community of historical black Americans—natives of Africa, the United States, and Jamaica respectively, each of whom lived in the United States for significant portions of their temporally disparate lives. This is one way in which *Free Enterprise* engages "a critical transnationalism" that, Giles asserts, "seeks various points of intersection, whether actual border territories or other kinds of disputed domain, where cultural conflict is lived out experientially" (65). This transnational perspective is perhaps most acute in the leper colony—an actual border territory—where the storyteller inhabitants, joined by Annie, manifest multidimensional time through their tales and form an actual community based upon physical and cultural survival. Many inhabitants of the colony, like Rachel, are members of groups who have histories of anticolonialist activism; although they claim divergent international backgrounds, their similar stories of oppression and resistance reveal their shared experience of colonialism. In a chapter entitled "Oral History," the storytellers become a kind of living history: beginning their narrative with stories they have inherited, each individual reaches back centuries, thus realizing a dialectic between imagined and actual communities.

An unnamed storyteller's essential conflation of his ancestor's history and identity with his own frames the United States in its transnational history of violent encounter and colonization. This man, who has repeatedly attempted escape from the colony, "trying to make his way back to Hawai'i, where his people were," begins his story with the landing of Captain Cook in 1778—long before, that is, US domination, exploitation, and annexation of the islands. He tells his story in the first-person narrative voice of his great-grandfather, a member of the party who slew Captain Cook. This Hawai'ian's way, then, of making it back to his people is to borrow the identity of an ancestor with which to impart his own transnational history and relation to the United States. His story reminds the reader of Hawai'i's relatively recent sovereignty, which he would personally remember, given that Hawai'i was annexed by the United States in 1898, just 22 years prior to his tale. This kind of critical transnationalism, according to Giles, "can probe the significance of cultural jagged edges, structural paradoxes, or other forms of apparent incoherence and illuminate our understanding of where the culture of the United States is positioned within a framework of global affairs" (65).

For Cliff in *Free Enterprise*, such critical transnationalism is the basis for telling the truth about US history. Like the Hawai'ian man, Annie's friend Rachel personifies a long history of Jewish cultural survival; beginning with her own story in Surinam, she recounts,

> Our floor was covered with sand. The floor of our temple. Even though we were hidden in the jungle...

...When we were in Spain, under the Inquisition, during the reign of Torquemada, we worshiped in hidden rooms, some underground, some at the ends of tunnels at the backs of houses. We worshiped in secret to save our lives, and used sand on the floor to muffle the sounds of the services....the sand quelled the sound and we carried this tradition with us into the New World. Some people think we needed a reminder of our exile in the desert. Others think, first came the tropics, then the sand. Not at all. It was a survival tactic, as usual. (59–60)

Tomás de Torquemada, grand inquisitor for all Spain from 1487 until his death in 1498, used the Inquisition to investigate and punish Marranos, Moors, apostates, and others on an unprecedented scale. Rachel's tale invites readers to view the central story of *Free Enterprise*—Mary Ellen Pleasant's historical role in US abolition—in a broader temporal and geographic context of underground resistance to colonization that precedes even Columbus's first voyage to the Americas. Reading such stories against one another suggests the colonialist forms of subjugation inherent in US slavery. Both the Hawai'ian man and Rachel adopt personas who travel between past and present to convey their respective narratives of communities that were displaced by historical events and yet that resisted the imperial forces oppressing them. The leper colony suggests the United States' historical refusal to recognize the human geography of those populations that have functioned as obstacles to its transnational projects of empire building. The nation can recognize such peoples only as pathology—by their deficiencies. Their personal and collective bodies need to be deteriorated in order to satisfy a nationalist history of America.

II CAPITALISM, FREE ENTERPRISE, AND "AMERICA"

Yet *Free Enterprise*'s portrait of US history informed by its transnational history is in dialectical relation to the traditional notions of "America" in which its protagonist is earnestly invested and which Pleasant's "tender comrade," Annie, foreshadows. Annie explains her flight from the subjugation of her Jamaican girlhood, her emigration to the States, and her joining the abolitionist cause "on the mainland": she believed "the island to be without hope" (10). Annie's "mainland/Island" description for the US/Jamaican relationship intimates the transnational perspective shared by all the novel's characters—whose political activism, migrations, and rhetoric tend to substitute an essential interrelation and transnationality for discrete nations. And yet Annie's disclosure of her motive in leaving Jamaica for the United States betrays a faith in the pursuit of freedom and justice within the United States when that faith is elsewhere extinguished, connoting a distinctly "American" creed. It is thus fitting that the introduction of Annie—a native of the Caribbean and a US abolitionist who lives among a community of transnational freedom fighters—precedes and contextualizes the reader's introduction to Pleasant, an "American" in both the transnational and the traditional senses of the word.

Cliff's interpretation of a wealth of historical facts about Pleasant's life renders the unremembered truth of Pleasant as a historical person-age. Whether she was born slave or free remains one of her life's many mysteries, but during her heyday, she was one of the most influential, powerful, and respected women in San Francisco (Hudson 19–26). Pleasant furthermore figures at critical junctures in US economic history, including the gold rush and the urbanization of the West. In addition to her covert investments that undermined the slave trade and helped further her race (Pleasant employed blacks, backed them in business, and sponsored their legal representation; and she harbored fugitive slaves and paid for their room, board, and escape fare), Pleasant donated large parts of her fortune. During the Civil War, she led the Franchise League, a civil rights group she helped form in the 1850s to dispel secessionists from California, and waged several court cases to test new civil rights legislation.[16] That historical materials on Pleasant are scarce is not surprising because it is only recently that historians have sought to study black women as serious historical subjects. Moreover, the traditional sources for such studies—church and city records, family and slave histories, female societies and clubs—are not the institutions where Pleasant is most visible. As the historian Lynn Hudson explains, "Pleasant operated in movements and milieus traditionally known for their male hierarchies and cultures. As an abolitionist and business-woman, much of Pleasant's work by its very nature remains secretive and hidden" (3). It is because, as Cliff declares, "Pleasant defeats every stereotype of an African-American woman in the nineteenth-century" that she was drawn to her as a subject. Pleasant was a successful capitalist and yet "always a revolutionary, and she never gave up the Cause, even after the failure of Harper's [sic] Ferry." ("Interview" 32).

When scant evidence fertilizes a legacy of power and influence from such an unconventional subject as a rich black woman in the nineteenth century, mythmaking flourishes. Pleasant has been a subject of US popular culture, including film, fiction, stage, and television, yet she remains virtually unknown. (Most recently, *House on the Hill*, *Mammy*

Pleasant's Story opened October 18, 2008, at the Playhouse Theatre in Los Angeles). These posthumous dramatizations have represented her as a voodoo queen, mammy, and jezebel. Cliff is cognizant of the way that these stereotypes have overshadowed Pleasant's role in the abolitionist movement, and her novel endeavors to recuperate and re-create Pleasant's legacy.[17] Her fictional Pleasant's reference to "the official version [that] entertains" suggests the novel's deconstruction of these stock types in favor of its nuanced portrait of Pleasant (16).

Cliff's expression of Pleasant's claims to and pride in her successful capitalist endeavors is rooted in Pleasant's history. In Pleasant's autobiography, observes Hudson, "keenly self-aware and near the end of a long life of deal-making, buying, and selling, Pleasant locates her knack for capitalist enterprise in her youth." As a girl, Pleasant worked in a shop that, she says, "very few people ever got by" without buying something from her. "Pleasant viewed those early years as formative in her development, and more specifically, her development as a capitalist" (Hudson 31; Pleasant quoted in Hudson 31). As an adult, Pleasant strived to protect her hard-earned capital and firmly believed it to be fundamentally connected to her citizen rights. A case that began in superior court in 1898, *Pleasant v. Solomons*, particularly illuminated this. Pleasant charged that her former attorney, Lucius Solomons, had committed an act of fraud and tried to cheat her out of one of the lots she owned on Sutter Street; she brought the suit so that she could recover the real estate. In a court statement, Pleasant explicitly links her free speech "rights as a free American citizen" to free enterprise and her wealth of private property (cf. Hudson 94), implicitly referring to the moral and material values inherent in the Declaration of Independence with its guarantee of "life, liberty, and the pursuit of happiness."

An imagined conversation between Cliff's Pleasant and John Brown wherein Pleasant justifies "slaves seizing" the properties for "which they had been held responsible" resonates with the same principle:

> "In this world, Captain, property, ownership equals power [and] freedom without the means to be self-supporting is a one-armed triumph....Without my particular expertise at ownership, property, there would be no thirty thousand dollars in gold, no rifles for our people. And that money was made in disguise, in the dark, so to speak. I would like to step into the open, for once."
> ... "So you see the profit motive as a measure of humanity."
> "I would say instead self-sufficiency. Simple." (144–49)

Pleasant's emphasis on African American ownership and the importance of "self-sufficiency" echoes Emersonian "self-reliance," an expressly American creed that was at least as influential during Pleasant's lifetime as it is today. Ralph Waldo Emerson's formulation of the self-reliant citizen supplied currency to the Horatio Alger story with which Pleasant's own life has been identified (Hudson 24–25). A contemporary of Pleasant, Emerson spoke in defense of John Brown—whom Pleasant abetted—and in opposition to the Fugitive Slave Law—which Pleasant subverted. Pleasant's articulation of Emersonian principles in this passage is both historically congruous and quintessentially "American." Her story of making her fortune "in disguise, in the dark," and her desire to "step into the open" are also unexceptionally a product of the United States in that they resemble the experiences of other historically marginalized US residents—both native and immigrant groups—for whom access to good jobs in commerce, business, and the public sphere has been limited. Consequently, members of these groups often prosper in underground ways.[18]

Cliff's fictional exchange between Pleasant and Brown also teases out the conundrum of the title she chooses for her novel. Cliff's portrait of the slave trade reveals the irony of the phrase "free enterprise": the principle of free enterprise is both central to the discourse of an enterprise—the Trade—that depended upon its product being unfree and what fostered its lucrative practice. In reaction to Brown's "devotion to communism, his notion of an African state as a christ-utopia," Pleasant reminds him, "Our people knew capitalism intimately, historically. Albeit from the wrong end—at least in the New World....in Africa commerce came easily to us, there were no communist states" (143). *Free Enterprise* stresses the way in which free enterprise—the development of industry and capitalism—relies, in the nineteenth century, upon slavery; yet the novel is foremost about the enterprise of freedom: abolition. Cliff's protagonist embodies the contradiction: Pleasant uses capitalism to undermine the trade that thrived by it in her time. Most significantly, Cliff represents Pleasant as a committed "New World" abolitionist—a representation that is emblematic of the America *Free Enterprise* portrays, in which the relation between the national and the transnational is dialectical and constitutive. This key dialogue between Pleasant and Brown is an important narrative moment that focuses this conceptual territory. Though an indissoluble relationship of political and economic freedom is vital to Cliff's heroine, here Pleasant locates African American apprehension of capitalist practices not with the United States—the nation in which such values are most dominant—but with all the "New World." Similarly, although this conversation closes with an oblique reference to Brown's famous raid on Harpers Ferry ("thirty thousand dollars in gold [and] rifles for our people"), which Pleasant materially promoted and which is readily identified in historical imagination with the US Civil War, *Free Enterprise* mentions neither the raid nor the war explicitly.

Furthermore, Pleasant rhetorically frames the slaves' battle as a New World struggle for abolition as well as for economic independence that involves slaves from all the Americas. Pleasant's transatlantic abolitionist sensibilities stem from her closest and longest-standing relationships. "The first woman Mary Ellen Pleasant had loved had been her mother, Quasheba," whose own mother convinces her daughter that "on a clear day from the highest dune [of the Sea Islands] you could see the Guinea Coast, and all the traffic in between. The skin of the globe tightened and over the curve ships came." Quasheba's frustration that the "transoceanic, African, eclipse-demanding, vengeance-hungry gods were helpless" to stop this traffic in African bodies is the seed that eventually blossoms into her escape from slavery, her becoming an accomplished gunsmith and abolitionist, and her passing down her ardent commitment to the Cause to her daughter, Mary Ellen (127–28). Pleasant's intimacy with the Jamaican American Annie most clearly situates Pleasant's abolitionism within the contemporaneous transnational war for the Cause. Pouring over Mary Ellen's letters, Annie explains to Rachel that their "plan was very simple. Arm the slaves." Ruing, however, the "chasm between the [Civil] war and what we planned," Annie concludes, "Our historical moment was lost, so our tapestry is dissembled.... Only with imagination could you draw it out" (191–93).

As the primary fictional character among this band of historical abolitionists, Annie functions to impel the imagination required to construct a politics of truth about transnational abolition. The dissembled historical tapestry to which she refers consists not only of Brown, Pleasant, and the Chatham Convention but of global accounts of the movement that traditional modes of history have segregated from stories of US abolition and the Civil War.[19] Annie's own role in Brown's raid is inextricable from her unrealized dream of "burning the great houses [of Jamaica] to the ground"; along with Pleasant and Rachel, her conviction that "there is no 'someone else's fight'" for abolition and racial equality underscores the Cause as essentially transnational (199). Although Cliff writes a constructive countermemory to the earlier one-dimensional narratives that have stood in for Pleasant, she also familiarizes Pleasant to contemporary recognitions of America—wherein the United States is one member of the Americas. This portrait is truthful in that it is rooted in a traditionally neglected yet a historically valid transnational abolitionism. Other aspects of Cliff's Pleasant, however, are historically misleading. For example, whereas Cliff represents Pleasant's fierce pride in her collaboration with Brown, her Pleasant also resents the fact that Brown received all the historical credit for the stand at Harpers Ferry ("I get very fed up with everyone referring to our enterprise as 'John Brown's Raid on Harper's [*sic*] Ferry,'" she says [137]). In fact, Hudson notes, "Pleasant considered herself lucky to have escaped; she was well-aware of Brown's hanging and the execution of many of his co-conspirators" (63). Cliff's concurrent acts of historical excavation and imagination are central to the politics of truth that the contemporary historical fiction represented by *Free Enterprise* asserts. Because subjugated historical subjects do not appear in the records and archives consulted by historians, we need to bring imagination to facts that remain in order to construct the truth of such subjects. This brings a visibility not only to black women's lives, which have been invisible in traditional historical sources, but to a historically transnational America, different from the nationalistic sense that prevails in all but the most recent studies of the antebellum United States. Yet to regard silences as an empty vessel for purely imaginative filling, without any historical support, is to replace a history of silences with a fiction of contemporary desire.[20] As in other contemporary truth-telling historical novels, significant research informs *Free Enterprise* yet remains unacknowledged in its pages. By withholding its equation of research and imagination, such fiction demands the reader's imagination of the history it writes and simultaneously invites the reader's investigation of historical remains.

Conclusion: A Transnational Comm(unity) of Abolitionists as Redemptive Counterhistory

Free Enterprise resituates the dominant political ideology of the slave trade era in its global economic context and, through its protagonist, transforms its eponymous ideology from a tool of oppression to a means of revolt. The novel significantly inscribes this revision within a spatial narrative and a multidimensional, redemptive temporality in its effort to figure political and cultural resistance to the hegemony of nationalist histories of abolition. *Free Enterprise* incarnates this form of narrative temporality multitudinously but perhaps most vividly in Mary Ellen's 1874 journey to Martha's Vineyard, site of her childhood schooling at the Free African School. Along the way, she has been "reflect[ing] on the past," writing a long letter to Annie—to her past, that is, given that she has not seen Annie since the failed raid on Harpers Ferry in 1859. While thus engaged, she has been kept company by a "hologrammatical man" who appears as a waiter in the Parker House where she breakfasts before her ship's departure, as well as in various postures aboard the ship that takes her back to her past. It becomes clear to the reader that the man, in whose "beautiful, as yet unborn eyes" Mary Ellen sees herself reflected, is Malcolm X; Mary Ellen "tried to locate him in the past, not know-ing he was an impression of the future" (76). The man's breathing is a "comfort" to her, and his spoken message to Mary Ellen—"I am with you always"—though unheard by her, contradicts her own idea that her collaboration with Brown in the armed rebellion of the slaves "has gone undetected, will go to the grave with her" (100). After the hologrammatical man leaves Mary Ellen, she arrives at the Vineyard, and temporal loci converge: "She is eleven, a girl waiting for her father's ship," and simultaneously "at the age of sixty," waving to "the girl standing on the dune, who thinks [her father] greets her. Everything is here, now" (154). *Free Enterprise*'s counterhistory—its revision that occurs in between displacing and embracing the nation's official record of history—reinscribes lost voices in a plural unity of the present, past, and future. Cliff's innovative narrative techniques resist erasure by Western history, which, according to Michel de Certeau, "begins with the differentiation between the *present* and the *past*" (2); such techniques furthermore illuminate the structures of orthodox history by providing a foil to them. If, as de Certeau argues, the writing of histories is an intercourse with death because the historically vanquished can speak no more nor do harm, counter-historical narratives such as *Free Enterprise* abet the resurrection of the historical dead.[21]

Free Enterprise thus conceives a spatial sphere through which different temporalities and related, though traditionally discrete, histories converge. The novel symbolizes this chronotopic history by the recurring pictograph, on various pages, of a Mesopotamian cosmogram—a cross surrounded at its four points with four circles. Its first appearance echoes the opening chapter's serpentine (rather than linear) presentation of history: the symbol occurs in a dream that Annie has in which a man asks her if she has forgotten Dan, the Rainbow Serpent, Damballah, Aido Hwedo, "who wrapped his body around the Earth to create a globe" (21). The figure materializes at first as etched on the snake's "dangling tongue," but then, as Annie looks at it, it becomes "suddenly disembodied" and is "repeated and repeated," like the oral histories the lepers tell. The cosmogram reappears severally in the book, as, for example, engraved in the wall of a slave cage in which Mary Ellen's father—an abolitionist ship captain who secretly ferries escaped slaves—is temporarily caught. Like Annie, Captain Parsons can make no sense of it, but its association with the snake circumscribing the globe, as well as its own graphical appearance and repetition, attaches a circularity to its meaning, as to the assorted narratives in the book. Repetition effects an abrogation of beginning and end, as does a circle. This symbol provides a visual image of the time-lag: an iterative, interrogative space, "the historical movement of hybridity as camouflage, as a contesting, antagonistic agency functioning in the time-lag of sign/symbol, which is a space in-between the rules of engagement" (Bhabha, "Postcolonial" 63). Although the symbol resists interpretation and thus creates a semiotic as well as a physical space, its presence throughout the narrative insinuates the countless abolitionists of multiple nations and times whose work was often camouflaged and always antagonistic to the formal laws of their lands. The cosmogram moreover suggests their shared purpose that transcended boundaries of historical temporality, nationalities, and languages. It replaces these with a circular temporality, or spatiality—suggested by the circles that enclose divergent linear temporal axes (represented by the cross circumscribed within the circles). The cosmogram connotes the multidimensional, redemptive temporality *Free Enterprise* creates throughout, suggesting the transnational comm(unity) of abolitionists it imagines, and with which it persuades us to reread US Civil War history.

CHAPTER 5

Transnational Empire and Its Exuberant (Dis)Contents: Bharati Mukherjee's *Holder of the World*

Through its erudite excavation of numerous primary sources that show the rich economic and cultural ties between Puritan Massachusetts through the revolutionary era and pre-colonial India, Bharati Mukherjee's *Holder of the World* (1993) also underscores the fact that America has been implicated in a global economy from its inception. With her historically deep look at these fertile connections, Mukherjee extends Michelle Cliff's focus on the United States' emergence as a nation-state in a global context to its transnational conditions as a colony nearly two centuries earlier. Like *Free Enterprise*, *Holder of the World* takes a long historical view of an America engaged in transnational crosscurrents and attempts to recover a sense of women overlooked by early American histories; it is thus that Mukherjee, in her own words, "extends the American mainstream" ("A Four-Hundred-Year-Old Woman" 34). And, with the other novels in this study, *Holder* excavates and envisions a national antinationalist history. Against the traditional grain of an insular Puritan city on a hill, *Holder*'s history turns on a colonial-era woman from the "cosmopolitan" port town of Salem, Massachusetts, who defines the American character and helps shape the nascent republic (*Holder* 40).

The novel imagines a fanciful Hannah Easton—a Puritan-born immigrant's daughter who, through two transoceanic voyages and a subcontinental near-death escapade, comes of age as the lover of Raja Jadav Singh (a noble Hindu warrior) on the Coromandel Coast of Southeast India: she is known as "the Salem bibi"—meaning "the white wife of Salem." On the heels of their torrid affair, war erupts between the Raja and Emperor Aurangzeb (the "Great Mughal," the "Seizer of the World" evoked by the novel's title); Hannah's beloved

Raja dismisses her from his suite to "the women's rooms," the "zenana" of the palace. Hannah returns to America with Raja Singh's child, "the quick, black-haired and black-eyed girl, Pearl Singh." There, with her "lively" love child Pearl, Hannah ekes out a living as a healer of various sorts—"nurse, veterinarian, even, on rare occasion, doctor"—remaining "in Salem until her death in 1750 at the age of eighty" where she "saw in her old age the birth this country, an event she had spent a lifetime advocating, and suffering for" (284–85). Beigh Masters (a 1980s Yale graduate and professional "asset hunter") narrates Hannah's story in 1993, interspersing her impassioned story of the adventurous, unconventional Hannah with the rational observations of her boyfriend Venn Iyer, an MIT researcher from India. Venn and his team are establishing a grid, an immense database of material from a singular, arbitrarily chosen day. "When the grid, the base, is complete, they will work on the interaction with a personality. Anyone. In five years, they'll be able to interpose me, or you, over the grid for upward of ten seconds. In the long run, the technology will enable any of us to insert ourselves anywhere and anytime on the time-space continuum for as long as the grid can hold" (6).

Whereas critics such as Lawrence Buell, Judie Newman, and Christian Moraru focus on Mukherjee's revision of that most canonical of American novels, Nathaniel Hawthorne's *The Scarlet Letter*, I wish to consider two conjoined elements of Mukherjee's frame tale— Beigh's historical pursuit of the Salem bibi and Venn's virtual reality (VR) program—as the central conceits of the novel. Considered together, their paired research projects illuminate not only Mukherjee's substantial intervention in the narrative of the American nation but also the novel's inventive contribution to a new form of the historical novel beyond historiographic metafiction. To such novels' individual and collective explorations of a historically heterogeneous America, Mukherjee adds a gendered and transnational frame to our early New England history. To their revisions of specific national mythologies, Mukherjee rewrites myths of American exceptionalism and Puritan origin. Moreover, with its multiple time frames and resourceful approach to history, *Holder*, like all the novels in this study, evinces a keen awareness of the problems with history that poststructuralist critiques target. Yet through the voice of the narrator-historian Beigh, *Holder* is the most metacritical in its poststructuralist sensibilities and its negotiation of the problems of traditional historiography. For critic Gita Rajan, the novel's multidimensional narrative temporality and self-consciousness "promises," but does not deliver, "a postmodern frame to the novel"; Rajan accuses Mukherjee of "plac[ing] Hannah awkwardly—entangled within the discourse of history and buoyed on the borders of two cultures, that, according to the narrator, can only be grasped by following a strict timeline of events" (294). As I will clarify, Rajan misreads *Holder* in large part because she locates it as "chronologically one of the latest examples of…historiographic metafiction," comparing it unfavorably to earlier writers who "move in an overtly fictional realm…into surreal, unimagined spaces" (294). However, *Holder* is at the forefront of a more recent development of the historical novel that strategically locates its counternarrative in a specific and significant period in national history, asserting, in Rajan's own words, a certain "vision of history," which stems from an alternative and rigorous approach to the archive and to concomitant interpretation.

Holder's feminist vision of an early transnational America as well as the novel's unique aesthetic—the content of its history and its narrative form—were inspired by an enigmatic historical artifact that Mukherjee viewed at Sotheby's in New York: "a 17th-century Indian miniature, a woman in ornate Mogul court dress holding a lotus blossom. The woman was Caucasian and blond." The portrait of an Anglo woman in a distinctly Indian setting confounds our notions of each colonial America and India. Mukherjee was struck by the paradox of both gendered and continental cultures: "I thought," she recalls, "'Who is this very confident-looking 17th-century woman, who sailed some clumsy wooden boat across dangerous seas and then stayed there? She had transplanted herself in what must have been a traumatically different culture. How did she survive?'" (quoted in Cincotti 7). To find her answer, Mukherjee studied not only Indian mercantile and military histories but also that of Salem and the Puritans, Hawthorne's biography, tales of pirates, the development of medical knowledge, and Indian Wars, among other sources (Newman 83). Yet to articulate her findings, Mukherjee writes not a history of this fascinating research but a historical novel in the "Mughal narrative aesthetic," embodied in the Mughal miniature itself.

In an essay published two years before *Holder of the World*, Mukherjee articulates an aesthetic ideal that, as a writer, she first realizes in *Holder*, and that, I argue, illustrates the defining structure of the novel and its unique historiography. "My image of artistic structure and artistic excellence is the Mughal miniature painting with its crazy foreshortening of vanishing points, its insistence that everything happens simultaneously, bound only by shape and color" ("Four-Hundred-Year-Old Woman" 38). Elsewhere, Mukherjee elaborates Mughal painting as "so crowded with narrative, sub-narratives, [and] meta-narratives, so taut with passion and at the same time so crisp with irony" (in Chen and Goudie par. 4[1]). Mukherjee internalizes this aesthetic and through it navigates the problems raised both by historiographic metafiction's limited use of history—definitively ironic and distanced—and by realistic mimesis employed in traditional historical narrative, fictive and academic. The novel evokes each of these approaches in Beigh's and Venn's respective historical projects. As a 1980s Yale graduate-school alumna, Beigh metacritically uses a history that is grounded in assiduous research and duly informed by the theoretical treatment of history that has proliferated in the last 30 years. As an elite MIT computer scientist, Venn builds a vast digital grid that incorporates exhaustive data. One approach is too narrowly academic; one is imperialist. Contrary to the popular interpretation of Beigh as "Mukherjee's transparent mouthpiece," her "alter ego," Mukherjee does not merely ventriloquize Beigh (Moraru 256). Nor, as other critics read, does she replicate Venn's approach to history (Onega 459). Instead, Mukherjee's historical vision mirrors the elaborately painted border of the Mughal miniature—a saffron-colored example of which constitutes the novel's cover. "The border shouldn't be dismissed as the artists' excessive love of adumbration," Mukherjee explains of Mughal painting (in C&G, par. 8). Rather, it creates, in essence, a lens that frames and unites the painting's plethora of narratives. Similarly, Mukherjee's historical vision is the "shape and color" that binds not only the novel's many intersecting stories from the past and present and a host of global regions—-*Holder*'s dense "narrative[s and] sub-narratives"—but also Beigh's and Venn's "meta-narratives." Like Beigh and Venn, Mukherjee's engagement of history is technical in terms of her specialized apprehension of historical sources but ultimately imaginative in its weaving this sundry material into a complex novel that encompasses as well as represents Beigh's and Venn's disparate, parallel approaches to history, along with the (hi)stories these contemporary "historians" reveal.

Beigh's historical quest together with the time-space continuum of Venn's machine climax at the novel's conclusion to constitute an interpretive model: first, for the novel's sense of an alternative historiography that depends upon extensive research to inform its self-conscious exploration of the historical record and its aporias; and second, for Mukherjee's vision of her readers "experiencing" history despite and cognizant of its mediations. In her work as an asset hunter, Beigh "unit[es] people and possessions...like matching orphaned socks through time" (5). Similarly, Venn qualifies his research to Beigh: "Not time-travel...Time-retrieval" (35). It is only the consideration of their conjoined projects of imaginative reconstruction of a lived historical reality—of connecting people through time as well as space—that evokes Mukherjee's. As it unravels "the tangled lines of Mughal India and colonial New England," *Holder of the World* inscribes this transnational historical sphere onto contemporary national mythology, manifesting Beigh's belief that "with sufficient passion and intelligence we can deconstruct the barriers of time and geography" (*Holder* 11).

Along with Cliff, Mukherjee reinvents historiographic techniques as a way to inflect national narratives with a gendered and transnational pitch. Both novels manifest a theory of history whereby past, present, and future interpenetrate in the same narrative space. What results is a redemptive narrative temporality in which, as in Cliff's novel, the past is not opposed to the future but coexistent with it, as with the present. Like *Free Enterprise*, Mukherjee's book "about the making of America and American national mythology" (Mukherjee in C&G, par. 96) figures the conceptual territory of the nation-space as located in multiple times and places that intervene in nationalist narratives, causing breaks in their action and enunciating countermemories in between and alongside traditional history. Where Cliff rewrites myths informed by the discourse of free enterprise and reforms a retrospective scrutiny of the official story of Harpers Ferry, Mukherjee appropriates the legacy of literary New England—from *The Scarlet Letter* to Mary Rowlandson's *Narrative of the Captivity*—and turns this inheritance into an open, mutable, diasporic space.

TRANSNATIONAL GEOGRAPHIES AND TEMPORALITIES

Published in 1993, the same year as *Free Enterprise*, *Holder of the World* anticipates the conviction Giles expressed in 2003 that "American literature should be seen as no longer bound to the inner workings of any particular country or imagined organic community but instead as interwoven systematically with traversals between national territory and intercontinental space" (63). Indeed, to the new spatial imaginaries of trans-American studies—the borderlands/*la frontera*, the Black Atlantic, and the circum-Caribbean—Mukherjee adds the Indian Ocean, connected in the late seventeenth and early eighteenth centuries by profitable trade to the thriving city of Salem, Massachusetts. Recovering the singular fact of Salem's prosperous maritime history between the 1780s and 1830s, Mukherjee recasts Salem as the major international port for the East Indies in this era. In "The Custom-House," Hawthorne's introduction to *The Scarlet Letter*, he emphasizes the 1850 decay of the Salem customhouse. "Poking and burrowing into the heaped-up rubbish," he "exerts [his] fancy...to raise up from these dry bones an image of the old town's brighter aspect, when India was a new region, and only Salem knew the way thither" (32). Immediately upon this brief allusion, however, Hawthorne happens upon the scarlet letter, which causes him to "skip over" Salem's recent history and to weave instead his famous tale of Hester Prynne of nearly two centuries prior. Before beginning it, moreover, he relates his own family history—ignoring the sea captains and tradesmen who dominate it through his present day in favor of an account of the stern Puritans William and John Hathorne. In fact, as Newman elaborates, Hawthorne's father was an East India sea captain who sailed to the East half a dozen times, including a trip to Bengal and Madras, on the Coromandel Coast, in 1800. Hawthorne grew up in the family of his mother, the Mannings, on Herbert Street, close to the wharves and customhouse where he worked. In its prosperous days to which Hawthorne fleetingly gestures, Salem's "city seal bore a palm-tree, a Parsee, and a ship with the motto, 'To the farthest port of the rich East.'...So extensive were Salem's contacts in India and the East Indies that some traders actually believed 'Salem' to be the name of a sovereign nation" (73–74). Central to the Salem Maritime National Historic Site today is the recently renovated Peabody Museum, featuring enormous collections of Asian art, porcelain, textiles, and precious objects, maritime collections, and a mass of souvenirs from the East.

Accordingly, in *Holder*, an unnamed Massachusetts seaboard museum with a cache of Indian art is a site especially ripe for Beigh's asset hunting that directly engenders her rich counternarrative to Puritan history, the tale of the Salem bibi. Yet Salem's mercantile history is occluded in the contemporary national imagination of Salem by association with its Puritan history and related macabre witch trials, perhaps largely courtesy of Arthur Miller and the emphasis of Salem's tourism board. Similarly, in "The Custom-House," as Newman points out, "The evidence of real history is left behind in favor of a fictional pre-Revolutionary artefact, and a myth of origins....Mukherjee spots the gap in the story, the space in-between the Puritan tale of origins and the decline which Hawthorne describes—the space of imperial expansion and Eastern plunder" (77–78). In its historically grounded rewriting of myths of American exceptionalism, *Holder* complicates the categories for which Mukherjee has been appropriated from the onset of her writing career—that is, as an immigrant or postcolonial writer—transgressing institutional as well as national boundaries that traditionally treat American and postcolonial studies as distinct and that omit the United States from historical studies of empire.[2] As

Buell observes, *Holder* exploits the Puritan myth of origin by connecting the remotest ends of empire.

However, the novel not only maps transnational geographies but connects disjunctive temporalities, fusing far-flung regions of the globe to various times and extending the recent focus in critical and literary theory on space and spatial metaphor to time. As Kirsten Silva Gruesz has recently noted, although the foundational work we associate with the paradigms of trans-American studies is resolutely historicist, "the temporal dimension remains undertheorized compared to the spatial one." *Holder*'s simultaneous interweaving of multiple time frames and places is elemental to its structure and voice that reflect the "complication, elaboration and sense of the interpenetration of all things," by which Mukherjee characterizes the Mughal aesthetic ("Four-Hundred-Year-Old Woman" 38). Unlike Hawthorne's "The Custom-House," which forms a separate and distinct introduction to the story of *The Scarlet Letter*, Mukherjee's frame tale recedes as the historical novel of Hannah develops but never disappears completely. Beigh's first-person voice dominates the first few chapters of the novel. When chapter 3 introduces Hannah's story in the third person, Beigh withdraws her first-person commentary for large portions of the story such that it reads like a traditional historical novel. By chapter 6 (page 44 of the 285-page novel) the reader is fully acclimated to a ca. 1680 Puritan world, in which an orphaned Hannah with her adopted family has moved from rural Brookfield to Salem. There, like Hester Prynne, Hannah "discovered in herself an obsessive love of needlework. Her needle spoke; it celebrated the trees, flowers, birds, fish of her infant days. Nostalgia...was augmented with fancy....Even at twelve, Hannah Easton's work was known" (43). The narrative describes in abundant detail a sampler of Hannah's, a verse that "emblazoned itself in colors so tropical that the threads Hannah used had to have been brought over from a mysterious place with a musical name: Bandar Abbas, Batavia, Bimilpatuam. The result is, for me, one of the great colonial samplers." Beigh's voice returns briefly here to relate the particulars of the scene woven into the sampler. Then suddenly a fragment interrupts the description:

> "The Utmost Parts" (Anonymous, Salem c. 1680) sold to an anonymous buyer on the open market at Sotheby's (Tokyo) in 1983 for $6,000. Besides me only one person in the world knows the names of both Anonymouses.

At this, the historical novel picks up where it left off, Beigh's voice describing the distinction of Hannah's sampler: "Thomas framed her handiwork in the finest cherrywood left over from a chest he had made for the fearsome old magistrate, the twisted John Hathorne (whose excesses in the witch trials would so torment his descendant, Nathaniel Hawthorne)" (44–45).

As in Mughal miniatures, in this passage, "everything happens simultaneously" through Mukherjee's yoking several disjunctive temporalities and "the utmost parts" of the world. The reader has been intimately acquainted with the atmosphere and setting in which Hannah embroidered the sampler at age 12 in 1680; in the same narrative moment, a contemporary museum label disorients the reader. It is only through piecing together information from various other places in the text—conveyed by Beigh in 1993—that the reader can understand that the 1983 buyer is Bugs Kilken, a Hollywood mogul and colonial American art collector who, that same year, flew Beigh out to Bel Air to hire her as his private art adviser and to enlist her services in his hunt for "the most perfect diamond in the world," called "The Emperor's Tear." Beigh and Bugs suspect that Hannah possessed the diamond in India and may have brought it back to America in 1701. This passage closes, moreover, with two more interrelated temporal frames: perhaps to purge his "torment" over his ancestor, Hawthorne writes *The Scarlet Letter* in 1850 and sets it in 1642–1649. This brief pastiche, like the Mughal miniatures as Mukherjee described, is "so taut with passion and at the same time so crisp with irony. Every separate 'story' in the miniature matters, every 'minor character' has a dramatic function. But all the strands and details manage to cohere" (in C&G par. 4). Another such key "strand" is that of the threads Hannah uses. The threads doubly register the ways in which even art is complicit in the rampant capitalist enterprise by which *Holder* chiefly links the seventeenth century to the present era. The description of the exotic threads firstly signals the East Indian trade by which a Salem citizen would acquire such material, providing a transnational economic context to a parochial view of the Puritan landscape; and secondly, juxtaposed as it is with the contemporary museum title, it underscores the imperial facets of both eras—from America to India and eventually Tokyo and back.

The closing reference in the passage to John Hathorne and his descendant Nathaniel Hawthorne not only interpolates Hannah into Hawthorne's genealogy and the environment of *The Scarlet Letter* but places her in the foreground of this literary history. Hawthorne and the resonances of his famous novel recede to the background of the woman's story. This is the first instance whereby Mukherjee reverses the cause-effect lineage of Hawthorne's story and her own: she

en(genders) Hawthorne's text. For the penultimate paragraph of
Holder reveals that when Hannah returned to Salem with her baby
and her mother (whom she found upon her return "in a workhouse for
the mad and indigent"), the previously named John Hathorne's son,
nine-year-old Joseph, "seemed to have found in [Hannah's] company,
doing odd jobs, running errands, a corrective to the orthodoxy of
his household. He even went to sea, driven from the taint of Salem,
drawn by the stories of the China and India trade that she related as
she sewed." This paragraph's final statement—"His great-grandson,
Nathaniel Hawthorne, was born in Salem in 1804."—insinuates that
it was Hannah's lived experience in the social margins of Salem, transmitted through generations of storytelling, that was the seed—and
Hannah herself the model—for Hawthorne's "morbid introspection
into guilt and repression that many call our greatest work" (284–85).
Beigh's metacritical interpretation and presentation of Hannah transform our recollection of Hawthorne and *The Scarlet Letter.*

At the same time, it is important to distinguish Mukherjee's
aesthetic from Beigh's voice: gesturing in each of these passages to
Hawthorne, Beigh's voice is distinctly in the historiographic metafiction register. Overtly fictional, it calls attention to *Holder*'s intertexts
as well as to the literary history into which *Holder* inserts itself, highlighting the joins between history and fiction and the gendered subjectivity that informs all narrative constructions of history—lived or
imagined. Ultimately of course, *Holder*'s detailed accounts of Hannah
and the rich cultural-historical pastiche of her life exceed that which
either Beigh or Venn (by virtual design) could possibly construct.
Mukherjee not only weaves together, from Beigh's deep historical
research, Hannah's unexpected historical globetrotting but vividly
imagines Hannah's thoughts, fears, and desires throughout decades
and across continents. "Bordering" Beigh's voice, then, Mukherjee's
Mughal-inspired aesthetic is implicit in the "interpenetration of all"
the details—temporal and spatial—that cohere in the *Utmost Parts* passage. The simultaneity of narratives and counternarratives distinctive
of the Mughal aesthetic, demonstrated in this passage, is also emblematic of what Homi Bhabha calls "dissemi-*nation*"—the "production
of the nation as narration." Such writing manifests "the structure of
cultural liminality *within the nation*" and elucidates the striking con-
gruity of the Mughal aesthetic for *Holder*'s (re)vision of national literary history. Bhabha writes that a "disjunctive temporality of the nation
provide[s] the appropriate time-frame for representing...residual and
emergent meanings and practices....Their emergence depends upon
a kind of social ellipses; their transformational power depends upon

their being historically displaced" (*Location* 148). Taking together
the seventeenth-century Mughal miniature of the blonde Caucasian
woman and Hawthorne's ellipses in the "Custom-House" as her
cue, Mukherjee figures the historical displacement suggested by the
Mughal portrait in Hannah Easton—whose needlework, independence, and desire evoke Hester Prynne and her shifting significations
within our cultural mythology.[3]

Atomizing an organic relation among gender, culture, and nation,
Holder's counternarrative to Hawthorne's urtext "contests the traditional authority of those national objects of knowledge—Tradition,
People, the Reason of State, High Culture, for instance—whose
pedagogical value often relies on their representation as holistic concepts located within an evolutionary narrative of historical continuity" (Bhabha, "Nation," 3). What is, for example, a Masterpieces of
American Literature course or a survey of American Literature Before
1900 without *The Scarlet Letter*?[4] *Holder*'s transnational (en)gendering
of Hawthorne's text is a political intervention in our national knowledge, claiming a place in that narrative and disrupting its historical
continuity. At the same time, the argument Moraru makes, that "what
unifies, what holds together the *Holder*...is the Hawthornian narrative body" (258), obscures Mukherjee's larger project to create "the
national mythology of...the post-Vietnam United States" (Mukherjee
in C&G par. 6). *The Scarlet Letter* is the backdrop to Mukherjee's
more insistent project of carefully unpacking history and its relation
to a cultural mythology provided by Hawthorne. Mukherjee's sedu-
lous research and her historio-cultural engagement of American identity unify *Holder*. Mukherjee withholds an explicit comparison of her
"real story of the brave Salem mother and her illegitimate daughter"
to Hawthorne's tale until nearly the last page of *Holder*, though her
novel evokes the *Scarlet Letter* tale from its onset. As Moraru shrewdly
observes, "Mukherjee demarcates—playfully repeats, reinscribes, or,
on the contrary, blurs, disfigures—the emblematic mark of the *Letter*:
the Hawthornian, ambiguous and dynamic 'A.'...The novel begins,
for example, with Beigh Masters tellingly reading *A&A*, namely, the
Auctions and Acquisitions magazine" (261).

But Mukherjee (de)situates this first "A"—this "purloined letter,"
as Moraru puts it, "of our foundational alphabet"—in the multiple
times and transnational setting of her story: "I live in three time
zones simultaneously," the novel begins in Beigh's voice,

> and I don't mean Eastern, Central and Pacific. I mean the past, the
> present and future.

> The television news is on, Venn's at his lab, and I'm reading *Auctions & Acquisitions*, one of the trade mags in my field. People and their property often get separated…Nothing is ever lost, but continents and cultures sometimes get in the way. (5)

Beigh's comment on her work anticipates the way in which, like Beigh, the reader is repeatedly made to straddle continents and centuries throughout the novel, beginning immediately: In *"A & A,"* Beigh learns that "a small museum between Salem and Marblehead has acquired a large gem" whose "inscription and provenance" interests her: "Anything having to do with Mughal India gets my attention. Anything about the Salem Bibi, Precious-as-Pearl, feeds me. Eventually, Venn says, he'll be able to write a program to help me, but the technology is still a little crude. He animates information" (5). Here as elsewhere in the novel, past, present, and future intersect not only through the three central figures of the story—the Salem bibi, Beigh, and Venn, respectively—but also, as Rajan notes, through the simultaneous confrontation of "dense media—print (past), television (present) and VR (future)" (294). Beigh's focus on fragments of time and place destabilize the mark of the *Letter*—"A"—the moment Mukherjee invokes it and pulls the reader instead into the multidimensional transnational world of her novel, "the immediacy of time as an experiential reality" (Rajan 294). If *The Scarlet Letter* is a key text through which Mukherjee "studies the nation through its narrative address," *Holder*'s use of *The Scarlet Letter*'s "A" "alter[s] the conceptual object itself. If the problematic 'closure' of textuality questions the 'totalization' of national culture, then its positive value lies in displaying the wide dissemination through which we construct the field of meanings and symbols associated with national life" (Bhabha, "Nation" 3). Beigh's introduction is the telling beginning of the novel's multiplying "transcontinental adumbrations" (230) of Hawthorne's celebrated romance and its evocations of sex and religion, gender and desire, taboo and national origins of our cultural mythology.

Mukherjee's achievement is thus to allow the cognitive map of her trans-American sphere to dissolve and re-form itself around a different set of historical circumstances. Not unlike Beigh—who for 11 years has tracked Hannah through her material history, including Hannah's exquisite embroidery; a series of seventeenth-century Mughal miniatures depicting the "yellow-haired woman in diaphanous skirt and veil" amid intricate Indian settings (15); and the Emperor's Tear—Mukherjee researched mercantilism in seventeenth-century India for

11 years. Yet it is Mukherjee's situatedness in the contemporary capi-
talist-driven United States as much as her study of "crucial new material on 17th-century trade, especially intra-Asian trade," published
in the early 1990s (in C&G par. 96), that informs her construction
of the 1695 scene into which Hannah Easton disembarks with her
merchant husband, Gabriel Legge, an English sailor/entrepreneur
whom she met and married in Salem, now in the pay of the East India
Company and dispatched to South India:

> The Coromandel was like Manhattan in the mid-eighties.... The chaos
> became exponential—a kind of late-stage capitalism such as America saw
> in the 1890s, or the 1920s, or...the late 1980s.... The chain of multi-
> national factories stretched up and down the Coromandel like condos
> on the Florida coast. And the wealth they generated!...Everyone grew
> rich—the shareholders back in London, the sharp-trading, black-mar-
> keting factors, the various local nawabs and, finally, the Great Mughal
> himself.... In the consultation books of the Company's factories and
> forts, the story of the Coromandel Coast is the story of Europe, of
> white nations battling each other in outposts paved with gold. It is the
> story of North America turned inside out. (160, 102)

In its recurrent strong connections between the economic boom and
raffish fortuity of the Coromandel Coast in the 1690s and that of Wall
Street in the 1980s and earlier decades, and between European imperialism on the subcontinent and in the Americas, *Holder*'s approach to its
transnational project charts an innovative cognitive map. Through its
determined crossing and exchange of temporal borders, alongside
its tracing "the uttermost shores" of empire, the novel irrupts the
transoceanic colonial enterprise and American sensibilities of the late
seventeenth century into the present, making the past newly relevant to
contemporary socioeconomic culture (*Holder* 285).

TRANSNATIONAL HEROINES FROM
EAST TO WEST AND PAST TO PRESENT

Against this imperial—and masculine—backdrop and in a similar
interplay and overlap of temporal axes, *Holder* reconstructs an early
trans-American heroine through the voice of the avowedly modern
and feminist Beigh. Through establishing as insistent a symmetry
among Hannah, Beigh, and Hester Prynne as it does among colonial America, Europe, and Mughal India as reciprocal hotbeds of free
enterprise, *Holder* reveals that, in Gruesz's words, "if new geographies
are heuristics for seeing relationships between places and cultures in a

fresh way, then new periods are no less vital for finding as-yet-invisible
links among the chaotic components of human experience." Indeed,
Mukherjee's comments that "I used two women characters, Hannah
the pre-America American, and Beigh, the post-deEuropeanized
American, to dramatize the need to redefine what it means to be an
'American' in the 1990s. . . . I'd like to think that the ideas and feelings
generated by my fiction will . . . provoke re-thinking of what citizenship
entails" (in C&G par. 96, 70) intimate the feminine and transnational
perspective that *Holder* brings not only to our literary history but to
our current moment. This "redefined" American sensibility—never
more urgent than in the violent wake of the Bush administration's
jingoistic and imperialist policies—is embodied in Hester Prynne
and belied by the parochialism associated with the Puritan society
that condemned her and by the insular nationalism associated with
Hawthorne as a foremost author of the "American Renaissance."[5] That
Hannah and her "closest friend, Hester Manning," live on Herbert
Street recalls together Hawthorne's Hester and the Hawthorne family history he elides in "The Custom-House," suggesting Mukherjee's
project of filling the gaps; as Beigh says, "nothing is ever lost, no gesture is futile" (51, 23). Readers will recall that in Hawthorne's novel,
"social ostracism sets [Hester] free from the narrow constraints of
Puritan ideology and she transmogrifies to some extent into a free-
thinker and an emblem of passion and rebellion" (Newman 70). In all
this, Hannah evokes Hester; but where Hawthorne punishes Hester,
Beigh celebrates Hannah.

Beigh reconstructs Hannah, calling her "the flower of the New
World Zion," in a trans-American sphere that irrupts Hannah into the
present: "Of all the qualities I admire in Hannah Easton that made her
entirely our contemporary in mood and sensibility," she says, "none is
more touching to me than the sheer pleasure she took in the world's
variety" (104). Beigh recognizes in Hannah traits that "a modern
woman can relate to: her curiousity, the awakening of her mind and
her own sense of self and purpose"—traits that also describe the contemporary asset hunter to a T and are central to Mukherjee's own sense
of the American dream: "that sense of discovering for yourself what
you believe and who you want to be" ("A Usable Past" 136). Of her
resourceful biography of Hannah, complete with its gaps of Hannah's
deep interiority and of certain portions of her life, Beigh laments, "Time
has made her free from me, just as an ocean passage made her free of
the watchful God who punished every venal sin" (89). That is, she resolutely moors her heroine's global life to the colonial epoch centuries
before her modern one and at the same moment unleashes Hannah

entirely from a conventional view of a Puritan woman. Hannah weeps and rages over her late discovery of Gabriel having a native mistress, a "bibi": it "was a matter that her pride would not permit forgiveness" (198). Before she can make her planned sail to London, a cyclone tears through the Coromandel Coast and "her piratical husband [was thought] to have drowned" (209) Hannah, too, nearly drowns, but the Raja's men pull her from the swirling river. Soon she accepts that "everything was in flux on the Coromandel coastline. The survivor is the one who improvises, not follows, the rules....What she had left Gabriel for just months before, she would accept from Raja Singh. She was no longer a wife. She was the bibi" (234).

Hannah's behavior is exceptional for a widow of Puritan or Indian origin; but her proclivity both to improvise and to reinvent herself is portrayed as characteristically American from the first immigrants onward. Hester Prynne was excoriated for succumbing to Dimmesdale after her husband, having disappeared for years, was thought to be dead; and the traditional and extant custom of Indian widow immo-lation is well known—Gabriel's and Venn's family each report the practice. That Beigh receives the stories with skepticism is no doubt informed by Hannah's memoir of her widowhood, in which, Beigh relates, Hannah wrote "so movingly of sexual passion [with the Raja] in a voice that is unique among her time and place" (76). After the Raja loses his right arm in battle, Hannah explicitly labels herself as an American who, by definition, recovers from cataclysmic events by remaking herself. Upon her failed plea to the Raja to come "home" with her to America—"Leave?" he replies. "It was an obscene idea, to alter one's fate, to abandon one's duty."—she defends her request with an ode to the American value of self-transformation. "My father was your age when he left England and came to America. He was a clerk, and he became a farmer. My stepfather was a farmer in the woods, and he became a carpenter in the city. My husband was a factor, and he became a pirate. I was once a respectable married English lady and look at me now—a bibi in a sari. We can all change" (256–57). Here, approaching the close of the novel, Hannah's voice recalls Beigh's early introduction of the heroine via her own family: "a chance for a rebeginning...like villages in Poland and Italy and Ireland emptying for America.... Case in point: my family" (21).

Beigh's ensuing explanation of how, "in the remotest of ways, Hannah Easton is a relative of mine" ensconces her association with Hannah not merely by scholarly interest but by genealogi-cal and cultural heritage. Hannah's maternal great-grandmother was a cousin of Beigh's Puritan ancestors, the "Musters/Masters of

Massachusetts"; "by 1653 Elias Walker, his wife and infant daughter, Rebecca [Hannah's eventual mother] leased from their distant relatives the Masters three hundred acres of prime Quabaug River bluff....by 1665, he had purchased the land outright. My direct Masters ancestors pocketed the cash and further dissipated their father's wealth" (21). To this quick making and unmaking of a fortune, Beigh contrasts Venn and acknowledges her own propensity to reinvention as inherent to the American character. "His family are all successful; there was never question of anything different. He grew up in a world so secure I can't imagine it, where for *us* security is another kind of trap, something to be discarded as dramatically as Rebecca stepped out of dog-blooded widow's weeds into a life of sin and servitude" (31, emphasis added). Recognizing her instinct to discard the "trap" of security, Beigh at once aligns herself with her Masters ancestors, Rebecca and Hannah. She refers here to the fact that following the untimely death of young Hannah's father, her mother Rebecca became beloved of a Nipmuc Indian. During King Philip's infamous 1675 siege of Brookfield, the two lovers stage Rebecca's murder, gallop away together, and abandon the five-year-old Hannah, whom a Nipmuc woman deposits on the threshold of a Puritan family's cabin; Hannah herself remains mute about the truth of her mother's desertion. Beigh's explicit identification with Rebecca and implicit identification with Hannah (who "suddenly married a man she recognized as inappropriate and untrustworthy...to expose herself to the possibility of life" [69–70]) conjoin her to Hannah and Hester as quintessentially American.

A Mutually Transformative Historiography

If Mukherjee (en)genders *The Scarlet Letter*, placing Hannah in a determinative position vis-à-vis Hawthorne's story, she similarly subverts Mary Rowlandson's *Narrative of the Captivity*. Mukherjee appropriates both canonized texts to write women's agency into a literary history of New England in which female desire, where it exists at all, is sublimated to God to reinforce patriarchal control over women's bodies. Beigh's active and insightful readings of Puritan texts to illuminate Hannah's untold story—and by implication, the obscured histories of most Puritan women—reflects and emphasizes Mukherjee's historiographic project in this sense. Mukherjee's historiography is mutually transformative: as we inscribe feminine agency on patriarchal history, we expand our sense of the past and at the same time revise our literary inheritance to bear on our present.

With the seminal tale of Rebecca's bold remaking of her life with a Nipmuc man during the same 1675 Indian raid that enslaved Mary Rowlandson, Mukherjee inverts the "original" captivity narrative—Rowlandson's 1682 account of her actual captivity during King Philip's war—to give a passionate, compelling voice to the female "captive." Because the striking account of Rebecca precedes the novel's later introduction of Rowlandson, the vivid sense of female agency paramount to Rebecca's story fundamentally informs the reader's apprehension of Rowlandson's. Moreover, as with *The Scarlet Letter*, the novel fragments Rowlandson's narrative in relation to Hannah's childhood and character. Hannah's friend Hester Manning reads *The Narrative* to the 15-year-old Hannah, insisting that "everybody, *everybody* [is] reading" it. Hannah's personal recollections of "her own dread-filled hour" along with third-person narrative speculations "that not all white women abducted were enslaved" repeatedly interrupt Hester's read excerpts. "There were sightings, sworn by respectable witnesses, of fair-headed and light-skinned women, English gentlewomen...moving with bands of Indians on the outer fringes of civilization" (52). This scene between the 15-year-old girlfriends brings the chapter to a halt as Hannah suddenly remembers Rebecca "initiating her daughter into a whispered, subversive alphabet, '*A* is for Act, my daughter!'"

> "*B* is for Boldness," Hannah pledged. "*C* is for character, *D* is for Dissent, *E* is for Ecstasy, *F* is for Forage..."
> And *I*, thought Hester, remembering the women who wore it emblazoned on their sleeves, is for Indian lover.
> "*I* is for Independence," said Hannah. (54)

Mukherjee's use of Rowlandson's *Narrative* in this scene is doubly transformative. Upon the sudden recollection, Hannah "miraculously recovers" from a month of bed rest during which she is given to "delirious babbling." At the same time, Mukherjee framing the *Narrative* within the powerful story of Rebecca's "betrayal" subverts both the captivity narrative and the dichotomous view of colonial-Indian relations that Rowlandson's narrative and the literary tradition of captivity narratives it spawned came to stand in for and define.

Such a mutual effect is vital to the novel's sense of an alternative, interactive historiography. It recurs additionally in Mukherjee's insistence on a "two-way transformation"—of Hannah herself "as an immigrant writer" and her readers—and it is a connotative dialectic for the long transnational history her novel recovers and irrupts into the present (in C&G par. 68, 70, 46). The novel's embedded historian, Beigh—who, unlike Mukherjee, writes up her copious research in a history—also figures such an interrelation. One of several examples of the way in which Beigh shapes the narrative of history is her presentation of a letter of marriage proposal to Hannah, written by William Pynchon on behalf of his son Solomon and addressed to Hannah's adoptive father, Thomas Fitch. Following the letter's full reprint in the pages of *Holder*, Beigh comments,

> This particular letter is well known and frequently annotated for the evidence of close attention paid to finances and practicalities and for the awkward display of passion in a Puritan context. The evidence of a dialogue, a response, however, has never been presented. (Hannah apparently was known both by her birth name of Easton and that of her adoptive parents, but scholars had never put the two identities together). Scholars have cited the letter as evidence of social mobility in Puritan New England; feminists have seized upon its implied sexism. (57)

Well aware that "the ideological sign," as Stuart Hall explains, "is always multi-accentual and Janus-faced," Beigh approaches history in a manner that reflects "a discursive conception of ideology" (9). Educated at the Yale Graduate School of History, Beigh flaunts her cognizance of the ways in which historians of different stripes appropriate the same piece of textual evidence for various interpretations that are driven at least as much by their subjective agendas as by empirical concerns.

She furthermore frames her subsequent interpretation of Fitch's response letter (which she alone, having "identified Hannah Easton as Hannah Fitch aka Precious-as-Pearl and the Salem Bibi," has pieced together with Pynchon's entreaty) as similarly subject to the "multiple contingencies [of] the universe we inhabit," self-consciously informed by contemporary critical theory along with a panoply of actual and fictional intertexts (60–61). Fitch declines the proposal on the basis of Hannah's "Disruptions of the Humours, Infections of the Very Soul," which he attributes to the trauma she experienced at losing, at a tender age, first her father and then her mother. Fitch insists that Hannah should remain under his family's care so as to spare Solomon "the Confusions and Sadness that caring for nervous Invalids must surely impose" (59). I quote Beigh's response at length because it is emblematic of her—and hence the novel's—metacritical approach to history, which reasons contingent interpretations while seizing upon facts:

> I want to think of Robert Fitch as a man ahead of his time, or at the very least, a decent embodiment of the tolerant forces in his age....He could not understand Hannah. What she had witnessed, what she suppressed. It is just that Hannah is a person undreamed of in Puritan society. Of course she must suffer "spells" and be judged an invalid. Outside forces—the devil, the forest, the Indians—must be blamed....
>
> Incestuous, obviously, my cynical self, my well-trained feminist half, reading these notes, has told me. The stepfather and stepbrother wanted her to themselves. They needed the money she brought in....
>
> She might have been a prisoner; they might have been her tender guardians. The fact is, she stayed in Salem with the Fitches through the famous witch trials, in which she played a small role as counselor of women who fled marriages and husbands they no longer under-stood....We know the Fitches feared their stepdaughter would be next, that she would personally intervene in some witch's trial, offer-ing testimony that could only implicate her or her family, and that she could not depend upon her childhood woes as a reliable indulgence before a judge like John Hathorne....They hid her wild embroidery; they barred entreaties; they monitored every visitor. Only the oldest friends, the Mannings, were allowed access. (59–61)

By explicitly raising several competing interpretations first of Pynchon's proposal letter and then of Fitch's reply, Mukherjee's novel implicitly interrogates the premises of realistic mimesis. Beigh's sympathetic reading of Fitch stems from the historicist conviction that, like texts, individuals are products of their historical social, political, and eco-nomic environments who cannot be understood unless one attempts to resituate them within those conditions. Her ensuing "feminist" interpretation displays a clever contemporary angle through which she could read Fitch's response, if she wanted to; and indeed such savvy informs her modern sympathetic understanding of the social margins in which so many women in Hannah's Puritan society suffered. Unlike the source of the proposal letter and the academic interpretations of it, Beigh does not provide the evidence for her concluding assertion of the Fitches' cautious protection of Hannah from the cancerous witch hunts, though her knowledge of Puritan history is so thorough that we are inclined to take her at her word. With the beginning phrase, "We know...," Beigh effectively dismisses the feminist reading as unsub-stantiated and favors her reading of Hannah, and to a lesser extent Fitch, in a vein counterhistorical to the fanatical witch trials, which she obliquely references by way of Hawthorne's maternal and paternal family. With Beigh's conclusion to her analytically plural interpretation of these material artifacts, *The Scarlet Letter* again becomes a means by which Mukherjee draws our attention to what Bhabha identifies as those "obscured but highly significant recesses of the national culture from which alternative constituencies of peoples and oppositional analytic capacities may emerge" ("Nation" 3). In *Holder*, these alternative constituencies of peoples range from the criminal and insane to the feminine and subversive.

Beigh underscores such an effective counterhistory, reflecting, in the midst of her interpretation,

> Looking at Hannah through the lens of history is like watching the birth of a nebula through the Hubble Space Telescope—a chance encounter that ties up a thousand loose ends, that confirms theories, upsets others. Her life is at the crossroads of many worlds.
>
> If Thomas Pynchon, perhaps one of the descendants of the failed suitor, had not written *V.*, I would call her a V., a woman who was everywhere, the encoder of a secret history. (60)

Beigh benefits from the retroactive knowledge of Hannah's life: that Hannah was previously raised in the woods by her mother along with a Nipmuc man whom she "knew as her inadmissible father" (they were "a frontier family"); later, about "the vow [Hannah] ma[de], bobbing in the arms of the nameless [Nipmuc] woman she has known all her life, to remain silent about this night, to sustain her mother in the ultimate lie, the ultimate unnatural crime of Puritan life, [that she kept] for sixty years" (27–31); and finally, that at 21 Hannah ventured oceans away to exotic worlds wildly different in character, color, climate, and values than her New England home. Through the telling "lens of history," that is, Beigh portrays Hannah as "a chiasmatic 'figure' of cultural difference," as Bhabha might say, "whereby the anti-nationalist, ambivalent nation-space becomes the crossroads to a new transnational culture" ("Nation" 4). For Hannah lived at the crossroads of a Puritan, parochial Salem and Salem the cosmopolitan port town in which "the world's races were represented, and a mini-congerie of languages" (*Holder* 39); at the crossroads of a British colony and a young state celebrating its membership in a whole new country; and, notably, at the crossroads of ancient Hindu-Muslim wars and modern transnational empire.

Beigh's reference to Thomas Pynchon is thus both connotative and provocative. Certainly it suggests Mukherjee's appropriation throughout *Holder* both of the Pynchonesque narrative voice that foregrounds alternative takes on historical records and of an intertextuality that juxtaposes overtly fictional sources with not-so-obviously authentic ones: thus Mukherjee doubly registers the manufactured lenses of history.[6] More specifically and to the point, however, Beigh's metaphor of "V." for Hannah, "the encoder of a secret history," speaks to the secret history of nameless, countless women throughout history trapped by narrowly defined nationally and religiously encoded gender roles, whose chafing against such codes of behavior were dismissed as hysteria or spiritual malaise, enciphered as "ill humours." This mostly invisible past to which the Mughal miniature and the imaginative figures of Hester Prynne and Hannah Easton gesture is at the core of Mukherjee's metahistorical project.

Imperial Designs and Virtual Reality

Although their common initials, crosscultural romantic bonds,[7] historical interests, and tenacity clearly figure a correlation between Beigh Masters and Bharati Mukherjee, less noted is the kinship between Venn Iyer and Bharati Mukherjee that is key to the novel's sense of an interactive historiography in which historian and reader alike can shape history and be altered by their experience of it (*Holder* 19). As members of the Indian diaspora, not only do Venn and Mukherjee share a common collective past, but in their contemporary moment, they are engrossed in a plethora of historical data and concomitant particular research projects. Like Venn, who is "out there beyond virtual reality, re-creating the universe, one nanosecond, one minute at a time," Mukherjee aims to create "miniature universes within the frame" of her novel, from Hannah Easton's colonial worlds—New England, British imperial, Hindu, and Muslim Indian—to Beigh and Venn's contemporary ones, in part through drawing on a mass of multinational sources from the seventeenth to the twentieth centuries (*Holder* 5; C&G par. 11). Venn's research involves the re-creation of a randomly chosen day, October 29, 1989, within which universe he can "stimulate sense responses—smell, touch, sound—in any subject properly equipped and programmed. But that didn't excite him. People will always respond to stimuli, but so will pond scum. The interesting problem," for Venn—and for Mukherjee—is "constructing an interactive model of historical or imaginative reality. Historical reality to begin with, since there was a data trail, indisputable facts to begin with" (34–35). Venn describes his "special kind of data and special kind of input" as "four dimensional" because it involves a

"time-traveler" who has punched in "the answers to a thousand personal questions…to construct a kind of personality genome" (7).
Each subject will thus experience a different virtual reality, even when
"traveling" to the same day, unique to the individual interaction with
the programmed data. Not unlike Venn, Mukherjee is uninterested
in "writing a historical novel that is simply a passive retrieval of past
data." Like Venn's subjects, she "need[s] to experience history and
have my readers experience history rather than be told historical
information" ("Naming Female Multiplicity" 300–301). Yet a comment on Venn's VR program evokes Mukherjee's unique challenge to
render the imaginative historical reality of the Salem bibi and a key
distinction between Mukherjee's and Venn's approaches to history.
"Because of information overload, a five-minute American reality
will be denser, more 'lifelike,' than five minutes in Africa" (7)—or
than a novel-span in Mughal India. As I have begun to elaborate, to
create this experiential—and remote—history, Mukherjee employs a
number of postmodern narrative techniques amid a wealth of historical complexity, imbued by both imagination and signposts as to the
limits of her project.

Venn's use of "overload" data, however, is subject to a critique in
the novel implied by the title itself—which is enigmatic, given that
the actual translation for Emperor "Aurangzeb" (for whom the novel
is ostensibly named) is "Seizer of the World." "Holder" implies something even more acquisitive than "Seizer," an insistent holding-onto.
The text's conflation of the appellation "Holder of the World" with
Emperor Aurangzeb—one of the most controversial and ruthless figures in Indian history, who, during his 48-year rule of India, expanded
the Mughal Empire to its greatest extent, leaving only the southern tip
of the subcontinent free from Mughal rule—insinuates the critique of
imperialism with which *Holder* is centrally concerned. This critique
recurs through various subnarratives—from Mukherjee's portrait of
the Coromandel Coast and its numerous transnational profiteering
factors connected to Salem in this context to her characterization
through Hannah's eyes of the Muslim General "more experienced in
conquering and acquiring than anyone but the kings of Spain, France
and England" (262). Hannah calls him a "despot" (264): "You cloak
your lust for vengeance and for gold and diamonds in the noble
words of duty and judgement and protection and sacrifice" (269).
Considered a tyrant by most Hindus, Sikhs, Shia Muslims, and other
non-Muslim Indians, Aurangzeb was remarkably pious and zealous,
unflinching in use of vast military might to attain his goal of strict
adherence to Islam and Sharia (Islamic law)—as he interpreted them.

Abandoning the religious tolerance of his predecessors, he defaced and destroyed many Hindu temples and converted many non-Muslims to Islam, both by inducement and by force ("Aurangzeb"). The novel's title is moreover conspicuous in that although to "hold the world" is impossible for any mere mortal, conquerors from the Great Mughal to the modern British and American empires implicated in *Holder* have attempted to approach this end in their ceaseless control of lands and nations.

Mukherjee extends her critique, by implication, to Venn, whose approach to history evokes such imperialist tendencies. His "research mean[s] the *mass ingestion of all the world*'s newspapers, weather patterns, telephone directories, satellite passes, every arrest, every television show, political debate, airline schedule... do you know how many checks were written that day, how many credit card purchases were made? Venn does" (6, emphasis added). Susan Onega's assertion that Beigh "gives the same historical value to all kinds of information" is misapplied (459); it is Venn who treats all data indiscriminately. As Venn's project begins to merge with hers, Beigh observes,

> Venn inputs data more boldly, more mischievously than I do. I watch my convoy of East Indiamen voyage across his computer screen, freed of space and time. He compresses by supercomputer Hannah, Gabriel, the schoolmaster, the maiden ladies from Lancashire, caulkers and coopers, soldiers and sailor makers, gunners, cabin boys, two two-headed freak dogs, horses, goats, hogs, sheep, geese, chickens, ducks, plum puddings, vats of pea soup, mutton pies, pork pies, chops, cutlets, potatoes, lemons, rum, beer, dysentery, scurvy, into a one-second long video model.
> Attaining Nirvana, for Venn, is attaining perfect design. (91)

In this sense, Venn resembles "His Imperial Majesty": "The Emperor was a builder of cities, a designer of human lives"; Venn is the "father of fractals and designer of inner space" (270, 19).

Venn's imperialist approach to his historical subject—his goal of "perfect design" and his simulation of the world—recalls the Jorge Luis Borges tale "On Exactitude in Science": "In that Empire the Art of Cartography attained such Perfection that... the Cartographers Guilds struck a Map of the Empire whose size was that of the Empire, and which coincided point for point with it. The following Generations... saw that the vast Map was Useless," and "they delivered it up to the Inclemencies of Sun and Winters. In the Deserts of the West, still, today, there are Tattered Ruins of that Map, inhabited by Animals and Beggars" (325). These current inhabitants, that is, confuse the map with the real thing. As Jean Baudrillard observes, this tale "bears witness to an imperial pride" (253). The "Map of the Empire" in Borges's tale bears an uncanny resemblance to "computer assisted time-reconstruction" in *Holder*, of which Venn claims, "It will be, literally, the mother of all data bases. It will be time on a scale of 1:1, with a new concept of real time. [Venn] won't call it time-travel. Neither we, nor time, will have travelled an inch, or a millisecond" (138). The program, nonetheless, simulates the experience of traveling to another place and time. Beigh recounts, "I put on the designer headgear and the electronic gloves and walked in virtual reality for ten seconds on a Boston street....I don't mean I watched them—I was with them; they responded to me. Those crowds on the Boston street parted to let me pass. I reached out and touched a faucet, touched the sleeve of a student beside me, and felt them both. When I walked up the stairs, I got winded" (138, 278). Venn produces a simulacrum of the world in the way that resembles the Cartographers' simulacrum of the Empire: their designs correspond to their respective historical realities 1:1, or point for point, effecting a confusion of the imaginary for the real. Baudrillard cites the Borges story as the "first allegory of simulation," the process of "substituting signs of the real for the real itself" to produce a "hyperreal...sheltered from any distinction between the real and the imaginary": history vanishes (253). Likewise, Venn's inputted data function as signs of the real, which produce a virtual reality that, tantamount to the Cartographer's tattered Map, effaces the real world: "Venn says I talked and the various monitoring devices showed I was physically reacting to virtual space, not to the lab" (278).

Moreover, in "freeing" Beigh's East Indiamen "of space and time," Venn totally dislocates them from any specific history, from any time and place. His proceeding "boldly," as if with "enough" data he can hold the world of a historical moment, ironically unmoors subjects from their historical contexts, creating a simulacrum: a "video *model*." Yet despite his thoroughness, Venn's "dense" data fails to produce a more "lifelike" American reality than Mukherjee's seventeenth-century India. Of her initial experience with Venn's program, Beigh relates, "I retrieved thirty seconds from lives I've never lived—but which I now have. But why did I intercept a lady in her yellow jacket demonstrating faucets in a Kansas City bathroom?" (279). Beigh formulates the paradox of "knowing" history—"retrieving lives I've never lived"—and implicitly questions to what degree and with what intimacy we can grasp histories, especially those of lives un(der) represented in the historical record—such as women and various peoples relegated to the social margins whom *Holder* (like a good many contemporary historical novels) imagines. Clearly, compiling exhaustive amounts of data—historical remains—alone does not ensure such access or understanding. In this respect, Venn mirrors the historian, who, poststructuralist critics claim, "at best, can point to actual remains that supposedly come to us from the past or to the sources historians use as evidence for their historical reconstructions," that is "the intertextuality that results" from "other 'histories'" (Berkhofer 149). In this sense, even "thorough research" such as Venn's yields a shallow representation of history, epitomized by the lady in her yellow jacket demonstrating faucets in a Kansas City bathroom. The context needed to make sense of this encounter—the emplotment and metaphor, as Hayden White would say—is absent. Without an historian to make meaning out of this raw data—to tell us, in essence, a story about it—we have no (hi)story, only a vacuous encounter with "remains." Thus Beigh answers her own question, suggesting the diacritical sifting and interpretive aspects of a Foucauldian genealogy—an attempt to emancipate historical knowledges. "I talk about asset hunting and the fact that data are not neutral," says Beigh. "There are hot leads and dead ends. To treat all information as data and to process it in the same way is to guarantee an endless parade of faucets in Kansas City" (279)—a caricature of history, that is, which merely positions the reader at an ironic distance from it.

Indeed, the endless parade of faucets functions identically to the "voyage" of Beigh's East Indiamen across the screen as simulacra, recalling Frederic Jameson's discussion of Andy Warhol's *Diamond Dust Shoes*. In contrast to Van Gogh's *A Pair of Boots*, whereby "these henceforth illustrious peasant shoes slowly re-create about themselves the whole missing object world which was once their lived context," we confront in Warhol's painting "a random collection of dead objects hanging together on the canvas like so many turnips, as shorn from their earlier life world as the pile of shoes left over from Auschwitz or the remainders and tokens of some incomprehensible and tragic fire in a packed dance hall" (8). Jameson's point in suggesting via simile these two radically different possibilities, of course, is that because Warhol's painting forestalls any historical context, it is impossible to know which or what event surrounds, produced, or informs the diamond dust shoes. Warhol's postmodern art, like Venn's virtual parade of faucets and East Indiamen, effects what Jameson calls a schizophrenic experience of the eternal present—"thrust before the eyes, which gaze with equal fascination on an old shoe or the tenaciously growing organic mystery of the human toenail" (10)—a "waning of historicity" (21). Like Beigh's voice elsewhere in the novel, Venn's approach to history, his production of simulacra, effects a critical distance from it, the identifying feature of historiographic metafiction.

However, it is vital to remember that neither of these diegetic characters constitutes the novel's approach to history as a whole and at the same time that the novel sustains a critique of both an imperialist approach to history like Venn's and an academic, wry approach like Beigh often takes as ultimately flat. Either of these approaches to history alone forecloses, in Jameson's words, "our lived possibility of experiencing history in some active way" (21). It is these aspects of *Holder* that perhaps cause Rajan to confuse it with historiographic metafiction such as Condè's *I, Tituba, Black Witch of Salem*, against which she continually compares Mukherjee's novel—only to tear it down for not showcasing "the pioneering work of postcolonial scholars," for example (292). Rajan explains, "I quote extensively from Condè to show the authority with which these characters conduct a dialogue in an imagined space in history. In other words, the timeline remains steady, but the circumstances, actions and reaction are situated in that space where anything could be imagined"—in contrast to *Holder*, which she disparages for "holding rigidly to history" (310, 295). *Tituba*, like *Free Enterprise* and *Holder* along with the other novels in this book, probes the conceptual borders of American identity, articulating it as hybrid and fluid. But where Condé employs flagrant anachronism to expose the subjectivity and contextualized nature of historical narrative and event, *Holder*, to borrow Bhabha's words, "engages the insights of poststructuralist theories of narrative knowledge ... in order to evoke the ambivalent margin of the nation-space." This margin must not be "seen simply as 'other' in relation to what is outside or beyond it [but] the problem of inside/outside must always itself be a process of hybridity, incorporating 'new people' in relation to the body politic, generating other sites of meaning" ("Nation" 4). Mukherjee retroactively reveals the concomitance of "new people" and regions—of the East—to the "boundary" of the nation, generating new sites of meanings around American origins and male-dominated cultural mythology.[8] Where Condé mocks the spare historical remains of her subject, Mukherjee stresses her extensive research stemming from her encounter of the seventeenth-century Mughal miniature as the grounds for her literary intervention into American history (C&G par. 96). Mukherjee's strategy, very much like Cliff's in *Free Enterprise*, is to draw upon recondite historical materials to respond to theorists of Western history even as she critiques that history and revises it. Rather than merely problematize the nature and status of our information about the past, as does historiographic metafiction, *Holder* makes counterhistorical truth claims to received versions of the past.

This provocative (dis)connection between Venn, the MIT programmer seeking to virtually retrieve a historical time, and Mukherjee, the historical novelist seeking to recover an experiential transnational history, is further highlighted by Sandra Ponzanesi's paper that focuses on "the cultural and ideological implications of the hypertext and [its relation] to the politics of diaspora." Ponzanesi reasons,

> The concept of diaspora refers to deterritorialised imagined communities which...despite their dispersal, shar[e] a collective past and a common destiny, and hence also a simultaneity in time as well as in cyberspace....Both cyberspace and diaspora convey a post-national space which is articulated by loosening the hyphen of nation and state and which dislocates previous notions of the centre/periphery divide. Cyberspace and diaspora are, in fact, nomadic and transnational concepts, able to traverse political boundaries and Western categories of thought. (396)

According to Ponzanesi, cyberspace thus serves as an apt "literary device to narrate a possible alternative historiography" (397). It is true that the intersection of cyberspace and diaspora in *Holder* is suggestive not only for Mukherjee's tracing, with the nomadic Hannah, her own diasporic journey west from India in reverse,[9] but for Mukherjee's recovery, through the figure of Hannah—who traverses national, sexual, and political boundaries—of the transnational aspect of colonial Salem and its crosscurrents with overseas British and Mughal empires. However, as we have seen, the historical vision rendered in Venn's program is deficient, two dimensional at best. As Ponsanezi herself points out, "the internet is based on the assumption that we can be disembodied...whereas many diasporic experiences are strongly marked by the 'enfleshment' of their experience" (399). Indeed, part of the appeal of cyberspace is its illusion of "freeing" the user from a precise geographical address as well as time. In this sense, cyberspace as a historical model is more apt for historiographic metafiction such as *Tituba*, which, like Venn's virtual reality program, unmoors its subjects from their historical contexts. For Mukherjee, in contrast, situates her Puritan female subject in a quite specific, heretofore obscure period of Salem's maritime history wherein the trajectory of her life is determined by its extensive East Indian trade.

An Experience of History

The distinction between Venn's and Mukherjee's approaches to history is again figured by the border of the Mughal miniature, which, Mukherjee elaborates, "forces you to view the work not primarily as a source of 'raw' sociological data, but as sociology *metamorphized*; that is, as a master-artist's observation on life/history/national psyche cast in the aesthetic traditions of the community and transmuted into art" (in C&G par. 8). This is why Beigh's tenacious pursuit of Hannah through her dense material history is the necessary complement to Venn's VR program, which *together* function as metaphor for the novel's sense of a historiography that, given the nationalist, gender, and class biases of traditional histories, must carefully consider sundry texts and bring to bear upon them a discriminating interpretation. These include not only literary as well as nonliterary texts but those that might moreover be excluded from the traditional canon of evidence, including texts from the domestic sphere—where information pertaining to a seventeenth-century woman's life, from embroidery to private letters and memoirs, might reside. As Onega notes, Beigh unearths "all kinds of records, from logbooks, annals, travel books, diaries and memoirs to paintings, poems," Native American as well as Indian "'captivity narratives,' embroidered samplers and orally transmitted tales or myths" (459)—an assiduous study that reflects Mukherjee's own research. One of *Holder*'s most striking features is its resolute historicism, and yet Mukherjee gives flesh and blood to the transplanted Anglo woman whom she viewed in the Mughal miniature. Her project is antithetical to the ironic distancing from history that chiefly characterizes historiographic metafiction and which the "endless parade of faucets in Kansas City" foregrounds. Through Beigh, the impassioned narrator-historian, Mukherjee engages her readers closely with Hannah, whom we come to know with increasing intimacy as Hannah herself comes of age, into a deeper knowledge of herself than we sense she could have in her stifling and stark Puritan environment.

Yet ultimately, it is through Beigh and Venn's VR program simultaneously, at the novel's climax, that Mukherjee most closely recovers a lived historical experience, brief excerpts of which I cite later. Preparing us for her virtual quest, Beigh explains, "It is necessary that I undergo the search [for the Emperor's Tear]; the program is interactive and when Venn tried it"—even after absorbing Beigh's "manuscript and all the documents, the travelogues and computer-ized East India records, the lavishly illustrated *namas*, or chronicles, of the emperors of the Mughal dynasty" into the database—"all he got was a postcard view of modern Madras. The program will give you what you most care about; your mind is searching through the program though you don't realize it...until it finds a place to jump in" (280–81). Articulating the subjectivity that informs any histo-rian's approach to her subject whether she acknowledges it or not, here as elsewhere Beigh engages the insights of poststructuralism—even as she pursues a "real" encounter with history. By "marrying" Venn's accumulation of data to Beigh's intimacy with her historical subject—"the union," in Foucault's words, "of erudite knowledge and local memories" (*Power* 85)—Mukherjee suggests a distinctive historiography in which, not unlike Patricia's genealogy in Morrison's *Paradise*, "creative imagination" is the vital supplement to fragmented historical remains. Explaining her claim that "technology serves the artist," Mukherjee says, "The technician downloads a statistics-rich experience; the artist, using the same program, wrests a vision" (in C&G par. 94). In *Holder*, both Venn and Beigh are, in different ways, "technicians" of history whose narratives Mukherjee "paints" onto her "Mughal miniature"—but Mukherjee is the artist who supplies the border that integrates and realizes an experiential history.

The moment that "Venn slip[s] the helmet, the goggles, the spe-cial gloves" on Beigh, the reader is catapulted into visceral contact with the very person of the Salem bibi at her defining moment in the bloody final battle between Raja Jadav Singh, her Hindu lover, and the Muslim emperor Aurangzeb, Seizer of the World:

> "Hannah!" I scream against the cannons and flying bullets. I can barely breathe from the sulfur clouds, my eyes burn and I reach out to hold her, my hand closes on her shoulder and she turns, my hand is brown, with a tinkling gold bangle. She is a beautiful woman, more Pre-Raphaelite than I had imagined, with crinkly golden hair. I try to pull her my way....
>
> He turns—I know that face from a hundred portraits of Aurangzeb, or "Alamgir, the World-Holder"—a look of demented satisfaction on his face....
>
> I scream with agony from the hot white flaming explosion in my shoulder that has spun me around and dropped me to the cool, wet soil. Hannah is on her knees, crying. Hester, Hester, Bhagmati, pray, pray, we must get back....I try to hold the diamond out, but it is slip-pery with my blood....

I plunge the knife deep in my belly, watch with satisfaction, and now with the mastery of my pain, the blood bubble from the beautiful brown flesh. More, I think, and plunge the knife deeper...and make a burrow inside me. I feel the organs, feel the flesh, the bowels of history, and with my dying breath I plunge the diamond into the deepest part of me.

Venn says he was about to pull me out of it, the screaming, the running, writhing, my tears, my adrenaline and heart rate and endorphins all indicated a near-death experience; even the plunge in my blood pressure and pulse was consistent with mortal trauma. He understood me—apparently I was shouting partially in his language, which, of course, I don't know. (281–83)

As I have suggested, Beigh's disparate experiences with Venn's VR program can be understood partly in relation to a Foucauldian effective history: "The immediate emergence of historical contents" that can result from "a multiplicity of genealogical researches" (*Power* 81). Foucault emphasizes the "rediscovery," "rude memory," and "reappearance" of buried historical contents made possible only by an invested genealogist such as Beigh (ibid., 83).

Yet it is Beigh's "sentient bodily interaction," in Eugene Gendlin's words, with the historical contents of this moment that lends an additional meaning to the "interactive model of historical or imaginative reality" the novel seeks to construct. "Postmodernism is right," notes Gendlin, "in that one can not claim to represent or copy experiencing"; the shortcomings of Venn's VR program demonstrate the limits to representing experience. But Gendlin shows that

the body is always in a fresh situational interaction that exceeds culture, history and language....Currently, some thinkers are searching for "emergent" concepts and knowledge. To find this requires finding the direct access to ongoing bodily experiencing [that] exceeds the common phrases....New facets of experiencing rearrange the implicit language and can generate new sentences. (101, 114)

Thus, although through the trope of virtual reality *Holder* maintains a postmodern aspect, Beigh's—and the reader's—new experience of Mughal history at this juncture "rearranges" the implicit poststructuralist language that elsewhere imbues the novel. Through Beigh's voice, which in this passage differs markedly from the rest of the novel, Mukherjee conveys a historical vision suffused with immediacy. Beigh uses the first person throughout *Holder* when speaking about her contemporary moment, but her first-person voice here is simply more vibrant and embodied:[10] she clearly speaks from within a body in palpable, emotional language, whereas elsewhere she sounds like the academic she is—removed a level from her own experience, narrating it from a learned distance. Additionally, Beigh has previously described imagined re-creations of this multifarious scene in the third person from a number of vantage points—from the Mughal painting's representation that she finds in the Massachusetts museum to Hannah's narration of it in her memoirs. Hence, by this penultimate chapter in the novel, the reader has been so thoroughly initiated to the cultural arena of this battle scene and its characters and layered conflicts—between the Muslim and Hindu warriors as well as among Hannah, her Indian servant/companion Bhagmati, and the fighting factions—that one instantly situates all of these sundry subjects in their historical contexts. *Holder*'s rich historicity prevents the "depthlessness," the "waning of affect" that occurs in Venn's simulated model as in historiographic metafiction (Jameson 9–10). Because the historian's work of storytelling and contextualizing has already been accomplished, the reader can be present (with) in Beigh/Bhagmati at this seventeenth-century Mughal moment in a way that reading a straight history would foreclose.

At the same time, unlike Venn's simulated history (and unlike a traditional historical novel), Mukherjee does not allow her readers to let go of the distinction between the imaginary and the real. Beigh's informed recognitions—of Hannah as "more Pre-Raphaelite" than she had imagined; of Aurangzeb whom she knows "from a hundred portraits"—remind the reader of the media-suffused contemporary moment that she and Beigh cohabit, characterized (in Baudrillard's words) "by the multiplication and saturation of exchanges" (*Illusion* 3). Here as throughout, Mukherjee resists "a realistic, mimetic voice" to produce instead a rich historical vision yet marked by an acute awareness of the constructive elements of history (C&G par. 18). For one way to read this scene might be Mukherjee suggesting that—to borrow the capitalist logic by which *Holder* links empire across centuries—with the proper investment combination of research and imagination, we can "experience" history despite all the mediating factors of historiography and the insights of poststructuralism that the novel engages throughout.

Yet Beigh's investment ("all my notes, the five hundred books consulted, the endless paintings, engravings, trade records, journals, the travel and the documentary picture taking" [269]) and sentient bodily interaction notwithstanding, her knowledge of Hannah is notably distinct from Hawthorne's access to Hester Prynne, granted to him by the material artifact of her history, the scarlet letter "A" that exerts his "strange interest": "While thus perplexed...I happened to place it on my breast. It seemed to me, then, that I experienced a sensation not altogether physical, yet almost so, as if a burning heat; and as if the letter were not of red cloth, but red-hot iron. I shuddered, and involuntarily let it fall upon the floor" (34). In this moment, Hawthorne, in a sense, becomes Hester. As he experiences the "red-hot" indignation that Hester herself, along with Dimmesdale, felt by the infliction of the letter of shame upon their breasts, he effaces her. Through his imagination and empathy, Hawthorne suggests, he can know history in a special way; his subsequent unmediated presentation of Hester's story ensues from this nineteenth-century sense of historiography. Although Beigh experiences physical sensations not unlike Hawthorne's in her digital trip to the Mughal battle scene, the most surprising aspect of her experience is that for all of her obsession with Hannah, she cannot know her directly, as Hawthorne does Hester. She enters Hannah's story in the "brown flesh" of Bhagmati at the penultimate moment of the servant's life, within mere minutes of Hannah's escape as "the light of extinguishment" spreads over Bhagmati. Mukherjee's complex portrait of Hannah Easton, her "reconstruction of a life through three continents and thirty years," culminates in this surprising encounter of Hannah in the flesh—yet still at a distance (*Holder* 279).

This dance of intimacy with her historical subject is simultaneously an imaginative recovery of a lived historical reality and an act of what Gayatri Spivak calls "ethical responsibility," the ethical stance of making discursive room for the Other to exist (269–70). Tellingly, after recovering from her near-death experience, Beigh muses, "Who can blame Hawthorne for shying away from the real story of the brave Salem mother and her illegitimate daughter?" (284). At the conclusion not only of a richly intertextual and highly mediated story of displaced (hi)stories but of a virtual experience of Hannah's history as an eyewitness whom she does not know nearly as well as Hannah, Beigh's question underscores the fact that Mukherjee has also shied away from the "real" story of Hannah and her "black Pearl." Unlike Hawthorne's determined representation of Hester, Mukherjee has not permitted Beigh to appropriate Hannah, for that would erase her—replacing Hannah's subjectivity with Beigh's own—the way that Hawthorne replaces Hester, the Cartographer's Map replaces the Empire, and Venn's simulacrum of dense data replaces history. In this sense, "shying away from the real story" is the only ethical way of rendering the (hi)story of a "Christian-Hindu-Muslim self,

[an] American-English-Indian self, [an] orphaned, abandoned, widowed, pregnant self, [a] *firangi* and bibi self" from the shards of the past (268).[11]

In this consummation of Beigh's and Venn's projects, Mukherjee most fully achieves her aim of her readers experiencing history—while at the same time maintaining a distinct sense of our prism-like access to it. She uses the unconventional tropes of virtual reality and asset hunting to negotiate between objectivism and subjectivism, between history and narrativity. These same tropes moreover enable Mukherjee to conceive a redemptive temporality through which *Holder* relocates and transforms literary, cultural, and historical topographies of colonial nineteenth- and twentieth-century America, interwoven with Mughal India. The novel's renovatory temporal logics model a new paradigm for trans-American studies, illuminating the (dis)contents of empire from the seventeenth century through the twentieth. My chapter title refers to the discontents of transnational empire that *Holder* evokes, for the novel expresses throughout the ways in which "a continent of opportunity is a continent of cruelty" (38). But it also refers to the (dis)contents of an imperial history from which women are dislocated—by silences and absences as well as by the distortions of male-dominated texts and worlds. As Mukherjee plumbs the time and space that Hawthorne—in *The Scarlet Letter* and particularly in "The Custom-House"—eclipses, a residual meaning of an American woman emerges who rises like the phoenix from the "rubbish" to which history and literature has dismissed her. *Holder of the World* constructs Hannah's/Hester's stories, giving them an eloquent voice and agency through which the women of early trans-American times resonate.

CHAPTER 6

Truth-telling Fiction in a Post-9/11 World: Don DeLillo's *Falling Man* and Julie Otsuka's *When the Emperor Was Divine*

Although this book focuses on a new kind of truth-telling histori-cal fiction that emerged in the 1990s, I have suggested throughout that the dynamic of amnesia and truth telling, which grew out of that decade's "turn towards truth," continues to be a vital strain of the current cultural climate. Like the fiction itself that evokes this dynamic, the cultural work of the novels must be understood in relation to so many recent events that manifest it: the 2006 Iran Holocaust denial conference and the international criticism of it; the disclosure of the Japanese army's use of "comfort women" during World War II and the ensuing documentary histories and victim tes-timonies that belie Japan's half-century of denial; the surge of interest in the historically neglected Bataan Death March and in the Pacific theater of World War II; newly formed truth commissions to redress histories of mass violence in a number of countries; and the paradig-matic shift in American studies to a transnational perspective of his-tory and a broader collective sensibility that reflects this. Positioning truth-telling historical fiction within this rich matrix reveals the many fields in which a paradox of denial and truth telling plays out.

To see this new form of the historical novel in light of a global cli-mate of truth telling extending from the 1990s into the twenty-first century, it is helpful to address the post-9/11 cultural and literary landscape. Pursuant to a post-9/11 climate marked by a politics of fear and evisceration of American civil liberties, we have collectively begun to uncover what the *New York Times* journalist Jane Mayer calls "the dark side" of the War on Terror and to reflect critically on it: as a number of recent books by journalists and former members of the Bush administration and the military reveal, a good deal of truth telling about the event and its aftermath remains.[1] In the wake of 9/11, the novel that attends to history continues to provide a psychological and empirical component to such official truth telling. By studying two important novels published since 9/11, Julie Otsuka's *When the Emperor Was Divine* (2002) and Don DeLillo's *Falling Man* (2007), this final chapter identifies some facets of the post-9/11 literary imagination and begins to chart the evolution of truth-telling historical fiction in this context. By situating these texts in a contemporary fiction that—although it remains invested in fundamental aspects of the postmodern—differs from its postmodern predecessors, I hope to show the structural and ontological threads between postmodernism, truth-telling historical fiction of the 1990s, and fiction of the current moment.

Emperor and *Falling Man* represent a plain shift away from a postmodern perspective marked by self-consciousness and formal fragmentation, instead treading an appreciably human psychological and emotional territory. In their narrative structures—which proceed according to the workings of memory—and in their recursive concerns with personal and cultural memory and forgetting, both *Falling Man* and *Emperor* write against the postmodern tendency of amnesia, extending the truth-telling project of the novels that inform this study. Yet these post-9/11 novels embrace neither the metahistorical scope and argument involved in *Americana, Underworld*, and *Paradise* nor the trenchant recasting of nationally ensconced historical periods such as the Civil War in *Free Enterprise* and the Puritan age in *Holder of the World*. Reflecting perhaps the humbling and ruminative effect of 9/11, *Falling Man* and *Emperor* work on a smaller scale: narrow and deep, private and utterly human. DeLillo and Otsuka write against amnesia, in part, by drawing on personal histories of their own families to focus 9/11 and Executive Order 9066 through a single New York and Japanese American family, respectively. Moreover, both novels tell their stories in short, episodic, loosely connected scenes—images, conversations, memories, interludes, and dreams—that shift between past and present and alternate points of view between different family members. With narratives, then, that work psychologically and evocative of visceral memory and trauma, *Falling Man* and *Emperor* trace the way the events of September 11 and the internment of Japanese Americans reconfigured the emotional landscape, memory, and perception of those directly affected. In this sense, these novels deepen our existing understanding of these aspects of US history largely unexplored in American fiction, telling intimate truths about their subjects that neither histories nor the historical truth commissions assigned to the respective events could.

Notwithstanding its formal departures from the 1990s historical novels on which the previous chapters focus, *When the Emperor Was Divine* is a lucid and compelling example of truth-telling historical fiction in the post-9/11 world. Set partly in San Francisco during and following World War II, it concerns the 110,000 Japanese Americans whom, through Executive Order 9066, President Roosevelt in 1942 reclassified as "enemy aliens" and ordered evacuated to crudely erected desert internment camps for more than three years. Published nearly one year to the day after 9/11 (September 10, 2002), *Emperor* is not a conscious response to 9/11 (one chapter was previously written as a short story); yet given its uncanny perspective on the Guantánamo prison camp—whose detainees are similarly classified by executive order as "enemy combatants"—and on the post-9/11 statist culture of fear, prejudice, and intimidation, it not only tells important truths about the notorious episode of American World War II history at its center but also evokes related truths about our current era. The selection of this heretofore unknown author's first novel for perhaps a record number of "one book" community- and city-wide reading projects and an even greater number of book clubs around the nation,[2] along with readers' responses to the novel, indicates the force of *Emperor*'s refracting this aspect of the War on Terror. *Emperor*'s haunting tale resonates powerfully in a post-9/11 world. In addition, more than any other novel included in this book, *Emperor*'s prose and structure manifest the national amnesia, denial, and truth telling that is its core story. As such, it serves both as a profoundly illustrative novel with which to conclude this study and a provocative example of how the truth-telling historical novel evolves in the post-9/11 moment.

Although not a historical novel in the traditional sense of its action set at least a generation prior to its issue, *Falling Man*, conversely, is a conscious response to 9/11. Set and structured specifically around the "day of the planes" in New York City through three years after, *Falling Man* studies the relationship between personal life and possibly the defining event of our time and in this sense reads not unlike an historical novel. At the same time, having begun this book with DeLillo's three historical novels that punctuate 26 years (1971–1997), I return here to DeLillo as a bellwether of contemporary fiction. More than any other living writer, DeLillo has always had his finger on the pulse of American culture. From *Americana*'s treatment of Madison

Avenue advertising culture (now resurrected in the popular television show *Mad Men*) to the subjects of his early novels (all contemporaneous stories)—college football and nuclear warfare in *End Zone* (1972); and sex, drugs, and rock and roll in *Great Jones Street* (1973)—and beyond, DeLillo followed through on his stated intent "to use the whole picture, the whole culture" of America. His novels that concern terrorist cells are chillingly prescient. In *Players* (1977), terrorists plot to attack "The Exchange"—the stock exchange—because it is the medium, symbol, and apotheosis of capitalism. Set in and around Wall Street, the newly constructed twin towers figure not only as the site of the Exchange but also, in an omen of 9/11, as a site of collective grief: a character who works for a counseling organization called the Grief Management Council muses, "It was her original view that the World Trade Center was an unlikely headquarters for an outfit such as this. But…Where else would you stack all this grief?" [18]). DeLillo tapped into the terrorist threats that arguably have come to define the twenty-first-century zeitgeist in *The Names* (1982; about US businessmen and terrorists in the Middle East) and *Mao II* (1991), which considers the increasingly commanding role terrorists play in the world and an act of terror as the only meaningful act of those who are powerless. The central event that disrupts the middle-American lives in *White Noise* is an "airborne toxic event": the novel was published the same month that the most deadly toxic leak in history, from a Union Carbide plant in Bhopal, India (on December 3, 1984), killed at least 3,800 people and caused significant morbidity and fatalities in thousands more. Likewise, *Underworld*'s paired concerns with the enormous garbage and nuclear waste problems the world faces—where or how to safely bury or destroy it?—predate the eco-consciousness manifest in currently widespread recycling and green programs and attempts to deal with global warming. (*An Inconvenient Truth* [2006] was released almost a decade after *Underworld*.)

Yet, post-9/11, the black-and-white dust jacket cover of *Underworld* is perhaps the most strikingly visionary element of DeLillo's oeuvre: in the foreground, a dark church with a cross atop its roof is set against the World Trade Center looming gray in the background. The twin towers are ghostlike in their faded tone; white clouds conceal the top of them, and a lone black bird to the towers' right flies upward and leans in toward them. Seen retroactively through the lens of 9/11, the white clouds presage the smoke and ash that attended their sudden crumbling, and the silhouetted bird evokes the spirit of the thousands who died in their midst. Given the author's prescience, *Falling Man* invites us to consider it in relation to the nearly 40 years of DeLillo's fiction that precede it. Widespread critical and popular responses to the novel suggest that, (like *Emperor*), it too struck a major chord among the reading public. Taken together, these novels adumbrate not only how the novelist responds to 9/11 and how a body of readers responds to 9/11 through the novel but, most importantly as the denouement to this book, what such practices of writing and reading tell us about the truth-telling historical novel in the present moment.

I begin with *Falling Man*, the direct response to 9/11, to introduce the literary and historical context for Otsuka's novel, which, for so many readers, chillingly evokes the post-9/11 political climate. DeLillo's exposure of the way in which official history is amnesiac by definition bears a particularly apt relation to the internment of Japanese Americans, a shameful aspect of World War II on the US home front that both mythic and popular histories of the war (such as the aforementioned Oscar-winning films *Saving Private Ryan* and *Pearl Harbor*) ignore. As we have seen, DeLillo's insistent use of the historical archive to deconstruct the very kind of mythic history these movies represent complicates postmodernism. Considering DeLillo—from *Americana* through his most recent work in the new millennium—gives both broad and deep insight to the trajectory of American literature from its emergent and complicated postmodern sensibility in the post-Kennedy and Vietnam eras through its psychological truth-telling sensibilities in the post-9/11 era. Appearing in a literary moment in which late-twentieth-century postmodernism stands in uncertain, inadequately investigated relationship to emerging literature of the twenty-first century, *Falling Man* allows us to explore the nature of that connection and also the departures therein. Specifically, taking the September 11 attacks on the World Trade Center as its starting point, the novel allows us to consider the effects of this traumatic experience on our individual psyches and collective culture, our relationships and means of conducting them, our past and future histories, our ideas about historicizing, and the capacity and limits of literature and language to document, understand, and heal from such traumatic experience.

"Falling out of the World": Memory, Intimacy, and the Post-9/11 Crisis of Meaning

If 9/11 underscored the enduring uncertainty and multiplicity of meaning fundamental to the postmodern, it also unearthed a humanism less visible in the postmodern. In the wake of 9/11, thrust into an unsettling combination of anomie and complex emotion, the scarred, dynamic characters of DeLillo's *Falling Man* long for, seek out, and ultimately discover human connection and intimacy. Although such humanism has been largely unrecognized by theorists of the postmodern, some readers of contemporary fiction have considered its strain. Wendy Steiner, for instance, distinguishes "stylistic" writing—characterized by "postmodern" experimental and metafictional narrative innovations—from "humanist" writing, which tends to "the imperative of individual pain…the indisputable reality of pain." Tellingly, Steiner cites the work of DeLillo as "one of the clearest examples of this fusion of stylistic and 'humanist' goals" (497). However, the themes on which Steiner focuses in *White Noise*—"domesticity, environmentalism, the family, the problems of a woman's fulfillment and a man's attunement to her"—DeLillo more fully develops in *Underworld* and the last, poignantly, in *Falling Man*. Steiner's claim about *White Noise*—that it is an "especially apt case of contemporary fiction, in that it merges existentialism, politics, and individual assertion" (498)—is especially true of *Falling Man*, the DeLillo novel that most significantly departs from postmodernism.

That *Falling Man* borrows structurally from the dense historical novels *Underworld* and *Libra* is not surprising given that the 2007 novel, set in increasing stages from the towers at the moment of the impact to three years after "the planes," is fundamentally about 9/11. The original trauma informs not only the characters and their experiences but also the unfolding of their stories. The novel turns on Keith, who, caught by the blast of the struck towers, manages (along with hundreds of others) to descend the stairs in smoke and walk away, blood-and-glass-strewn, to the home of his estranged wife, Lianne, and their son, Justin. The narrative approaches the event not as isolated by time and space or as self-consciously figured by the narrative act but rather as reconstructed from a present perspective—a view that postmodernism abstracts. In this, *Falling Man* resembles *Underworld*'s and *Libra*'s approaches to the Cold War and the Kennedy assassination, respectively. Yet where *Underworld*'s metahistorical perspective deconstructs (in Molly Wallace's and Kathleen Fitzpatrick's words) "commodified" and "reified" histories and where *Libra*'s metafictional Nicholas Branch embodies a postmodern ironic distance from history, *Falling Man*'s characters experience the past more like Sethe of Toni Morrison's *Beloved*. It haunts them; it hangs over them. Says Florence, a fellow survivor of Keith's burning tower, "If I live to be a hundred, I'll still be on the stairs." Mulls Keith, "These were the days after and now the years, a thousand heaving dreams, the trapped man, the fixed limbs, the dream of paralysis, the gasping man, the dream of asphyxiation, the dream of helplessness" (230). Similarly, years after the gaping terror and unredeemable losses, Lianne concludes, "She was ready to be alone, in reliable calm, she and the kid, the way they were before the planes appeared that day, silver crossing blue" (236). Not unlike Sethe's final uncertain moments in *Beloved*, these last words of Lianne's narrative beg the question, is this healing? Or regression?

Unlike the quintessentially postmodern *White Noise*—populated, according to the querulous Bruce Bawer, "by epigram-slinging, epistemology-happy robots" (42), characters who, another critic rants, "talk and act like the aliens in *3rd Rock From the Sun*" (Myers 9)—the individuals in *Falling Man* are palpably real. They are without, for example, the fraught surreality of the mysterious Mr. Tuttle of *The Body Artist* (DeLillo's previous novel that dealt with grief and emotional trauma, albeit on a purely individual level). American airliners flying into the World Trade Center, the firestormed-then-collapsing towers—one, then the other—was surreal in itself. Rather than requiring imagination equal to body artist Lauren's deeply inner grief, 9/11, as DeLillo put in an essay published four months after, was "so vast and terrible that it was outside imagining even as it happened"; the event "was unreal...too real, a phenomenon so unaccountable and yet so bound to the power of objective fact that we can't tilt it to the slant of our perceptions" ("In the Ruins of the Future" 8). So the novel slants the writer's perception to the too-real event, to the folds within and between human experience of it. The visceral quality of *Falling Man* no doubt stems in part from DeLillo's personal proximity and strong connection to New York and from the actual experience of his nephew, Marc, stranded for a spell in his smoking, ash-covered apartment building two blocks from the World Trade Center. "When the second tower fell, my heart fell with it," writes DeLillo of his anxiety about Marc that morning ("Ruins" 4). This rare first-person disclosure is the rawest revelation DeLillo has written in any essay.

But it is not just those who populate *Falling Man* that set apart the novel as a form of contemporary writing with "humanist" concerns. Although formally resembling *Underworld* and *Libra* (both of which are nearly universally claimed for "historiographic metafiction"), *Falling Man*'s structure, uniquely adapted to its central event, marks a certain evolution from its postmodern antecedents. Two chapters set in *Underworld*'s contemporaneous 1990s (Part 1, "Long Tall Sally 1992," and the epilogue, "Das Kapital") frame the novel's backward flow from the present to the 1950s. From the prologue on, several of *Underworld*'s 37 chapters can be read as stand-alone short fiction; like the unforgettable account of the famous 1951 Dodgers-Giants playoff game, a handful were published as short stories prior to the novel's 1997 issue. In a related fashion, the first and last chapters of *Falling Man* portray the cataclysmic attack on the towers and the immediate aftershock backward: a man's emergence *from* the World Trade Center into "not a street [but] a world, a time and space of falling ash and near night" (3) *to*, in the novel's final pages, him high inside it. "An instant before the aircraft struck the tower, heat, then fuel, then fire, and a blast wave passed through the structure that sent Keith Neudecker out of his chair and into a wall" (239). Like *Underworld*, the body of the novel intervenes in this long dramatic space. Composed of linked stories and multiple voices—segments ranging from a paragraph to a few pages that can also be read as independent pieces—the text advances roughly toward the future, the human fallout of the event. Keith and Lianne's progressively rich narrative web—including the threads of Keith's fleeting affair with Florence; the writing group of men and women in the early stages of Alzheimer's disease that Lianne facilitates; Lianne's dying mother, Nina, and her mother's lover, Martin—extends by increments of days and then years into the post-9/11 world. Simultaneously, DeLillo weaves a sketch of Hammad, one of the 19 Muslim plotters, from months prior to 9/11 to his fatal plane ride on that morning. This intertext then—albeit transposed—also moves inexorably forward, in short slices that intersect the New Yorkers' passages and that converge with Keith's experience of the plane's crash into his office tower in the novel's gripping climax. The formal interrelation of these coupled stories moreover parallels *Libra*'s coupled chapters that alternately develop Lee Harvey Oswald and follow the CIA plotters—tales that merge in the Kennedy assassination.

Falling Man's narrative structure, however, proceeds according to the workings of memory, trauma, and emotional healing. By tracing Keith's journey from his exit from the combusting tower to the days and years after—and then, finally, to the cataclysmic moment when the planes hit the towers—the narrative unearths Keith's memory, traces his trauma, and reveals his emotional healing. And unlike *Underworld*'s reverse order of distinct chapters, which work progressively to unmake the mythic history of the Cold War, *Falling Man* unravels not in a measured chronology of neat chapters but evocative of the way visceral memory floods the present; and stories overlap. For example, Keith's shock-laden migration from Ground Zero concludes in chapter 1 with him accepting a lift: "It wasn't until he got in the truck and shut the door that he understood where he'd been going all along" (6). Yet the novel introduces a number of characters and perspectives of 9/11 over the ensuing weeks before chapter 6 depicts Keith's arrival at Lianne's apartment: "When he appeared at the door it was not possible, a man come out of an ash storm, all blood and slag, reeking of burnt matter, with pinpoint glints of slivered glass in his face." This page-and-a-half scene closes with Lianne cleaning the dust, ash, and blood from Keith's face, hands, and head, realizing, "It was not his blood. Most of it came from somebody else" (87). Following an inch of blank page, the chapter fast-forwards to weeks after the planes, Keith at Florence's apartment, their second meeting, which ends with Keith "crawl[ing] out of his clothes" (93). Progressive empty spaces punctuate several other disparate scenes that occur in the same chunk of time.

If the mere white line between settings and voices implies fragile, intersecting lives, then the two major narrative strands that steadily approach each another emphasize human interconnection across geography and culture. At the same time, in that the New Yorkers' timeline moves away from 9/11 while Hammad and his brothers-in-arms' moves grimly toward it, 9/11 is the implicit, traumatic center of the narrative, the defining moment in terms of which all else (as Keith says) is "these after-days....Everything now is measured by after" (138). Eventually regular flights into the professional gambling world—days-long, otherworldly poker tournaments in Vegas, LA, Atlantic City—characterize Keith's "after-days." Alongside, on the late-night phone call in New York, Lianne insists to Keith, "There's the other thing and that's the family....we need to stay together, keep the family going. Just us, three of us, long-term, under the same roof, not every day of the year or every month but with the idea that we're permanent. Times like these, the family is necessary....This is how we live through the things that scare us half to death" (214). *Falling Man* details many individuals' coexistence on this definitive temporal axis, a shared new world in which only intimacy and community ensure survival and growth.

All this and more situates DeLillo's most recent novel within a contemporary literature that, although it inherits the stylistic innovations of its predecessor, is categorically distinct—chronologically, aesthetically, culturally, and politically—from postmodernism. For, other than the ongoing bitter argument between Nina and Martin as to whether "God" or "history," "politics and economics" is the motivating force for the 9/11 attacks (47), the event itself is not "postmodern" in nature: not marked, that is, by uncertainty. Indeed, in

Falling Man's inevitable subject of so much death and loss, little in the novel is uncertain. All but one of Keith's weekly poker buddies has died in the towers; Nina will die before the novel's end; she is dying, Lianne realizes six days after the towers: "It was difficult to see her...resigned and unstirring, the energetic arbiter of her daughter's life, ever discerning, the woman who'd given birth to the word *beautiful*...All this dwindling to a human breath" (48). So, too, are the Alzheimer's group members to whom Lianne has grown so attached: "The truth was mapped in slow and certain decline...the crime of it, the loss of memory, personality and identity, the lapse into eventual protein stupor" (125). Although DeLillo suspends the original moment of trauma—Keith's reeling from the impact of the plane, the immediate harrowing aftermath and claustrophobic escape down the stairs—until the novel's last pages, the drama of the story (what *is* uncertain, what the reader waits to find out) is not 9/11 itself. It is what will become of Keith and Lianne's marriage, broken the year prior to the planes and ambiguously renewed on 9/11. Keith's wish to tell Lianne about Florence underscores the multiplicity of meanings therein.

> He would tell her about Florence. She would say she knew something was going on but in view of the completely uncommon nature of the involvement, with its point of origin in smoke and fire, this is not an unforgivable offense....
>
> He would tell her about Florence. She would get a steak knife and kill him.
>
> He would tell her about Florence. She would enter a period of long and tortured withdrawal.
>
> He would tell her about Florence. She would say, After we've just renewed our marriage. She would say, After the terrifying day of the planes has brought us together again. How could the same terror? She would say, How could the same terror threaten everything we've felt for each other, everything? I've felt these past weeks....
>
> He would tell her about Florence. She would want to be convinced that it was over and he would convince her because it was true, simply and forever.
>
> He would tell her about Florence. She would send him to hell with a look and then call a lawyer. (162)

In fact, Nina and Martin's standing argument along with the layered Al-Qaida plot, quickly discovered after the attacks, underscore that 9/11 did not share, as DeLillo tells it, "the shattering randomness of the [Kennedy assassination]" with all of its "ambiguity and chaos" ("Art of Fiction" 299, "An Outsider in This Society" 287). The assassination, as many have argued, was perhaps the definitive postmodern event—both in that it continues to signify uncertainty in American mythic history and (as *Libra* highlights) that it was the first postmodern media event, caught on camera and immediately broadcast such that Americans largely know where they were "when Kennedy was shot" by their multiplied personal recollections of watching "reruns of the shooting...over and over" on television (*Libra* 445). It "surely," in DeLillo's words, "began to give us a sense of something coming undone....We felt the shock of unmeaning" ("The American Absurd" 32). September 11 and its discontents, however, quickly came into focus. As DeLillo wrote in his December 2001 essay, "In the Ruins of the Future," "The sense of disarticulation we hear in the term 'Us and Them,' has never been so striking, at either end" (2). Further, although "the events of September 11 were covered unstintingly,...The raw event was one thing, the coverage another" (8). And rather than the "psychic disorientation" and "rootless[ness]" that ensued from Kennedy's murder, after 9/11, Americans (and New Yorkers especially) dig in and cleave together. When Lianne told people she wanted to leave the city, "They said, Leave the city? For what? To go where? It was the locally honed cosmocentric idiom of New York, loud and blunt, but she felt it in her heart no less than they did" (*Falling Man* 69). *Underworld* implies the postmodern character of the Kennedy assassination—media-suffused seclusion—by articulating its difference from the 1951 Dodgers-Giants playoff game: "When JFK was shot, people went inside. We watched TV in dark rooms and talked on the phone with friends and relatives. We were all separate and alone. But when Thomson hit the homer, people rushed outside. People wanted to be together. Maybe it was the last time people spontaneously went out of their houses for something. Some wonder, some amazement" (94).

Albeit in horror, 9/11 engendered something similar—shock and awe—and also fusion, a seeking and finding togetherness. September 11 was not private, either in the nature of the event or in American collective response to it. *Falling Man* portrays the spontaneous and ongoing gatherings that followed 9/11. "These three years past, since that day in September, all life had become public. The stricken community pours forth voices and the solitary night mind is shaped by the outcry" (182): poetry readings; confluences in churches and parks—unscripted memorials of left mementos, flowers, photos, candles; and eventually the long walk, Lianne and Justin's, "with five hundred thousand others, a bright swarm of people ranging sidewalk to sidewalk...a march against the war, the president, the policies" (181). Such actions foster collective memory, to which the novel returns in broad and small brushstrokes. The Alzheimer's group members' "storyline sessions" take "on a measure of intensity" after 9/11. "There was one subject the members wanted to write about, insistently....They wanted to write about the planes" (31). The members thoughtfully tend the past: they recover, reconstruct, and read their memories aloud to each other. "This was their prayer room," says one.

Together with the many public recollections of 9/11, the group's practices stress that memory is sacred and is made more so by sharing it with others. Through the sessions, individual memories become collectively cradled. Their weekly meetings in a room within a large downtown community center—where "a steady bang and clatter bounded off the hallway walls"; "children raced around, adults in special classes"; "people played dominoes and ping-pong, volunteers prepared food deliveries to elderly people in the area"—are the antithesis of people alone in secluded rooms watching TV after JFK was shot. Lianne fears the members' "halting response, the losses and failings, the grim prefigurings that issued now and then from a mind beginning to slide away from the adhesive friction that makes an individual possible. It was in the language, the inverted letters, the lost words at the end of a struggling sentence" (29–31). The novel emphasizes written expression against forgetting, against ineluctable loss: at lunch weeks after, the only project Lianne's publisher mentions—a sprawling book that predates 9/11 by years yet seems to predict the event—"was precisely the one not intended for Lianne and precisely the one that Lianne needed to edit" (139–40). In another instance of written recording, Justin does Nina's portrait; his old-world means of capturing her image is a striking contrast to the digital technological world that earlier DeLillo fiction penetratingly refracts. Justin loves to sharpen his pencils from all over the world in an old-fashioned pencil sharpener in his room—"crank and blow, crank and blow" (39). With the pencil-drawn portrait, Justin strives to preserve Nina's visage before her imminent death.

At the same time, there is a pervasive sense in the novel that human life is ineffable; the dimension of memory and experience exceeds the potential of its recording. Although Lianne's advanced computer search of the recently deceased performance artist known as Falling Man reveals a dozen or more pictures of his various safety-harness-suspended falls, there are "no photographs" of the fall she unexpectedly witnessed nearly three years ago, beneath elevated train tracks. "She was the photograph, the photosensitive surface. That nameless body coming down, this was hers to record and absorb" (223). Most deep memories are not written down, after all. From Keith's involvement with Florence to Lianne's recurrent recollection of her father—who, victim to Alzheimer's disease, shot himself—memories remain profoundly private. Several facets of this, Lianne's defining memory, surface throughout the novel, triggered by aspects of her "after-days" and provoked and nourished by her work with the writing group. She "know[s] that one memory at least is inescapably secure, that day that has marked her awareness of who she is and how she lives" (218). In this sense, we can only experience the past through the present. As Lianne's after-days allow her to approach the bittersweet memory of her father, Keith's after-days—his asymmetrical intimacies with Florence, his bond with Justin and especially with Lianne—allow him, the novel's organization suggests, to release the original trauma with which the pages cease.

Moreover, *Falling Man* intimates, the self is vitally defined in terms of others. Of seeing one's face—in a photo, in a mirror—Nina says, "What you see is not what we see. What you see is distracted by memory, by being who you are, all this time, for all these years". That is, not only can we only experience the past through our present; we can only experience the present through our past. Our surfeit of memory indelibly informs our view of the present: "Your face is your life," continues Nina, "but it is also submerged in your life. That's why you don't see it. Only other people see it" (115). This is the ultimate and the strongest humanist claim of the novel: one can only grow—can only heal—through relationships. During Keith and Florence's four or five encounters over 15 weeks, they share "crossing memories, brought down out of the tower....They drank tea and talked...and he understood that they could talk about these things only with each other, in minute and dullest detail, but it would never be dull or too detailed because it was inside them now and because he needed to hear what he'd lost in the tracings of memory" (57, 91). The need is wholly mutual. As their liaison draws to an end, she tells him, "You saved my life. After what happened, so many gone, friends gone, people I worked with, I was nearly gone, nearly dead in another way....Then you walked in the door. You ask yourself why you took the briefcase out of the building. That's why. So you could bring it here. So we could get to know each other. That's why you took it and that's why you brought it here, to keep me alive" (108–9). Years after, Lianne similarly tells Keith, "You were stronger than I was. You helped me get here. I don't know what would have happened....You were the one in the tower but I was the berserk" (215).

The wounded mend by drawing near to others. Weeks after the planes, Florence goes to St. Paul's, she says, because "I wanted to be with people, down there in particular. I knew there would be people there" (89). Years after, Lianne, an atheist, takes a long walk uptown to find the church of one of her former group members. "It was not something godlike she felt but only a sense of others. Others brings us closer. Church brings us closer" (233). She and Keith "spend nights in bed with the windows open, traffic noises, voices carrying.... Words, their own, were not much more than sounds, airstreams of shapeless breath, bodies speaking.... On these nights it seemed to her that they were falling out of the world" (212). Because of 9/11, but also in spite of it, they fasten and bend together, sealed off time and again from global politics, unloosed from malaise. In its keen attention to memory as well as to human connection, *Falling Man* eschews the postmodern inclination not only of amnesia but of fragmented isolation. In the face of the anxiety and fear that persist in the post-9/11 world, the novel suggests that memory—bred, sustained, and nurtured by community and intimacy—is a means both of historicizing traumatic history and of healing from it.

"Everything You Have Heard Is True": The Dialectic of Denial and Revelation

Like *Falling Man*, *Emperor*'s intense focus on one family's experience of a historical trauma conveys the psychological dimensions of that trauma at large. But unlike *Falling Man*'s encounter with 9/11, the recent event that is so vividly and (thanks to TV and the Internet), visually embedded in our collective memory, *Emperor* insistently remembers an episode vaguely recollected in the American mythic memory of World War II, the internment of Japanese Americans. Perhaps because of this difference, the humanist strain in *Emperor* is marked not by connection, intimacy, and healing but by the quiet suffering of rejection. The characters' tangible loneliness ensues firstly from being forcibly removed from their community—and then, upon their return years later, from their community's ongoing denial of their exile, a collective refusal even to recognize them, an omission of the truth of their experience. In this, *Emperor* too is a telling example of a post-9/11 turn toward humanist concerns and away from a postmodern self-consciousness of the history it probes. It offers private, immediate revelations of individual memories drawn from survivors that counter a collective amnesia of the trauma and surrounding disgrace.

As historical fiction, however, *Emperor* bears a unique testimonial relation to the milieu of official truth seeking against which the emergence of this new form of the historical novel occurs. The novel's subject of internment is the same as that for which the Commission on Wartime Relocation and Internment of Civilians was established by the US Congress in 1981. Significantly, this was the first-ever "historical truth commission." In contrast to truth commissions that serve as part of a political transition to look into recent abuses, historical truth commissions, Hayner explains, inquire "into abuses by the state that took place many years earlier [to] clarify historical truths and pay respect to previously unrecognized victims or their descendants. The events investigated [are] generally not those of widespread political repression, but targeted practices that may have affected specific ethnic, racial, or other groups." Historical truth commissions thus "are likely to document practices that are largely unknown to the majority of the population" (17). Yet the most pronounced public effect of the commission's 1982 report, *Personal Justice Denied*—which officially acknowledged the US government's wrongdoing in interning Japanese Americans 40 years earlier—may have been internment apologists' contentious reaction to it.[3] Notably, the report did not act as a catalyst for former internees to share their stories, for Japanese American reticence about the experience has persisted through to the present generation.[4] As Sau-ling Wong observes, in *Reading Asian American Literature* (1993), "despite the enormity of Japanese American internment, there is as yet no single book-length treatment of it comparable in range and intensity to Joy Kogawa's novel on Japanese Canadian relocation *Obasan*. And no one quite knows why" (128). In this sense, *Emperor* is a breakthrough novel that, through the singular voice of a descendant of internees, performs a cultural work of truth telling that the US commission could not. As the first Japanese American–authored novel on the internment experience to be widely read and to have generated a large-scale collective dialogue about its subject, the novel has, in a very real sense, unsilenced the topic.[5] At the same time, the delays between: the internment and the truth commission (40 years); the truth commission and the novel (20 years); and internment and the novel (60 years) suggests two simultaneous and related phenomena: the traumatic nature of internment, along with the collective taciturnity that has attended it; and the post-9/11 environment, ripe for a daughter of wartime internees to give voice to the internment experience. The American public has responded to the narrative in the context of the War on Terror through which the US government again, "in the interest of national security," declared a group of people "enemy combatants," exiled them to prison camps, and stripped them of habeas corpus. Not unlike the September 11, 2001, attacks that unleashed a strain of anti-Muslim sentiment and Arab profiling and suspicion, the December 7, 1941, attack on Pearl Harbor loosed an anti-Japanese frenzy in both the United States and Canada; in both cases, what began presumably as a matter of "national security" quickly escalated into an unconscionable set of practices targeting a minority population on the basis of race. Between the bombing of Pearl Harbor and before the passing of Executive Order 9066 on February 19, 1942, "enemy aliens" were subjected to certain orders and restrictions—from the prohibition of firearms, short-wave radios, and cameras to a strict curfew. What Executive Order 9066 did was to expand the rules of "military necessity" to suspect citizens, thus making it possible to subject Japanese American citizens to the same regulations required of (mostly Japanese) "aliens." Indeed, one month after President Roosevelt signed Executive Order 9066, Public Proclamation No. 3 extended military regulations to "all persons of Japanese ancestry"; evacuation orders for the same shortly followed, resulting in 120,000 Japanese Americans interned, approximately 65 percent of them US born and thus citizens. Although "extraordinary rendition" affected fewer innocent civilians than internment,[6] that both practices invoked national security to abrogate the legal rights of a particular group of people, and were conducted mostly in secret and in locations far removed from the majority population, implies their shared violations of constitutional law and the prejudicial zeitgeist of both historical moments. Initially, the United States, like Canada, had planned to exclude "all persons of Japanese ancestry" from their coastal regions and to allow them to resettle where they liked in the interior regions. However, explains Nancy Peterson, in her book's chapter on *Obasan*, "both countries soon realized that anti-Japanese feeling was so strong among whites that the 'evacuees' would need to be 'resettled' and 'protected'" in "military areas" designated by the secretary of war (142–43). Surrounded by barbed wire and gun towers and supervised by armed guards, the "relocation centers" were in fact concentration camps.[7] In excruciatingly small quarters, privacy was nonexistent and camp rules and regimens—from waking to the blast of a siren to lining up for meals, mail, and coal, to shower, or to use the latrine—ordered every moment of daily life (*Emperor* 125).

Similar to denouncing the bombing of Afghanistan or Iraq in the immediate post-9/11 political climate, to denounce the camps was to invite questioning of one's own patriotism; little public, cultural, or even legal support was available for those who wished to voice their opposition. In 1943, Ansel Adams, America's best-known photographer, documented the Manzanar War Relocation Center, a collection of hundreds of tar-paper barracks hastily built to house more than 10,000 people. Adams published his photographs in 1944 in a book entitled *Born Free and Equal: The Story of Loyal Japanese Americans*; it made it to the *New York Times* bestseller list and at the same time was publicly burned en masse in San Francisco. The case of *Born Free* exemplifies the public milieu of the 1940s in which, although there were sympathetic Anglos who actively imposed internment, war-driven anxieties and racism drowned out their protests. Adams did not renew the copyright and gave the prints and negatives to the Library of Congress. Like the 120,000 interned Japanese Americans Adams wanted to make visible, his book disappeared before the war ended. Also in 1944, two important court challenges to the curfew and exclusion orders, *Hirabayashi v. United States* and *Korematsu v. United States*, argued that the orders were unconstitutional because they discriminated on the basis of race. Ruling that wartime measures and military necessity justified the orders, the Supreme Court rejected these arguments. A third case, *Ex Parte Endo*, is significant both legally and in the contemporaneous context of Otsuka's novel because, like challenges to the Bush administration's suspension of habeas corpus to Guantánamo detainees, it arose from a habeas corpus petition. In July 1942, Mitsuye Endo—a Nisei (US-born Japanese American and thus an American citizen) who, like 100,000 other Nisei, was summarily dismissed from her job as a stenographer and relocated to a segregated Utah camp—filed a petition for a writ of habeas corpus. When the US District Court denied her petition, she appealed, remaining confined at Topaz camp for two years without charge. In December 1944, the Supreme Court ruled in her favor; following the ruling, the exclusion orders were suspended and Japanese Americans were allowed to return to their homes. Historical accounts of this era often conclude that, following the Allied victory, the hysteria of the war years dissipated; yet distrust of Japanese Americans haunted the postwar years. Indeed, although the Wartime Relocation and Internment Commission Report concluded, in 1982, that internment was thoroughly unjustified, it was immediately met with protests claiming that Japanese Americans were actually a threat to national security during World War II.

Less visible, however, was the wounding effect of these egregiously discriminatory policies on Japanese Americans. The Japanese phrase *shikatago-nai* ("it cannot be helped") is often invoked to explain the postwar silence of the internees themselves. Shame, likewise, prevented internees from sharing their painful histories. Thus many children of internees have grown up knowing little to nothing of their parents' or grandparents' traumatic experiences. The historical narrative outlined earlier adumbrates the traumatic nature of internment and the ensuing lack of narratives about it. As Peterson reasons, "the public hysteria and oppressive policies, the silencing of oppositional voices, along with the consolidation of military, executive, and judicial authority in the 1940s produced a peculiar and perverse 'logic' that defied...comprehension"—and thus, one might add, sustained prose treatments of it (152). The abrogation of Japanese American civil rights, the wartime executive classification of civilians as "enemy aliens," and the consequent suspension of habeas corpus all reverberate in the current context of the War on Terror, extraordinary rendition, and Guantánamo. Yet whereas recently released books, memos, and testimonies inform a current public debate on these still-raw issues, Japanese American internment to this day remains on the fringes of American collective memory.

As the historical novels *The Sun Also Rises, Absalom! Absalom!*, and *Beloved* (concerning World War I, the Civil War, and slavery, respectively), among others, show us, writers have an especial capacity to articulate, expose, and reckon with large-scale traumas to which victims can seldom fully testify or convey. The cultural work of such literature is often therapeutic, political, and artistic all at once; and scholars of twentieth-century mass atrocities, from the fields of history, law, and transitional justice, have begun to recognize the role of art and literature in particular to truth telling and potential healing. Early in *Between Vengeance and Forgiveness*, Minow notes, "The striking prevalence of therapeutic language in contemporary discussions of mass atrocities stands in contrast to comparable debates fifteen years ago.... Therapeutic purposes contrast starkly with political ones, although in practice the two influence one another" (22). Considering then what contemporary Western art may provide or suggest for victims healing from mass crimes, she invokes the Holocaust historian Saul Friedlander, who asserts that it is "imperative" to "render as truthful an account as documents and testimonials will allow" and crucial "to introduce individual memories and individual voices in a field dominated by political decisions and administrative decrees" (24). Yet, given the nature of trauma, individuals' voices of such memories are often not forthcoming. Explains Dori Laub in *Testimony: Crises of Witnessing in Literature, Psychoanalysis, and History*, "The fear that fate will strike again is crucial to the memory of trauma and to the inability to talk about it." Moreover, "if one talks about the trauma without being truly heard or truly listened to, telling might itself be lived as a return of the trauma" (67). For internees, it is clear that, as Peterson points out, "there has been a crisis in witnessing similar to what Dori Laub has identified as a terrible crisis for Holocaust survivors" (7).[8] As I will show, *Emperor*'s portrait not only of the community's refusal to recognize their returning neighbors, three years after their forced relocation, but also of the racial torment Japanese Americans face upon "coming home" underscores the trauma inherent in the evacuees' silences on the topic; certainly there was no ear to hear or listen to their tale of intense dislocation, isolation, and psychological, physical, and material loss. The novel also conveys the way in which the internment experience took place, to borrow Laub's words,

> outside the parameters of "normal" reality, such as causality, sequence, place and time. [This] puts it outside the range of comprehension, of recounting and of mastery....To undo this entrapment of a fate that cannot be known, cannot be told...a therapeutic process of constructing a narrative, of reconstructing a history and essentially, of *re-externalizing the event*—has to be set in motion. This re-externalization of the event can occur and take effect only when one can articulate and *transmit* the story, literally transfer it to another outside oneself. (69)

Like most evacuees who, upon their return from the camps, preferred to bury "the shame," Otsuka's mother (who was 11 when she went to the camps) and her grandmother spoke little about their experiences. "Also, culturally," Otsuka notes, "you just don't really complain; you endure" ("A Conversation with Julie Otsuka").

Yet that "the subject of the internment—but even more than that, the emotions behind it[—]resonated with" Otsuka and "kept resurfacing in [her] writing" suggests Otsuka's crucial role in this process of reexternalizing the internment and the cathartic dimension of the novel. Provoked by her mother's "humorous" stories of internment and her family's elisions of their ordeal (her grandmother "was not so forthcoming") and anchored by "a lot of research" ("Conversation"), Otsuka's issue of *Emperor* and its reception reveal the novel as a necessary psychological and emotional supplement to the truth-telling work of the 1981 Commission on Internment. The historic commission and concomitant absence of evacuee narratives[9] implies the lacuna that the novel begins to fill. In this sense, *Emperor* is especially redolent of the cultural work of the historical novels that inform this study. As I demonstrate, *Emperor*'s narrative is a symptomatic revelation both of the workings of denial that cloud gross crimes against humanity and of individual truth telling against amnesia. Moreover, in conveying a personalized experience of internment generations after the event, the novel not only imparts a sense of the trauma associated with it, but—as *Emperor*'s readers relate—serves as a timely commentary on contemporaneous issues.

A slim, taut novel—composed of five distinct chapters each narrated from one of four family members' points of view before, during, and after their three-and-a-half-year internment and one from the collective perspective of the two children upon their return to their indelibly changed San Francisco home—*Emperor* immediately drops the reader into the interior world of its characters. The first chapter, "Evacuation Order No. 19," belongs to the mother, who tells her story in a matter-of-fact manner that almost belies the injustice of the chapter's driving action invoked by its title—the only place in the novel the word "Evacuation" is ever mentioned. In fact, as Otsuka does not reveal the text of the order—its wording or instructions—the reader must infer its detail and certainly its historical and ethical implications. Yet the order's mere ubiquity underscores its severe authority: "The sign had appeared overnight," the book begins simply.

> On billboards and trees and the backs of the bus-stop benches. It hung in the window of Woolworth's. It hung by the entrance to the YMCA. It was stapled to the door of the municipal court and nailed, at eye level, to every telephone pole along University Avenue. The woman was returning a book to the library when she saw the sign in a post office window. It was a sunny day in Berkeley in the spring of 1942 and she was wearing new glasses and could see everything clearly for the first time in weeks.... She read the sign ... wrote down a few words on the back of a bank receipt, then turned around and went home and began to pack. (3)

The quotidian elements of daily life (from returning a library book to going to the bank) and the family's credulous response to the evacuation order not only mark the opening passage but dominate the entire chapter. In this way, the chapter obliquely reveals the evacuation order referenced by the chapter's title—President Roosevelt's Executive Order 9066—as well as the action that preceded this moment: the FBI's mass nighttime arrests of Issei men (first-generation Japanese immigrants) alleged to be spies yet never criminally accused. Until midway through the novel, that the family has suffered their father's midnight abduction is barely visible. Here in the opening chapter, the mother discloses it merely in practical terms, in relation to undone chores: "The woman had not mowed the grass for months. Her husband usually did that. She had not seen her husband since his arrest last December.... Every few days he was allowed to write her a letter.... On the back of every envelope was stamped "Censored, War Department," or "Detained Alien Enemy Mail" (10).

Not only the mother's mundane tone and actions but those of the whole community in which they live—who seem tacitly united to suppress the treachery being committed against all their Japanese American neighbors—grate against the fragmentary evidence of what's occurring. *Emperor*'s opening chapter thus effects a tremendous situational irony, which is yet so subtle that readers must scratch for it. The family's blithe daily practices in preparation for the coming week undermine the assertion that "the woman could see everything clearly." For at the same time, readers learn, "Tomorrow she and the children would be leaving," the woman tells "the girl it was time to practice the piano for Thursday's lesson," and the girl "practic[es] her prime numbers for Monday's test"—which she will never take (8, 16–17). Likewise, the hardware store owner— who surely has seen the omnipresent sign—exchanges niceties with the woman that simultaneously hide and forebode her impending departure.

> "Nice glasses," Joe Lundy said the moment she walked through the door....
> "How's your roof holding out?...
> "It's been a wet year."
> The woman nodded. "But we've had some nice days."...
> He pushed the quarters back toward her across the counter but he did not look at her. "You can pay me later," he said. Then he began to wipe the side of the register with a rag. There was a dark stain that would not go away. (5)

His refusing eye contact as well as her money dimly reveals what the persistent "dark stain" emphasizes: their unspoken mutual knowledge that there will be no "later" time for her to pay him.

In this characteristically symptomatic manner, the suppressed information regarding the FBI arrests of Issei men and the curfew and exclusion orders permits the reader to remain only vaguely aware of the factual background to the story—and of the father's absence at all—reflecting the collective mindset of US citizens at the time, who, like Joe Lundy, pretend to ignore their neighbors' plight. This stands until, at precisely the center of the novel, the longest chapter (belonging to the boy) disabuses the reader of this (un)comfortable ignorance. That this central chapter shares the book's title, "When the Emperor Was Divine," moreover suggests it holds a key to the novel. Although the boy mostly conveys the daily, tedious, and sad life in the crude desert camp, flashbacks to life in his Berkeley suburb shortly before the family's evacuation are interspersed among the present-tense narration:

> A man stopped him on the sidewalk in front of Woolworth's and said, "Chink or Jap?" and the boy answered, "Chink," and ran away as fast as he could. Only when he got to the corner did he turn around and shout, "Jap! Jap! I'm a Jap!"
> Just to set the record straight.
> But by then the man was already gone.
> Later, there were rules about time: No Japs out after eight p.m.
> And space: No Japs allowed to travel more than five miles from their homes.
> Later, the Japanese Tea Garden in Golden Gate Park was renamed the Oriental Tea Garden.
> Later, the signs that read INSTRUCTIONS TO ALL PERSONS OF JAPANESE ANCESTRY went up all over town and they packed their things and left. (76)

Such recollections not only slowly fill in the historical details of the story but also convey piece by piece the painful experiences, shot through with prejudice, that haunt the boy.

In this way, the text itself is evocative of the trauma of internment and sutures the reader to the subjectivity of the family members who struggle to survive their present conditions by stuffing away, for limited periods of time, the anguish and unfairness that split their family and forced their exile. Likewise, boy's poignant expression of his father's deeply felt absence sharpens and sensitizes the reader's nebulous sense of, and numbness to, the father. Through the son's innocent voice, the reader experiences the emotional wound the family has suffered from the father's disappearance: "'Does he ever think about us?' asked the boy. / 'All the time'" (61). Tender memories flood the boy's mind, revealing his nagging emptiness and longing for his father: "Whenever the boy knocked on his door his father would look up and smile and put down whatever it was he was doing. 'Don't be shy,' he'd say. He read the *Examiner* every morning before work and knew the answers to everything" (62). When they arrive at the Utah desert camp—"a city of tar-paper barracks behind a barbed-wire fence on a dusty alkaline plain" that clearly resembles nothing more than a prison—the boy thinks he sees his father everywhere: "wherever the boy looked he saw him: Daddy, Papa, Father, *Oto-san*." In response to the boy's calling out, "Papa," during a meal, "three men with thick metal-rimmed glasses looked up from their plates and said, *Nan desu ka?*"

> What is it?
> But the boy could not say what it was. (50)

That the traumatized boy cannot speak his father's absence implies the unspoken nature of the event itself—from the mass arrests of the Issei men to the internment of their children and fellow Americans of Japanese descent. The memory of his father's arrest comprises more space—that is, demands more of the boy's attention (and by extension, the reader's)—as the chapter proceeds:

> They had come for him just after midnight. Three men in suits and ties and black fedoras with FBI badges...The Christmas tree was up, and the whole house smelled of pine, and from his window the boy had watched as they led his father out across the lawn in his bathrobe and slippers to the black car that was parked at the curb.
> He had never seen his father leave the house without his hat on before.... If they had only let him put on his shoes then it all might have turned out differently.... Later the boy remembered seeing lights on in the house next door, and faces pressed to the window...Elizabeth Morgana Roosevelt had seen his father taken away in slippers. (74)

That the text withholds the details of the father's arrest until after showing the boy's pained yearning for him notably makes the emotional wound the context for the arrest. This approach—that is, *the narrative of internment as trauma*—counters historical treatments of the subject, imparting vital psychological and emotional truths about internment that histories cannot. In this vein, even the single "historical" fact of this scene, the arrest itself, as seen through the boy's eyes, is characterized by an affecting sense both of the father's forced removal from his family's Christmas celebration and of the boy's memory of the indignity with which the FBI took his innocent father at midnight. This sad resonance marks the boy's trauma of the event, for it is the image that recurs, again and again, fragmenting the chapter's anecdotes of daily camp life: "He'd be thinking these things, and then the image would suddenly float up before him: his father, in his bathrobe and slippers, being led away across the lawn. *Into the car, Papa-san*" (83).

Emperor works simultaneously to fill a part of history that previously has defied naming and to illustrate the forgetting and namelessness that surrounds the event. While in the desert internment camp, the boy—whom, along with the rest of his family, the novel never names—senses his being unseen and begins to lose a sense of himself. "Nobody's looking at me," he tells his sister. In response to her comment that in the desert, "water is just a mirage," he thinks, "A mirage was not there at all" (58). Such passages imply the large-scale dynamic of internment, by which the US government ensured the success of evacuation by ferrying away a swath of its citizens to undisclosed desert locations, facilitating an out-of-sight, out-of-mind mentality that, we soon see, the family's former friends and neighbors internalize. As such, Otsuka's gripping novel only begins to trace the hidden history of internment. Because the family remains unidentified for the whole of the text, these characters whom we come to know intimately through their first-person voices otherwise remain a mere shadow of a mostly unwritten history. Indeed, everything about the family defies naming. "One evening, before [the boy] went to bed, he wrote his name in the dust across the top of the table. All through the night, while he slept, more dust blew through the walls. / By morning his name was gone" (64). This image of a vanishing history that occurred in the deserts of Utah reappears. When his father returns from the internment camp, "the handwriting in his notebook grew smaller and fainter and then disappeared altogether" (137). The failure of these characters to record their stories or even their names seems to close them out of the pages of history in exchange for racial slurs written on the wall of the bedroom by the squatters in their house—which, the children say, "for years we could not get out of our heads" (111). Even upon the evacuees' haggard return from the camps, the majority population's convoluted version of history (informed by the national war effort against the Japanese) has already been written over the Japanese American experience during World War II.

Otsuka portrays the collective denial of this event that has ensued since 1942 as incipient in the evacuation process itself—and in the family's return after the war's end. That in the postwar years this denial develops into a vague collective amnesia of internment illuminates the reciprocity between denial and amnesia: denial of an injustice facilitates forgetting. When, after three bitter years in the sun-baked internment camps, the mother and children return to their Berkeley home, they are confronted by a paradox of silent denial and accusation by their community. "In the windows of the houses on our block we saw the faces of our old friends and neighbors. . . . They had all seen us leave, at the beginning of the war, had peered out through their curtains. . . . But none of them came out, that morning, to wish us goodbye, or good luck, or ask us where it was we were going (we didn't know). None of them waved. . . . Now when we ran into these same people on the street they *turned away and pretended not to see us*" (114–15, emphasis added). Friends at school reflect this "neighborly" denial. "Not a single one of our old friends from before— friends who had once shouted out to us, Your house or mine? every afternoon, after school, and whose backyards we had dug holes and built forts[—] . . . came up to us to say, "Welcome back," or "Good to see you," *or even seemed to remember who we were*" (121, emphasis added). This seeming *forgetting* of the children's identity and concomitant willful or complacent ignorance of the mass wrong Japanese Americans have suffered for the past three-plus years attempts to disguise the public denial that "greets" the returning internees.

Emperor reveals a telling aspect of the workings of amnesia regarding gross crimes against humanity that informs this book: the characteristic denial of the injustice suffered by one's neighbors—and citizen complicity therein.[10] The result (for the victims of Otsuka's story) is likewise a strong desire to forget, which, along with the reserve for which Japanese culture is known, helps to explain the national amnesia of internment. Neither the guilty nor the innocent— the American government and its citizen majority nor the imprisoned victims—wish to tell anyone what happened. (Hayner notes that truth commissions struggle not only "with rampant lies, denials, and deceit" of perpetrators [typically state agents] but also with "the painful, almost unspeakable memories of victims to uncover still-dangerous truths that many . . . resist" [23].) The father finally returns an aged and utterly broken man who does not resemble at all the successful businessman and charming and caring father who was suddenly taken from his wife and children nearly four years ago. When at last his train arrives back in Berkeley after the war,

> all we could do was stare down at our shoes, unable to move. Because the man who stood there before us was not our father. He was somebody else, a stranger who had been sent back in our father's place. . . . Our father, the father we remembered and had dreamed of, almost nightly, all through the years of the war, was handsome and strong. He moved quickly, surely, with his head held high in the air. . . . The man who came back on the train looked much older than his fifty-six years. (132)

The father's essential malady—his utter ruin—is not the government's, his perpetrator's, concern, so it remains neglected and thus undiagnosed, untreated, unnamed. His symptoms, however, mirror those of post-traumatic stress disorder suffered by war veterans, including an implacable paranoia ("He was convinced someone was watching the house. He did not like to use the telephone—You never know who might be listening—or to eat out in public" [134]). That he can neither work nor communicate results in painful adjustments to poverty for his children and his wife, who must take the only job available for a Japanese American woman at the time, a maid. "He never said one word to us about the years he'd been away. He never talked about politics or his arrest, or how he had lost his teeth. . . . We didn't want to know. We never asked. All we wanted to do, now that we were back in the world, was forget" (133). The father's essential losses—in his physical body, mind, character, and spirit—insinuate terrible truths, mostly untold, about the US government's rank treatment of Issei men and their families during World War II.

At the same time, the text counters the appreciable denial and insidious amnesia of the event with testimony of the family's personal experiences as victims of racism and violence in the World War II era. As a "crucial mode of our relation to the traumas of contemporary history," testimony, according to Shoshana Felman, is "composed of bits and pieces of a memory that has been overwhelmed by occurrences that have not settled into understanding or remembrance" (5). By the time the children return home, the reader has witnessed so much through their eyes—from the train to camp and finally back at their house—that the pervasive community denial can veil neither the crime committed against them nor the secrecy that enabled it. When a soldier on the train instructs the passenger-prisoners to lower the shades, the girl reflects,

> A man walking alongside the tracks would just see a train with black windows passing by in the middle of the day. He would think, There goes the train, and then he would not think about the train again. . . . She knew it was better this way. The last time they had passed through a city with the shades up someone had thrown a rock through one of the windows. (29)

The racial violence against Japanese Americans is, however, more flagrant upon their return: squatters not only occupied their house but horribly defaced it, destroyed their belongings and stole others; the family now can afford one cotton mattress on which they take turns sleeping in the front room "until the night the whiskey bottle shattered the window." Yet they fare better than some: "One man's house had been doused with gasoline and set on fire while his family lay sleeping inside. Another man's shed had been dynamited. There had been shootings in the valley...unannounced visitors knocking on doors in the middle of the night" (112). Rather than offer protection, the government encourages such scapegoating by its ongoing criminalization of the former internees. "The War Relocation Authority had sent each person home with train fare and twenty-five dollars in cash. 'It doesn't add up,' our mother had said. 'Three years. Five months. Twenty-five dollars...' We later learned [it] was the same amount given to criminals on the day they were released from prison" (118).

Emperor is the first widely received book to detail not only what happened from a Japanese American perspective—albeit, as the father's muteness on his imprisonment reveals, partially—but also the painful psychological and emotional dimensions of that truth, each for the imprisoned Issei men and the interned, including (significantly) children. In revealing the innocence, confusion, and internalized racism with which the children respond to the ordeal of internment, *Emperor* conveys a weighty aspect of internment that nebulous collective memory generally forgets: of 110,000 Japanese Americans who were so removed, two thirds were Nisei, US-born Japanese American children, and thus American citizens. The novel traces the damaging effects of racism on children; the boy mistakes the guilt that shrouds their imprisonment as his. He wakes up in the camp, "crying out, Where am I?" and worries that "he'd done something horribly, terribly wrong....It could be anything. Something he'd done yesterday—chewing the eraser off his sister's pencil...– or something he'd done a long time ago that was just now catching up with him" (57). This guilt insidiously causes the children to internalize the racism that clouds their young lives. When they return, they "kept up with the stories in the papers....We looked at ourselves in the mirror and did not like what we saw: black hair, yellow skin, slanted eyes. The cruel face of the enemy...We were guilty....On the street we tried to avoid our own reflections wherever we could...shiny surfaces and storefront windows" (120). Their guilt, their father's silence and fear, and their own all help explain why so much of the internment experience (as Toni Morrison says regarding slavery) "never came down." That "something untold, unsaid...some deliberate calculated survivalist intention to forget certain things" indicates the large-scale trauma that ensued from this national crime ("Profile of a Writer"). In this sense, drawing on her familial and cultural background along with her own research and imagination, Otsuka attempts to convey victim experiences—"acts that," as Felman explains, "cannot be constructed as knowledge nor assimilated into full cognition, events in excess of our frames of reference" (5).

Although *Emperor* is noteworthy for its singular revelation of these obscure truths, it also illuminates the mechanisms of their having been, heretofore, largely undisclosed. Whereas it shares such revelations with all the truth-telling novels in this book, it is distinct in that it does not express its historiographic concern self-consciously. In this sense, little is "postmodern" about the novel; nothing in it draws attention to its process as a narrative—that characteristic that Linda Hutcheon summarized over two decades ago as emblematic of postmodernism: "process made visible" (*Narcissistic Narrative* 6). *Emperor* proceeds by realistic storytelling—which, moreover, in its stark objective description, is often documentary in nature. Anchored in clear detail of a world that directly corresponds to a historical reality, the text withholds all self-awareness until its final terse chapter, a mere five pages in which the father directly addresses the reader. And yet Otsuka's insight into the hidden nature of the particular history that concerns her is no less keen than novels that self-consciously address the silences that have marked their historical subjects.

Rather, *Emperor*'s story is itself symptomatic of the fact that much of the history of Japanese American internment has long remained suppressed, as it was in 1942–1945. With the father's letters to his family, Otsuka underscores that essential information about the event remains a mystery; that her effort to tell about it is limited; that palpable omissions—like those in her mother's and grandmother's stories—and excisions remain. "Every few days the letters arrived, tattered and torn, from Lordsburg, New Mexico. Sometimes entire sentences had been cut out with a razor blade by the censors and the letters did not make any sense. Sometimes they arrived in one piece, but with half of the words blacked out. Always they were signed, 'From Papa, With Love'" (59). The blacked-out sentences and cut-out words are a synecdoche for the larger history of Japanese Americans during World War II, particularly that of the imprisoned Issei, and for the incomplete evidence and testimonies from which Otsuka sketches her story. Instances of such gaps in the history recur throughout the novel. Although many Issei, like the father in Otsuka's tale, "disappeared" psychologically and emotionally as a result of their imprisonment, others did not return at all.

> On a warm evening in April a man was shot dead by the barbed-wire fence. The guard who was on duty said the man had been trying to

escape. He'd called out to him four times, the guard said, but the man had ignored him. Friends of the dead man said he had simply been taking his dog for a walk. He might not have heard the guard, they said, because he was hard of hearing. Or because of the wind. One man who had gone to the scene of the accident right after the shooting had noticed a rare and unusual flower on the other side of the fence. It was his belief that his friend had been reaching out to pick the flower when the shot had been fired. . . . *One false move, pal, and you're dead.* (101–2)

Like another man who "disappeared [from the internment camp] and was found frozen to death three days later, ten miles west of the mountains" (88), this pithy anecdote in the midst of the boy's chapter figures the disappearance not only of individual internees and their personal histories but that of countless Japanese Americans who were lost or permanently traumatized by their years of internment and imprisonment. These elisions, combined with the father's reticence, suggest that the whole of the internees' experiences is unattainable; like the suppositions as to the murdered man's death, much of what remains from the internee's experience are partial, possible versions of it. Like the father's psychological and physical wounds that do not translate to words, the individual and collective trauma of internment does not lend itself to full exposition but solicits the reader's perception and halting experience of the event.

In this sense, *Emperor* shares with the other novels in this study a poststructuralist sense of history—which is manifest, however, not metacritically but in the tenor and structure of the narrative itself. The novel's sparse form and chapters—each from a different point of view—underscore its fragmentary revelation of internment and at the same time holds and intimates a palpable power. The reader detects a heavy emotional and psychological weight beyond what the characters can individually convey—beyond even the most bitter of these, the father, whose fulmination ends the story. In the novel's last, brief chapter, the father not only speaks for the first time but addresses the reader head-on, dramatically shifting the voice, tone, and style of the novel. His physical, then emotional and psychological, absence throughout the narrative, juxtaposed to his blunt voice in the final chapter, is a profound metaphor for the dynamic of amnesia and truth telling that is *Emperor*'s most striking revelation—and itself emblematic of the cultural work of the truth-telling novels of this study. This concluding chapter, "Confession," is a truth-telling counterpoint to all of the secrecy that surrounds the Japanese American experience—from the father's abduction and censored letters to his prolonged absence and the train window shades that shield the internees from their fellow Americans. Because the father (as the children disclose) will not speak about his experience, Otsuka fills the scant testimonies of the imprisoned Issei men with her imagination of his vivid voice—the innermost outrage, no doubt, of so many so unjustly treated:

> Everything you have heard is true. I was wearing my bathrobe, my slippers, the night your men took me away. At the station, they asked me questions. *Talk to us,* they said. The room was small and bare. It had no windows. The lights were bright. They left them on for days. What more can I tell you? My feet were cold. I was tired. I was thirsty. I was scared. So I did what I had to do. I talked.
>
> All right, I said. I admit it. I lied. You were right. You were always right. It was me. I did it. I poisoned your reservoirs. I sprinkled your food with insecticide. I sent my peas and potatoes to market full of arsenic. . . . So go ahead, lock me up. Take my children. Take my wife. Freeze my assets. . . . Ransack my house. . . . Hand over my lease. Assign me a number. Inform me of my crime. *Too short, too dark, too ugly, too proud. Put it down in writing.* (140, 143, emphasis added)

As Tina Chen argues, this sudden shift to second-person point of view transmutes what "comfortable empathy" the reader may have experienced in the rest of the novel to "an engaged accountable critical sympathy" that reorients the self in respect to the Other. Indeed, the father's anger and pain, nakedly expressed at last, puts the reader in an "antagonistic" position (169).

Yet this surprising rhetorical shift emphasizes the novel's stake in claiming to tell an *unwritten* truth about American history—a counternarrative to the official "writing" of internment. "Everything you've heard," this chapter begins, "is true." Although, as we have seen, the novel is not "postmodern" in its self-consciousness, these words put the text—and the reader's consideration of its story—in dialogue with what one knows, or does not know, about the history of Japanese American internment. Unlike the situational irony of the opening chapter, the verbal irony of this last chapter is likewise more characteristically postmodern. The father's "admission" to a litany of crimes against humanity are so excessive as to be patently untrue; and at the same time, his false confession chafes against his statements that the reader, by this conclusion of the novel, knows to be true: the gross violation of this Issei man and his family and property and, by extension, of the citizen rights of "ALL PERSONS OF JAPANESE ANCESTRY" in 1942. By speaking directly to the reader, *Emperor* finally collapses the distance between the world of the novel and the world "outside" it, probing the truth and lies of the history that is its subject.

Simultaneously, the novel casts an uncanny light on the egregious abuse of state power coincident with its 2002 publication—including the ongoing assault of civil liberties under the 2001 Patriot Act (from broad wiretapping of US citizens to airport and border searches of people and baggage). Contemporary rationalizations of these state violations echo the mantras the government repeated to the internees in 1942: "It was all in the interest of national security. / It was a matter of military necessity" (70). *Emperor*'s narratives invoke, among other current comparisons, the May 2008 release of Sami al Hajj, the Al Jazeera cameraman and only journalist whom the United States imprisoned at Guantánamo for nearly seven years, never charged and yet classified as an enemy combatant. Although he was subjected to 130 interrogation sessions, the United States never published its allegations against him. Likewise, the United States detained Maher Arar, a Canadian engineer, during a stopover in JFK airport in 2002 and, on suspicion of terrorism, deported him to a Syrian prison where he was tortured, interrogated, and kept in a tomb-like cell for almost a year. Three years later, a Canadian commission cleared him of all terrorist charges. Arar is pursuing a federal lawsuit charging that the US government violated his constitutional right to due process, among other rights. In a recent interview with Terry Gross, Arar confessed that during torture interrogations, "you will say anything to get them to stop." In this sense, the unwarranted midnight arrest of the father in *Emperor*, his interminable imprisonment, the interrogation tactics he recalls, and his ensuing hollow "confession" all mirror what we have learned in recent years about the false-confession effects of torture, about the wrongful detention of innocent citizens, and about Guantánamo and other remote prisons to which the United States deports detainees.

The father's detailed, eruptive confession is the language of testimony; together with the novel's prior narratives, it transforms the past, even for readers who were never there, into a present experience. In this, *Emperor* is a psychological complement to the purely empirical work of the historical truth commission that, 20 years prior to the novel, investigated its subject and to the written apologies and $20,000 checks issued in 1990 to each surviving individual of internment. Given the nearly half-century that had passed from the original injustice, tens of thousands of the original adult internees never lived to witness or receive this retribution. Of course, the apology and money (even for those who did survive to receive it) cannot erase, fully alleviate, or even give authentic or empathetic voice to the suffering internment imposed on its victims nor the long-term trauma from it. In its personally informed imaginative detail of the internment and its aftermath, however, *Emperor* adds an essential psychic component to these material acts of retributive justice.

Epilogue: Looking Back Is Looking Forward

In the cultural milieu that shapes this book, Otsuka's novel offers a constitutive counterpoint to two instances of obscene state abuse of human rights contemporaneous to *Emperor*'s subject and to its publication, respectively: the Japanese Imperial Army's incarceration, rape, and abuse of "comfort women" during World War II; and the Bush administration's excesses of the War on Terror abroad and at home in flagrant defiance of constitutional and international law. Though a half-century apart, both events are marked not only by the type of nationalist justifications of unchecked power in a time of war that Otsuka's novel invokes but also by the dynamic of official denial and public calls for truth telling that underlie this book as a whole. As I write, a maelstrom surrounds the documentary evidence of torture under the Bush administration that has alternately been withheld, destroyed, released, and redacted. At the same time, the nation awaits a response from the Obama administration to calls for a congressional investigation into the abuses of the Bush-Cheney administration—indeed, for a federal truth commission. The heated conflict suggests the force of this extant dialectic of denial and truth telling, the salience of this new form of the historical novel in the current moment, and the fertile ground for the cultural work of such novels in the future.

Indeed, the current debate on torture is an emblematic instance of official denial and public attempts at truth telling of historic significance. One might locate a beginning of this tug-of-war between state suppression of truth on the one hand and revelation and public insistence of truth on the other to October 2003. At this time, to determine whether the US government's interrogation policies were consistent with domestic and international law, the American Civil Liberties Union (ACLU) with several other organizations, under the Freedom of Information Act (FOIA), filed a request for documents concerning the treatment of detainees held by the United States overseas. The Bush administration initially stonewalled. Even after the graphic photographs of US military abuse of prisoners at Abu Ghraib prison in Iraq sparked outrage around the world in April 2004, President Bush himself in June 2004 maintained, "The United States remains steadfastly committed to upholding the Geneva Conventions," and, said FBI director George Tenet in April 2007, "We do not torture people."[1] Meanwhile, the ACLU filed a lawsuit to enforce its request for documents. The court, clearly influenced by the Abu Ghraib photographs, ordered the government to respond to the ACLU's request. Since that ruling, the FOIA litigation has yielded more than 100,000 pages of documents, which collectively show that the abuse and torture of prisoners was systemic and not limited to Abu Ghraib, that over 100 prisoners have died in US military custody—dozens of these ruled homicides (that is, prisoners were tortured to death)—and that many others have disappeared into the CIA's secret detention system. These newly declassified memos, communications, and testimonies make undeniably clear that those at the very highest level of the Bush administration authorized, encouraged, or tolerated the mistreatment. The most keen and persuasive narrative of these facts may be the *New York Times* journalist Jane Mayer's *The Dark Side: The Inside Story of How the War on Terror Turned into a War on American Ideals* (published July 15, 2008). A meticulously researched account of the administration's nefarious actions in the name of the War on Terror, *The Dark Side* is among nearly two dozen books published in 2008 alone that belie the administration's denials of torture.

In the wake of this flood of revelation of the government's violation of domestic and international law and two days prior to the historic 2008 US presidential election, Nicholas Kristof, in the *New York Times*, called for the new president to "start a Truth Commission to investigate torture and other abuses during the 'war on terror'" (12). On his second day in office, President Obama issued an executive order mandating that Guantánamo—which had increasingly become a symbol of American lawlessness and human rights violations—be closed. Within weeks, invoking the president's executive order as a "first step" to "restoring the rule of law" and "returning government to the people," Senator Patrick Leahy on February 9, 2009, proposed a truth commission to investigate Bush-Cheney administration abuses, including the treatment and torture of terrorism suspects, the authorization of warrantless wiretapping, extraordinary rendition, and executive override of laws.[2]

In that the proposed truth commission would look into recent state abuses, along the lines of the 1990s Latin American truth commissions and South Africa's TRC, it is fundamentally unlike the only two truth commissions the United States has previously established, historical inquiries into internment during World War II and AEC-conducted human radiation experiments during the Cold War. A number of legal advocacy groups including Human Rights First and New York University's Brennan Center for Justice, both of whom earlier proposed similar ideas, supported Leahy's proposal. And on March 4, 2009, the bipartisan Constitution Project submitted a statement to the Senate Judiciary Committee calling for President Obama to appoint a nonpartisan commission to examine the legality of Bush policies related to detention, treatment, and transfer of detainees. Entitled "Getting to the Truth Through a Nonpartisan Commission of Inquiry" and signed by 18 different organizations and a range of former government officials, it concludes with a compelling case for "uncovering hard truths":

> It is certainly tempting to move on without investigating [and] to ignore this chapter of American history....But we cannot allow these detainee policies to become an indelible mark of shame on our democracy. Our obligation to reveal the truth should not be seen as a distraction from the serious challenges our country currently faces. Understanding our past is a crucial step to building a better future free of these same mistakes. (Monroe 2)

As "Getting to the Truth" suggests, at the crux of the debate over an investigation of abuses under the previous administration is President Obama's stated, reiterated intent "to look forward, not back"[3]—a proposition that many, in the words of the director for the ACLU's National Security Project, "reject as a false choice" (Jaffer). This seeming opposition between telling the truth about the past and moving into the future recurs as documents from the War on Terror are alternately released and withheld. Executive Director Anthony Romero of the ACLU criticized, for example, Obama's May 12, 2009, reversal of his April 23 decision to release detainee prison photographs: "We cannot fulfill the president's stated desire to restore the rule of law, to revive our moral standing in the world and to lead a transparent government" if that government is "complicit in covering up" egregious abuse and violations of the rule of law. "*Only by...acknowledging the crimes of the past* and achieving accountability *can we move forward* and ensure that these atrocities are not repeated" (ACLU press release May 13, 2009; emphasis added). Not only do these rationales for a US truth commission from various sources echo one another; they echo the reactions of citizens and survivors of brutal regimes around the world—the lessons, that is, of healing from a dark history, both for individuals and for the national psyche.[4] As Patricia Hayner, in her book on truth commissions, summarizes, "In some countries 'the past' is often the first and most contentious item on the agenda. Elsewhere, the new government has confronted the issue, with accountability for past crimes often one of the most pressing issues before the new administration" (5). Clearly, this is the case for the young Obama administration. In this regard, for a great many Americans, looking back is looking forward; indeed, we base our criminal justice on this very premise.[5]

The same premise underlies the truth-telling historical novel. Arising as it has from the widespread "turn towards truth" in the 1990s and proceeding, in Toni Morrison's words, by "literary archaeology," it excavates, imagines, and articulates formerly suppressed truths about the national past—particularly the human dimension of that past—for which its contemporary audience and cultural milieu is ripe. Indeed, Otsuka's attention to censored and severely blacked-out letters from the father in *When the Emperor Was Divine* evokes the state of the recently released memos and communications from the War on Terror. A joint PEN Center/ACLU event on October 13, 2009, made vivid these documents and the role of writers in reflecting on the responsibility for crimes committed in the name of their nation. Entitled "Reckoning with Torture: Memos and Testimonies from the 'War on Terror,'" and occurring in the Great Hall of the Cooper Union in New York City, the event featured authors (Don DeLillo, Paul Auster, Eve Ensler, Art Spiegelman, and others), a former CIA interrogator, and an ACLU attorney who read from these materials to the fully packed Great Hall. The ACLU and PEN Center's shared belief, which was used to publicize the event, expresses the same essential conviction that informs this book: "Writers have a crucial role to play in examining crimes committed in the name of their country, and in helping the nation face, understand, and reckon with these terrible acts" (PEN e-mail announcement, September 16, 2009). Presented as an invitation to "start with the evidence" and begin reckoning, the event was dedicated to galvanizing support for a public call to "meaningful accountability" and "transparency": the disclosure of all torture files that remain secret and a Justice Department–appointed criminal investigation of the Bush administration's torture program. Two aspects of the evidence stressed how much of "the dark side" of the War on Terror remains unknown: the vast number of documents that the CIA continues to withhold or has destroyed altogether and the heavily censored nature of the material that has been released.

Five-plus years after accounts of torture and prisoner abuse at Abu Ghraib came to public attention, the CIA still retains hundreds of thousands of documents and photos related to the War on Terror. Yet as disturbing is how little has been done in response to the information that has been released. For although the grim revelation on March 2, 2009, that the CIA destroyed 92 interrogation videotapes makes chillingly clear that we will never know the full historical truth of "what really happened," the materials now publicly accessible provide excruciating, if partial, accounts of what those tapes captured.

At the same time, the heavily erased information within those documents intimates experiential and psychological truths that require a writer's imagination and talent to tell. That is, this (dis)information and the intense conflicts around "meaningful accountability" and "transparency" adumbrate the cultural work of truth-telling historical fiction in future years. Of all the declassified "torture memos" read at the PEN event, the most revealing and also occlusive in this regard was an excerpt from an 18-page paper prepared by the CIA for the Justice Department. Don DeLillo read from the simultaneously detailed and—where he explicitly noted and I indicate below in upper case—substantially redacted account of the agency's detention, interrogation, and rendition programs:

> This paper provides further background information and details on High-Value Detainee (HVD) interrogation techniques....
>
> A. **Initial Conditions**. Capture, REDACTED contribute to the physical and psychological condition of the HVD prior to the start of interrogation. Of these, "capture shock" and detainee reactions REDACTED are factors that may vary significantly between detainees. SEVERAL LINES REDACTED....
>
> 1. Rendition.
> a. The HVD is flown to a Black Site REDACTED....During the flight, the detainee is securely shackled and is deprived of sight and sound through the use of blindfolds, earmuffs, and hoods. REDACTED....
> b. Upon arrival at the destination airfield, the HVD is moved to the Black Site under the same REDACTED conditions....
>
> 2. Reception at Black Site. The HVD is subjected to administrative procedures and medical assessment upon arrival at the Black Site. FIVE LINES REDACTED the HDV finds himself in the complete control of the Americans; SIX LINES REDACTED....
> a. The HVD's head and face are shaved. REDACTED...

Transitioning to Interrogation—The Initial Interview.
...The standard on participation is set very high during the Initial Interview. The HVD would have to willingly provide information on actionable threats and location information on High-Value Targets at large—not lower level information—for interrogators to continue with the neutral approach. THE REMAINING HALF PAGE IS REDACTED.

C. Interrogation. SEVERAL LINES REDACTED.
...2. Conditioning techniques. The HVD is typically reduced to a baseline, dependent state...to demonstrate to the HVD that he has no control over basic human needs.... The specific conditioning interrogation techniques are:
a. Nudity. The HVD's clothes are taken and he remains nude until the interrogators provide clothes to him. REDACTED.
b. Sleep Deprivation. The HVD is placed in the vertical shackling position to begin sleep deprivation.... The detainee is diapered for sanitary purposes, although the diaper is not used at all times....

Following these "conditioning techniques," the paper next details "corrective techniques," including "the *insult slap, abdominal slap, facial hold*, and *attention grasp*"; within each paragraph description of each of these techniques that follows, several lines are redacted.

Among much worth probing in this and other torture memos is the consistent substitution of "HVD" for the personal identity of each and every detainee; along with the significantly redacted lines, this results in a nagging tension between explicit and implicit information. This tension between the clinical, detached language of the memos and the human element of torment they imply—but leave out—is the domain of the writer willing, as Morrison puts it, to "reconstruct the world the remains imply" and to convey a counterhistory that tells a kind of truth the cold facts refuse. One source and sliver of the humanity missing in the official record of torture is the video testimony of former detainees with which the PEN event closed.[6] "Justice Denied Video: Voices From Guantánamo" features 4 of the 775 men detained at Guantánamo, most of whom—by the US government's implicit admittance in eventually releasing 560 of them[7]—are innocent. Their testimonies correspond to the "conditioning" and "corrective" techniques the torture memos outline; and they tell of other sordid, "unofficial" torture they experienced. From suffering the sexual abuse of female soldiers to eventually—from repeated waterboarding—becoming incontinent, the men, in the words of one, were "physically and psychologically broken" (Ruhal Ahmed, "Justice Denied"). Like the vast majority of their fellow prisoners, they lost years of their life at Guantánamo subjected to such torture and were then summarily released without being charged with a crime—actions that reiterate the US government's stripping Japanese American detainees of habeas corpus during World War II. As in 1942–1945, Congress circumvented the US Constitution's provision of habeas corpus by passing a federal act—the Detainee Treatment Act of 2005, which eliminated habeas corpus for all detainees—that the US Supreme Court eventually overruled (in this case on June 12, 2008). Such personal testimony as the former detainees in "Justice Denied" provide just begins to flesh out what the official record has omitted and erased.

Although the statist language represented in the CIA paper excerpted earlier denies the human dimension of torture, it is the role of the writer to imagine the lives of detainees (and of their interrogators). Clearly, we are only beginning to grasp the extent and nature of the trauma wreaked by the War on Terror, both on individual victims of state abuse and torture and on the national psyche. One began to get a sense of this trauma at the PEN/ACLU event, particularly in the different responses to the evidence. After several authors read memos from the War on Terror—all of which evinced that the Bush administration authorized torture—Eve Ensler read from George W. Bush's June 26, 2004, speech commemorating the United Nations Day in Support of the Victims of Torture. In light of the preceding documents, it was clear that the speech was rife with lies. One could only hear, then, Bush's stated commitment to "lead the fight to eliminate torture everywhere" with damning insight. Yet, though Ensler read with a thickly ironic tone, glancing up with a smirk throughout, seeking audience members to join her in smug derision, the room remained silent and grave. Of striking contrast was the profound empathy Kwame Anthony Appiah expressed, in his opening remarks but most poignantly following the video testimony that exposed the naked agony the Guantánamo detainees endured at the hands of "our" government.[8] The first to speak after the video ended, Appiah broke down in tears, needing some moments to gather himself before completing his concluding remarks.

Like the vast majority of audience members present, neither could I laugh with Ensler at Bush's prevarications and the torture program they concealed; the truth the evidence revealed was so intensely disturbing that it had shattered any comfortable distance irony—the chief trope of the postmodern—might provide. As the stunned silence in the auditorium was palpable throughout the evening, I sensed that Appiah's reaction was cathartic for many individuals witness to the event. I point to this contrast (between Ensler's and Appiah's responses to the evidence) to suggest the complicated path of healing the nation faces in the wake of these abuses and to suggest that, to do so, we as a nation must own some of the trauma the victims experienced and by which they will be haunted for the rest of their lives. To borrow Toni Morrison's words concerning the trauma of slavery, "there is so much more to remember and to describe. For purposes of exorcism...things must be made...some*thing* where these things can be released. But the consequences of [traumatic historical events] only artists can deal with. And it's our job" ("Profile of a Writer"). The historical and cathartic facets of these experiences will constitute, no doubt, vital territory of truth-telling historical fiction in years to come.

NOTES

PROLOGUE

1. From Robert Faurison, a lifelong Holocaust denier from France, to
   David Duke, the American white supremacist politician and former
   Ku Klux Klan leader, who contended that no gas chambers or extermination camps were actually built during the war on the grounds
   that killing Jews by that method would have been cost-prohibitive
   and much too bothersome. "The number of victims at the Auschwitz
   concentration camp could be about 2,007. The railroad to the camp
   did not have enough capacity to transfer large numbers of Jews," said
   another speaker. The conference included an exhibition of various
   photos, posters, and other materials meant to contradict the accepted
   version of events, that the Nazis murdered millions of Jews and other
   "undesirables" in death camps during the war. Some familiar photos of corpses at the camps bore new captions in Persian arguing
   that they were victims of typhus, not the German state. This discussion of the Holocaust denial conference is based on "Iran Hosts
   Holocaust Deniers," Associated Press, December 12, 2006; Nazila
   Fathi, "Holocaust Deniers and Skeptics Gather in Iran," *New York
   Times*, December 11, 2006; "Rogues and Fools," Editorial, *New
   York Times*, December 15, 2006; Tammy Bruce, "This Weekend:
   Iran's Holocaust Denial Conference." Blog. : <http://tammybruce.
   com/2006/12/this_weekend_irans_holocaust_d_html>; "Hatred
   on Parade," Editorial, *Daily Camera*, December 14, 2006.
2. Minow 123. For an extended discussion of various manifestations of
   justice ensuing from trials, truth commissions, and reparations, see
   Minow 123–33.
3. In 1995 Queen Elizabeth II became the first British monarch ever
   to make an official apology. In the presence of the Maori queen,
   Te Arikinui Dame Te Atairangikaahu, she signed into New Zealand
   law a bill in which the Crown apologized to the largest Maori tribe,
   the Tainui people of Waikato, for sending imperial forces into their
   land in the 1860s and for the subsequent devastation and injustice.
   In 1997 Prime Minister Tony Blair apologized for Britain's role in
   the Irish potato famine; French bishops apologized for silence over
   French collaboration during the Holocaust. In 1998 alone, the
   Japanese prime minister Tomichi Murayama apologized for suffering

inflicted in World War II; East German lawmakers for the Holocaust; Pope John Paul II for violence during the Counter-Reformation and, partially, for the Church's role during World War II; the Canadian government to its native aboriginal population for past governmental actions that suppressed their languages, cultures, and spiritual practices; and President Jacques Chirac of France to the descendants of Alfred Dreyfus, the Jewish army captain who was falsely arrested, convicted, and degraded for spying in the 1890s. As well that year, Australia instituted an annual Sorry Day, held on May 26, the anniversary of the release of the best-selling human rights report *Bring Them Home*, which documents the government's long-standing policy of stealing some 100,000 Aboriginal children from their parents to be raised by white families and in orphanages.

4. In 1998 President Clinton awarded Fred Korematsu, a leading figure in the movement to make official amends for the Japanese American internments, the Presidential Medal of Freedom, the highest civilian honor. More than a decade earlier, the District Court judge Marilyn Patel had not only granted Korematsu's petition for the rarely used *coram nobis* (which, 40 years after the fact, wiped from the record his 1942 conviction for refusing to obey the executive relocation order) but also used the occasion to afford a public acknowledgment of the harm done and a public warning against future harms. Korematsu's case and the larger movement for reparations inspired other US citizens to seek redress for group-based injustices. Of these, following the example of the Japanese Americans reparations movement and bearing the most success, Native Hawaiians pressed in the 1990s for redress of the overthrow of the Hawaiian monarchy. In 1993 Clinton signed a joint congressional resolution apologizing to Native Hawaiians for American's role in the overthrow of the Kingdom of Hawaii.

5. See Leslie T. Hatamiya, *Righting a Wrong: Japanese Americans and the Passage of the Civil Liberties Act of 1988* (Stanford, CA: Stanford UP, 1993). Recent years have again witnessed more official apologies: in 2004 the South African president Thabo Mbeki apologized for failing to intervene in Rwanda, and the BBC apologized to the government over Andrew Gillian; in 2005 the Pope apologized for injustices against indigenous people in the South Pacific, and Tony Blair apologized to the Guildford Four and the Maguire Seven. Nonetheless, official denial of inhuman violence persists perhaps most notably in the case of Japan's half-century denial of the imperial army's rape and abuse of "comfort women" during World War II, with which this prologue concludes.

6. Quoted in Hayner 18. See also Danielle Gordon, "The Verdict: No Harm, No Foul," *Bulletin of the Atomic Scientists* 52, no. 1 (1996): 33; Michael D'Antonio, "Atomic Guinea Pigs," *New York Times*

Magazine, August 31, 1997: 38–43; Timothy Garton Ash, "Ten Years After," *New York Review of Books*, November 18, 1999, 18.

7. Hayner distinguishes these far less common "historical truth commissions" as "present-day government-sponsored inquiries into abuses by the state that took place many years earlier (and that ended years earlier). Such an inquiry is not established as part of a political transition . . . but serves instead to clarify historical truths and pay respect to previously unrecognized victims or their descendants. . . . The events investigated [are] generally not those of widespread political repression, but targeted practices may have affected specific ethnic, racial or other groups. These historical truth commissions document practices that are largely unknown to the majority of the population, and their reports can thus have a powerful impact despite the years that have passed" (17).

8. Vidal devotes his whole book to detailing many examples of such amnesia. Here he rebukes the predictable reaction to his proposal for all drugs to be legalized "and sold at cost to anyone with a doctor's prescription": "horrific." "Brainwashing on the subject begins early, ensuring that a large crop of the coming generation will become drug addicts. Prohibition always has that effect as we should have learned when we prohibited alcohol from 1919 to 1933, but happily, for the busy lunatics who rule over us, we are permanently the United States of Amnesia. We learn nothing because we remember nothing. The period of Prohibition . . . brought on the greatest breakdown of law and order that we have ever endured—until today, of course." We forget, Vidal reminds us, that in 1970 England, with a population of 55 million people, "had only 1,800 heroin addicts. With our 200 million people we had nearly a half-million addicts," because rather than criminalizing the addict, England "required him to registers with a physician who then gives him, at controlled intervals, a prescription" (7–8).

9. Bertman devotes his entire first chapter, "Cultural Amnesia," to a thorough eponymous display, citing over 100 statistics such as these: "More American teen-agers can name the Three Stooges than the three branches of government"; "80 percent of eighth graders were found unable to do seventh-grade math"; "only 48 percent of Americans know that the earth goes around the sun once a year"; "fifty-eight million Americans couldn't tell east from west" on a map issued by the National Geographic Society. Each fact comes from organizations such as the National Science Foundation, the US Department of Education, the National Endowment for the Humanities, the Gallup Organization, the *New York Times*, and the US Congress, who conducted the dozens of national and international studies, polls, and surveys from 1988 to 1998, with the majority carried out between 1992 and 1998.

10. My initial discussion of this book is from its collectively authored introduction (1–13). As the authors Roy Rosenzweig and David Thelan write separate primary chapters, I later cite the individual author as appropriate.

11. The pilot survey, conducted by Arizona State University graduate students, convinced COHMIA that they "needed to pay attention to how we introduced our topic. *History* is the word that scholars privilege to describe how they approach the past. But in Phoenix *history* conjured up something done by famous people that others studied in school.... *Trust* was the concept that best captured how people viewed sources of information about the past.... what mattered to them in the past could be elicited by the concept of *connection*" (6).

12. They cite among other such pundits Lynne Cheney, who, as chairman of the National Endowment for the Humanities (NEH), had issued in 1987 a pamphlet called *American Memory*, which began with the declaration, "A refusal to remember...is a primary characteristic of our nation." In turn, Cheney is among the exponentially more sources that inform Bertman's decade-later irrefutable testimony of cultural amnesia. Bertman's premise deals with the collective loss of core knowledge—i.e., the category of "history" that COHMIA strategically circumvented—but his central concern is "education's larger purpose," to teach why geography, history, and literature are "worth knowing," "the cultural whole to which the parts belong" and "their interconnections" (16).

13. "Many respondents said they fear being manipulated by people who distort the past to meet their own needs—whether commercial greed, political ambition, or cultural prejudice. In their desire to strip away layers of mediation, respondents trust eyewitnesses more than television or movies.... They feel unconnected to the past in history classrooms because they don't recognize themselves in the version of the past presented there" (13).

14. Here Patell draws from Sacvan Bercovitch's introduction, which explains that this volume of the CHAL "redraw[s] the boundaries of the field" of American literary scholarship (672).

15. "Frequently lost in the historical preoccupation with disorder and conflict" of the 1960s and 1970s, reminds Bodnar, "was the fact that the period began and ended with two large celebrations that attempted to foster order and national unity. The language and activities of these celebrations seldom referred directly to arguments over civil rights or Vietnam, for instance. Rather, the celebration of the Civil War Centennial between 1961 and 1965 and the American Revolution Bicentennial in 1976 were heavily influenced by government officials who urged widespread citizen participation, respect for patriots who died for the cause of national unity, and loyalty to the nation." Officials who planned these national commemorations "desperately wanted to interpret the past in ways that would reinforce

citizen loyalty to a nation-state.... These contemporary political goals transformed the interpretation of the past to such an extent that [these] acts of outright rebellion against political authority became dramatic stories in which great men made irrevocable decisions that now deserved praise, and ordinary people deferred to higher authority and fought heroically for political dogmas" (206, 243).

16. In a chapter of *The Presence of the Past* that "explores the terrain that lies between individual uses of the past and the collective and national themes most of us studied in school" is a subtitled section, "'The Government Was a Bunch of Liars': Is National History Weakening?" which Thelan summarizes thus: "The lessons baby boomers learned from the 1960s left them considerably skeptical about the nation-state" (130–35).

17. Most indicative is the contentious—and emotional—debate over the final design of the Vietnam Veterans Memorial (VVM), dedicated in November 1982, a compelling story that constitutes Bodnar's prologue and which I detail further in chapter 2. Because many ordinary people had been so accepting of official control of public memory "for a very long time, the original design for the VVM came as something of shock" to some of the Washington D.C. veterans who had originally planned the memorial and felt the design was "anti-heroic." The VVM "represented the triumph" of a vernacular expression of comradeship with and sorrow for the dead over official ideals of patriotism and nationalism and raised the possibility that vernacular interests might be more powerful in the future (9, 20).

18. Implicit in public memory, writes Bodnar, "is an argument about the interpretation of reality" (15) that is immediately recognizable in the voices of the African Americans and Native Americans surveyed by COHMIA, for whom "orally transmitted history—as well as particular trusted books, films, and museums—competes with an 'official' version of the past that is often distrusted.... Although every group we interviewed rated high school history teachers, nonfiction books, and movies and television as the least trustworthy historical sources, Native Americans ranked them significantly lower than anyone else," and African Americans also judged them "as significantly less trustworthy than did whites" (Rosenzweig 168). This collective distrust of sanctioned historical sources reveals the way in which the argument inherent to public memory, an "aspect of the politics of culture," is rooted not simply in a time dimension between the past and the present but ultimately "grounded in the inherent contradictions of a social system: local and national structures, ethnic and national cultures" (Bodnar 14).

19. In 1990 rumors of sexual slavery by the Armed Forces before and during World War II began to circulate; in 1991 the first of many comfort women went public with her testimony. Japan, however, officially and repeatedly denied any governmental forced draft of comfort women,

even following the January 1992 public disclosure, by a Japanese history professor, of documents obtained from the Library of the National Institute of Defense that reported the widespread wartime organization of comfort stations. Finally, nearly two years later, in August 1993, Japan admitted deception and coercion and official involvement in the recruitment of comfort women. Yet despite international investigations from Korea and the Netherlands to the International War Crimes Tribunal on Military Sexual Slavery and the UN along with concomitant demands for an official apology from the state of Japan, Japan to this day refuses to apologize. Minow 105; George L. Hicks, *The Comfort Women: Japan's Brutal Regime of Enforced Prostitution in the Second World War* (New York: Norton,1997); Yuki Tanaka, *Japan's Comfort Women: Sexual Slavery Prostitution during World War II & the US Occupation* (London: Routledge, 2001); and Yoshiaki Yoshimi, *Comfort Women* (New York: Columbia UP, 2002) are among the sources on the topic. Nora Keller's *Comfort Women* (1997) and Chang-rae Lee's *A Gesture Life* (1999) are two haunting novels on the lives of comfort women, the former inspired by the testimony of a comfort woman that Keller heard at a symposium on human rights at the University of Hawaii in 1993.

I INTRODUCTION

1. I refer to the extraordinary success of histories such as those by Stephen Ambrose and David McCullough, whose best-selling books *Band of Brothers* (1992) and *John Adams* (2001), respectively, (among dozens of other best-selling nationalist histories between these two authors alone) were subsequently made into hugely popular "HBO Miniseries Events." The *John Adams* miniseries (2008) has won more Emmy awards, 13, than any other miniseries and four Golden Globe awards.

2. *Ragtime* refuses to situate the reader explicitly in the present, "symbolically cutting its moorings" and thus figuring "some new world past historical time whose relationship to us," Jameson says and Hutcheon agrees, "is problematical indeed" (22). The novel also resists "instituting a narrative dialectic between what we already 'know' about" its historical subject and what that historical subject "is then seen to be concretely in the pages of the novel" (23). For Hutcheon, these characteristics are sources of the novel's strengths because they stress "the narrativity and textuality of our knowledge about the past" (136). My argument that DeLillo forces a confrontation between contemporary American history and traditional American mythologies, in contrast, depends upon the relationship DeLillo sets up between the protagonist's present in the late 1970s (and eventually, in 1999) and his past, rooted in his 1950s childhood and his 1960s coming-of-age. Unlike

Ragtime's deployment of what Jameson calls "incommensurable" characters that are both historical and fictional, as well as intertextual, *Americana*'s characters are purely and clearly fictional. Yet—as plain—the violence and terror that fractures the inherited national mythologies are historical. (These include the Bataan Death March and POW camps of World War II and US pilots' bombing of Vietnam villages during that war.) In *Americana* (as in *Underworld*), the past, rife with both personal and national sin, always returns in the form of memory to invade the consciousness of DeLillo's "heroes," fracturing the myth of the essentially innocent American Adam who possesses a hope "unspoiled by memory."

3. Experiencing the past in this way is crucial given that, as *Shoah* filmmaker Claude Lanzmann has argued, understanding the Holocaust—like understanding the horrors of chattel slavery—is an "absolute obscenity." Quoting Lanzmann, Felman insists that "the refusal of understanding" such atrocity is "the only possible ethical attitude" (Lanzmann and Felman quoted in Caruth, 154–55). Benn Michaels likewise argues, "What the Holocaust requires is a way of transmitting not the normalizing knowledge of the horror but the horror itself" (8). As do Sommer, Lanzmann, Benn Michaels, Paul Gilroy, Michel R. Trouillot, and others, I find the analogy between the Holocaust and slavery in the Americas worthwhile. Sommer points out that "trauma on a national scale occurs in many places. Jews don't have a monopoly on violent dislocation and guilt-ridden survival" (178).

4. "Unisonance" occurs when "a special kind of contemporaneous community which language alone suggests" characterizes the nation; Anderson offers the example of the singing of national anthems (quoted in Bhabha, *Location*, 132–33).

5. The Obamas scripted the American dream narrative explicitly at the 2008 Democratic National Convention with the video biography of Barack's life, another featuring Michelle's mother and older brother, and Michelle's personally delivered testimony that concluded, "The American Dream endures." All of these narratives conveyed the story that their hardworking parents gave each of them the great gift of superb educations, which, along with their own hard work and ideals, led them to the highest office in the nation and indeed in the world. In addition to the deep hunger for hope and change that fueled Obama's successful bid for the US presidency, the immense energy his campaign generated showed the broad transnational investment in the American dream—a powerful mythology that transcends race and even (as the fervent international enthusiasm for Barack Obama showed) nation.

6. One reason the idea of America and the politics of canon formation changed so radically in recent decades is that it is primarily in the last century that the majority of marginal cultural populations

has become part of what Anderson would term the "monoglot mass reading public" that shares English as a national language and even more recently that their members have become—as the COHMIA survey demonstrates—critical readers and writers of national mythic history. Contemporary historical fiction by and about resident groups that historically were excluded from membership in the nation—both legally, through denial of citizenship, and practically, through lack of access to reading, writing, and publishing—renders, not surprisingly, a nation in which such perspectives absented from traditional histories collide with and revise national mythologies.

7. I discuss Jean Baudrillard's analysis of "the disappearance of history" in subsequent pages. In addition to the claims of "historical amnesia" that my prologue details, critical discussion of the "disremembering " and "selective remembering" of contemporary American cultures can be found in, e.g., Kammen, "Nostalgia, Heritage, and the Anomalies of Historical Amnesia" and "Disremembering the Past While Historicizing the Present" ("Prolegomenon" and chapter 18, part 4 of *Mystic Chords of Memory*).

8. Intellectual historian Dominick LaCapra, for instance, brought the issue of "truth claims" in history and in literature to bear on the discussion of "reference" that ensued from Satya Mohanty's July 1, 2003, lecture at Cornell University's School of Criticism and Theory, "Why I Am Not a Strategic Essentialist." Mohanty deconstructed the first of what he claims are the two tenets of strategic essentialism, that "we need to abandon the idea of reference to an extra-textual reality." LaCapra questioned the relation of truth claims to Mohanty's assertion that there are instances in which reference both is complex and makes an epistemic advance. Through its attention to such representational issues, all the novels that compose *Telling the Truth* implicitly bear on such contemporary debates about history, narrative, and truth.

9. See Roland Barthes, "The Discourse of History," trans. Stephen Bann, in *Comparative Criticism: A Yearbook*, vol. 3 (1981), 3–28; and Hayden White, *Metahistory: The Historical Imagination in Nineteenth-Century Europe* (Baltimore: Johns Hopkins UP, 1973); *The Content of the Form: Narrative Discourse and Historical Representation* (Baltimore: Johns Hopkins UP, 1987). *Metahistory* was White's groundbreaking work, in which he demonstrated that the historiography and philosophies of history current in the nineteenth century shared the same rhetorical structures as Northrop Frye had discerned in the Western literary tradition.

10. Bryan Palmer, Fredric Jameson, David Harvey, and Jean-François Lyotard, among others, also define postmodernism in this way. David Harvey, in *The Condition of Postmodernity: An Enquiry into the Origin of Cultural Change* (1990), presents a complementary account to Fredric Jameson's *Postmodernism* of the remaking of a

capitalist cultural order of the late twentieth century. Lyotard, in *The Postmodern Condition* (1984), links the arrival of postmodernity with the emergence of a postindustrial society—theorized by Daniel Bell and Alain Touraine—and famously defines postmodernism as "an incredulity towards metanarratives" (especially scientific knowledges, which can no longer claim the imperial privilege over other forms of knowledge to which it had pretended in modern times). Astruadur Eysteinsson's *The Concept of Modernism* (1991) details this debate by recounting and then deconstructing various conceptions of the postmodern as distinguished from the modern. Similarly, Alex Callinicos, in *Against Postmodernism: A Marxist Critique* (1990), argues that postmodernity does not exist as some sharp and fundamental break from "the modern."

11. Although Palmer (like Jameson, Eagleton, and others whom I engage in this introduction) relies on a Marxist formulation of history, he notes, "It is perfectly plausible to accept that the late twentieth century has witnessed a series of shifts in the cultural arena, even perhaps in the realm of political economy, without, of course, seeing this as a fundamental transformation of the mode of production" (106).

12. Norris notes that American deconstructive methods forego "the kind of consequential argument and analytic rigour that one finds in Derrida's essays on Plato, Kant, Hegel or Husserl" and ignore much of Derrida, who "is far from endorsing Richard Rorty's proposal that we should drop the idea of 'philosophy' as a discipline with its own particular interests, modes of argument, conceptual prehistory and so on, and henceforth treat it as just one 'kind of writing' among others, on a level with poetry, literary criticism and the human sciences at large. In fact [Derrida's] recent essays have laid increasing stress on the need to conserve what is specific to philosophy, namely its engagement with ethical, political and epistemological issues that cannot be reduced *tout court* to the level of an undifferentiated textual 'freeplay'" (91–92).

13. Although Benjamin cites Flaubert (who is in turn talking about his historical novel *Salammbo*, which treats the Carthaginian empire and the Punic Wars), the example of resuscitating Carthage is particularly apt for Benjamin's point, given that vast populations were conquered in the immense extension of the Carthaginian empire. By subjugation of the Libyan tribes and by annexation of older Phoenician colonies, Carthage in the sixth century B.C. controlled the entire North African coast from the Atlantic Ocean to Egypt as well as Sardinia, Malta, the Balearic Islands, and part of Sicily. The maritime empire of the Carthaginians enabled them to extend their settlements and conquests, forming a scattered empire devoted to commerce. The cannibalizing character of the Carthaginian empire is perhaps revealed by two interesting facts concerning Carthaginian art and religion. Carthage produced little art. Most of the Carthaginians'

work imitated Egyptian, Greek, and Phoenician originals. In literature, only a few technical works appeared. Religion in Carthage involved human sacrifice to the principal gods, Baal and Tanit, the equivalent of the Phoenician god Astarte. Later religious patterns of the Carthaginians adapted the Greek gods Demeter and Persephone and the Roman goddess Juno.

14. Although Norris refers to myths circulating in Britain in the late 1980s and early 1990s regarding Hitler's rise to power and Fascism, his statement resonates in light of the Bush administration's 2001-launched "War on Terror," which justified—among other violations of justice and law—the military invasion of Iraq on the state-issued myths that Iraq supported the terrorists responsible for 9/11 and housed weapons of mass destruction.

15. Of her research on slavery for the purpose of writing *Beloved*, Morrison says that she was surprised at how little information there was. "Now that may sound odd because there's a lot of books written," but, for example, "there's almost no reference to the ships"; most African Americans, Morrison continues, "don't remember, or, remember a little bit…because you can't remember if you want to get up and go to work in the morning." *"Profile of a Writer: Toni Morrison."* Dir. Alan Benson. Ed. Melvyn Bragg. R. M. Arts. Home Vision, 1987. Videocassette. Morrison relates one of many examples of what I mean by "collective amnesia." Of note in this context is the disparate domestic gross box office receipts for two critically acclaimed Steven Spielberg–directed films that hit the market only six months apart: *Amistad* (December 1997) and *Saving Private Ryan* (July 1998): $44,229,441 and $216,540,909, respectively. Along with the success of Spielberg's previous historical film *Schindler's List* (1993. $96,065,768 gross box office receipts), the comparative nonevent of *Amistad*—the first major motion picture to confront directly the historical memory and experience of slavery—was striking. Given the arguable fact that America's favorite cathartic national pastime is going to the movies, *Amistad*'s lack of popular success suggests, I think, an ongoing collective inability or unwillingness to remember—through movie-going—the crisis that divided the nation well over a century ago.

16. A survey of students or of citizens on the street betrays the amnesiac ignorance to which I refer. Jay Leno's regular survey of citizens on the streets of Los Angeles is a prime example. Approximately bimonthly, *Late Night with Jay Leno* viewers are entertained by watching Jay take to the streets to ask one passerby after another basic questions about contemporary and recent historical events and facts, which are consistently met not with stupefaction but with radically wrong answers delivered with an air of complete and feigned aplomb.

17. Baudrillard proposes three processes by which the phenomenon he calls "leaving history to move into the realm of simulation" occurs. (1) The "modern media has created, for every event, story and image a simulation

of an infinite trajectory" such that "every political, historical and cultural fact" is propelled into a "hyperspace where, since it will never return, it loses all meaning…in the shape of our computers, circuits, and networks—we have the particle accelerator which has smashed the referential orbit of things for once and all." (2) The "vanishing of history" is produced "by the multiplication and saturation of exchanges" such that "events follow one upon another, cancelling each other out in a state of indifference. The masses, neutralized, mithradiated by information, in turn neutralize history." In this situation, "political events already lack sufficient energy of their own to move us; so they run on like a silent film for which we bear collective irresponsibility. History is being buried beneath its own immediate effect, worn out in special effects, imploding into current events." Or, lastly, (3) like "that famous feedback effect which is produced in acoustics by a source and a receiver being too close together and in history b y an event and its dissemination being too close together and thus interfering disastrously—a short-circuit…casts the event in radical doubt" (*Illusion* 2–7).

18. Himmelfarb delineates the various aspects of this crisis: "Historical Methodology," the course that was "once the centerpiece of the graduate programme [in history], is now obsolete because the idea of any 'methodology,' let alone a uniform, obligatory one, is regarded as 'authoritarian' and privileged.' The absence of such a course, the lack of any training in what used to be confidently called the 'canon of evidence'—even more, the disrespect for such a canon—is itself a fact of considerable importance in the training (or non-training) of young historians. It has even affected some older historians, including some traditional ones, who now feel sufficiently liberated to dispense with such impediments to creativity as footnotes. This methodological liberation has done more to transform the profession, making it less of a 'discipline' and more of an impressionistic 'art' (171)." Himmelfarb also notes, "Few historians go so far as Simon Schama, who introduced entirely fictional characters and scenes into what might appear to be a conventional work of history (*Dead Certainties*), identifying them as 'pure inventions' only in an 'Afterword.' But many historians who shy away from any suggestion of fictional or even 'metafictional' history welcome the invitation to be 'inventive,' 'imaginative,' 'creative.' Where once we were exhorted to be accurate and factual, we are now urged to be imaginative and inventive. Instead of 'recreating' the past, we are told to 'create' it; instead of 'reconstructing' history, to construct or 'deconstruct' it" (165).

19. I use mythic history to stress the integral derivative relationship that the myths on which I focus have to history. Mythic history is distinguished from history in that it is one aspect of collective memory that may overlap with, but is not coterminous to, the historian's account. Although myth is usually opposed to history because it is seen as unchanging and archetypal, some contemporary critics of myth define

myth as essentially related to history. For Richard Slotkin, "Myth is the primary language of historical memory [that is]...used to summarize the course of our collective history and to assign ideological meanings to that history" (*Gunfighter Nation* 70). Similarly, Roland Barthes sees myth as a language, "undoubtedly determined by history," that naturalizes "ideological abuse" (*Mythologies* 11). See also Michael Kammen, who wrote, "All of history cannot be remembered; and collective memory must be used with discrimination by the historian" (9); mythic history is a repository of collective memory.

2 "THE DOWNFALL OF THE EMPIRE AND THE EMERGENCE OF DETERGENTS": UNDERHISTORY IN DON DELILLO'S HISTORICAL NOVELS

1. In 1955, R. W. B. Lewis persuasively detailed a mythology of quintessential American innocence in *The American Adam*, a study of literary heroes from 1820 to 1860. Lewis identifies "a native American mythology" that yielded up "the authentic American as a figure of heroic innocence and vast potentialities, poised at the start of a new history." A solitary individual free from ancestry, he thus embodies a state of innocence: free from the "burden of history." Lewis's study does not address the relationship of this amnesiac innocence to the bloody aggressions of the nineteenth century—notably slavery, American Indian Wars, and Indian Removal. His readings make clear that the creation of innocent subjects actually encourages the kind of violence demanded by nation building, what historian Richard Slotkin calls "regeneration through violence"—the unofficial American policy that, Slotkin's landmark *Frontier* trilogy shows, recurred from 1600 through Vietnam. Vietnam and the embittered aftermath of the 1960s initiated a cultural crisis of public myth that produced an American environment ripe for myth revision—in which, I submit, DeLillo is a key player. DeLillo recasts the trope of the American Adam's fall from innocence; in DeLillo's late-twentieth-century world, innocence functions as a mythology—a deceptive signifier of what it means to be "American."

2. Although the irony in *Americana* centers on a misplaced faith in the image as a source of redemption, the need for redemption in the world of *Americana* is absolutely genuine. David's thirst for salvation—"The city was full of people searching for the man or woman who would save them" (110)—and repeated characterization of the image as "religious" foregrounds his self-destructive worship of it. From his assertion that "Burt [Lancaster] in the moonlight was an icon of a new religion" to his promise that the trip will be "a religious journey" because "cars are religious," it is clear that David is on a spiritual quest for his self. David Cowart also notes the sincerity of David's quest; he calls Bell "a confused seeker after the truth of his own tormented soul and its relation to the larger American reality" (611).

3. Dyess writes, "The stench of the place reached us long before we entered it. Hundreds of the prisoners were suffering from dysentery. Human waste covered the ground....Maggots were in sight everywhere....The Japanese...ordered the Americans to drag out the bodies and bury them....As the earth began falling about the American, he revived and tried to climb out....Two Jap guards placed bayonets at the throat of a Filipino on the burial detail....The Filipino raised a stricken face to the sky. Then he brought his shovel down upon the head of his American comrade, who fell backward to the bottom of the grave. The burial detail filled it up" (83–93).

4. The first of many memoirs eventually to be published by survivors of the Bataan Death March over the years, *The Dyess Story*, according to the introduction to the Bison Books edition, "remains the premier narrative of the Death March, the prison camps," due in part to its primacy and its revealing "the unique escape of Dyess" and two fellow soldiers. "The book has helped other writers of memoirs complete their own stories and has provided useful background information to editors of survivor accounts and to compilers of oral histories. Writers of secondary narratives, both popular and scholarly, have all begun their research with prisoner-of-war memoirs, usually starting with *The Dyess Story*, before consulting documentary and other material" (xv–xvi).

5. This book, by Hampton Sides, *Ghost Soldiers: The Forgotten Epic Story of World War II's Most Dramatic Mission* (New York: Doubleday, 2001), was also retitled in its paperback edition, published by Anchor Books (New York: 2002), to *Ghost Soldiers: The Epic Account of World War II's Greatest Rescue Mission* (emphasis added). Notice that the retitle emphasizes a heroic conclusion to the story of Bataan and at the same time "forgets" that the original story of Bataan has indeed been "forgotten"—i.e., in this case, removed from the original title. *Esquire*'s review of this edition—"the greatest World War II story never told"—gestures to the forgotten aspect of Bataan in World War II history. Yet in any case, this focus on the story of the group of soldiers who, in a daring raid near the end of the war, liberated 500 starving, tortured, and diseased POW soldiers obscures (if only superficially) that these 500 were a fraction of the nearly 20,000 prisoners who suffered gruesome deaths along the Bataan Death March itself and following in the internment camps ruled by arbitrary brutality. The 2005 film *The Great Raid* also tells this liberation story. This is a minor instance of the American predisposition to amnesia and mythic history against which truth-telling historical fiction writes.

6. The invasion of Normandy was the largest seaborne invasion at the time, involving over 850,000 Allied troops crossing the English Channel from the United Kingdom to Normandy in less than a month; securing Normandy began the Western European campaign and the downfall of Nazi Germany. The two aerial-wave attack on Pearl Harbor—a rare surprise attack against the United States—was

a clear tactical victory for Japan but a grand strategic failure, notable both for its large-scale destruction and for its effecting the United States' involvement in World War II.

7. Clint Eastwood's two 2006 films, *Flags of Our Fathers* and *Letters from Iwo Jima*, bring attention only recently to the battle of Iwo Jima; as I explain shortly, their narratives are counterhistorical. Paul Fussell's "Thank God for the Atomic Bomb," an essay in his 1990 essay collection of the same name, though likewise a tough-minded memoir of the war in the Pacific, is even less well known and "read" than Eastwood's film, which garnered relatively little box office revenue.

8. The Bataan Death March of April 1942, involving the forcible transfer of 75,000 American and Filipino prisoners of war captured by the Japanese in the Philippines from the Bataan peninsula to prison camps, was characterized by wide-ranging physical abuse and murder and resulted in very high fatalities inflicted upon the prisoners and civilians along the route by the armed forces of the Empire of Japan. Beheadings, cut throats, and casual shootings were the more common and merciful actions—compared to bayonet stabbings, rapes, disembowelments, numerous rifle-butt beatings, and a deliberate refusal to allow the prisoners food or water while keeping them continually marching for nearly a week (for the slowest survivors) in tropical heat. Falling down or being unable to continue moving was tantamount to a death sentence, as was any degree of protest or expression of displeasure. Prisoners were attacked for assisting someone failing because of weakness or for no apparent reason whatsoever. Strings of Japanese trucks were known to drive over anyone who fell. Riders in vehicles would casually stick out a rifle bayonet and cut a string of throats in the lines of men marching alongside the road. Accounts of being forcibly marched for five to six days with no food and a single sip of water are in postwar archives including filmed reports. Postwar Allied reports tabulated that only 54,000 of the prisoners reached their destination, and thousands more died in the internment camps.

9. On August 18, 1945, The Japanese Ministry of the Interior ordered the Ibaraki Prefectural Police Department, whose jurisdiction is just northeast of Tokyo, to "set up sexual comfort stations for the occupation troops.... Police officials and Tokyo businessmen established a network of brothels under the auspices of the Recreation and Amusement Association (RAA), which operated with government funds.... Though arranged and supervised by the police and civilian government, the system mirrored the comfort stations established by the Japanese military abroad during the war." A December 6, 1945, military memo "shows US occupation forces were aware the Japanese comfort women were often coerced" (Talmadge). Seiichi Kaburagi, the chief of public relations for the RAA writes, "The worst victims were the women who, with no previous experience, answered the ads calling for 'Women of the New Japan'" (quoted in Talmadge).

10. *Flags*, the story of how the three surviving flag raisers photographed by Rosenthal were used as propaganda tools by the US government, shows the long-term effects of the war on the veterans and how they suffered for the rest of their lives. (Like Terrence Malick's 1998 *The Thin Red Line*, an account of the Guadalcanal campaign in the Pacific theater of World War II, adapted from James Jones's 1962 novel of the same name, Eastwood's films received critical acclaim but not commercial success.) The critical acclaim of these films in tension with their under-performances at the box office speaks directly to the dialectic of amnesia and truth telling that constitutes the cultural milieu of this book. For instance, although *Flags* has drawn the ire of a small number of veterans groups, the film critic Richard Roeper reviews it as patriotic "because it questions the official version of the truth, and reminds us the super-heroes exist only in comic books and cartoon movies" (*Chicago Sun Times*, October 10, 2006). Similarly, a reviewer of *Letters* writes, "In *Letters*, the glossy romanticism of history crumbles before our very eyes." (Robert Humanick, "Us and Them, Then and Now: Eastwood and Milestone's Lessons of the Past." *SLANT Magazine*, February 8, 2007, http://www.slantmagazine.com/house/2007/02/us-and-them-then-and-now-eastwood-and-milestones-lessons-of-the-past/).

11. David's journey in *Americana* begins in the "innocent" 1950s as a child and ends in the heart of the postmodern age, 1999, the year that David writes the story for us and in which historical moment he com-pares himself to Prufrock: "I am wearing white flannel trousers" (a comparison that has also been noted by Cowart [610]). Like Prufrock, David is aging alone on the beach and sees himself as a split man, "con-templating his celluloid adventures as a young man" and suffering the loss of romantic dreams and possibilities (DeLillo, "Notes Toward a Definitive Meditation (By Someone Else) on the Novel 'Americana'"). Prufrock is lost because he sought satisfaction in banal sensualities and in the social sphere, rather than choosing the riskier path of meaning-ful enlightenment. David is lost because he is never able to recover from the fragmentation of his own mythopoeia and romantic self-conception.

12. Some reviews of the novel, as the interviewer Anthony deCurtis notes, "evaluated [DeLillo's] theory of the assassination almost as if it were fact and not fiction" or, in DeLillo's words, "reviewed the assas-sination itself, instead of a piece of work which is obviously fiction" ("An Outsider" 58).

13. The Zapruder film is a silent, color motion picture sequence shot by private citizen Abraham Zapruder with a home-movie camera as U.S. president John F. Kennedy's motorcade passed through Dealey Plaza in Dallas, Texas, on November 22, 1963, thereby unexpectedly capturing the president's assassination. It was an important part of the Warren Commission hearings and all subsequent investigations of the assassination and is one of the most studied pieces of film in

history. Of greatest notoriety is the film's depiction of a fatal shot to President Kennedy's head when his limousine was almost exactly in front of, and slightly below, Zapruder's position.

14. Henry Nash Smith's famous elaboration of "The American West as Symbol and Myth" in *Virgin Land* (1950) places Frederick Jackson Turner's hypothesis—that "the existence of an area of free land, its continuous recession, and the advance of American settlement westward explain American development"—in an intellectual tradition that begins in the eighteenth century with St. John de Crèvecoeur and Benjamin Franklin and subsequently continues with Ralph Waldo Emerson, Abraham Lincoln, Walt Whitman, and "a hundred others" (Turner quoted in Smith 291, Smith 3). This intellectual tradition explains the Western "myth of the garden," out of which, Smith argues, Turner's hypothesis developed (292). For Walt Whitman—"the poet who gave final imaginative expression to the theme of manifest destiny"—the Atlantic Seaboard "represented the past," overflowing with history, and the West was the place where "would grow up the truly American society of the future," unfettered by history. The hope that Americans have invested in westward movement is based on the belief in what Whitman called "a free and original life there," nourished by the expanse and beneficence of nature (Smith 48, Whitman 183). American mythologies of westward migration and innocence intersect in the figure of Whitman, for he is also the poet whom Lewis argues provides the fullest portrayal of the New World's representative American Adam, "the new unfallen Adam in the western garden" (50). The American mythic hero thus moves away from history and toward the garden in his migration west. An early essay version of this chapter further reads *Underworld* through this myth; Marni Gauthier, "Better Living Through Westward Migration: Don DeLillo's Inversion of the American West as 'Virgin Land' in *Underworld*," in *Moving Stories: Migration and the American West, 1850–2000*, ed. Scott E. Casper. Nevada Humanities Committee Halcyon Series 23, 131–52 (Reno: U of Nevada P, 2001).

15. Michael D'Antonio, "Atomic Guinea Pigs," *New York Times Magazine*, August 31, 1997.

16. A Utah sheep herder's 1984 description of his life first echoes and then diverges from Whitman's idea of Western life: "It was a clean and healthy life. It got in your blood. One thing about it, you wasn't breathing the air someone else was breathing. It was fresh air. But not when the bomb was there, it wasn't fresh then" (quoted in Gallagher 378).

17. The waste represented throughout *Underworld* is both the irreducible wrapping and the core of American consumerism on a national scale. DeLillo concentrates on this theme on a personal scale in *White Noise*. In a scene that foreshadows *Underworld*'s theme of waste, Jack Gladney peruses the family garbage in search of the discarded bottle

of Dylar. As he picks through the items, he feels he is "uncovering intimate and perhaps shameful secrets." The objects of refuse do, in fact, bare various family secrets, as the waste in *Underworld*, as a whole, evokes national secrets. The national refuse betrays the toxicity and dangerous permanence of the consumer economy spawned in the 1950s; the waste material of the bombs—what remains after the product is used up—is an invisible debris (fallout) that registers its physical effects on the bodies and landscape on which it precipitates. Of the family garbage, Jack asks, "Does it glow at the core with personal heat, with signs of one's deepest nature, clues to secret yearnings, humiliating flaws? What habits, fetishes, addictions, inclinations?…Was this the dark underside of human consumer consciousness?" (259). The answer to these questions in *White Noise* and more insistently and seriously in *Underworld* is, emphatically, yes.

18. *White Noise* is like *Americana* in that the irony in both novels centers on a misplaced faith in sources of redemption (in technology and the image, respectively). In *White Noise*, all of the objects produced by technology in which the characters at one time or another place their faith—from the sophisticated Dylar tablets (called "a super piece of engineering" by neurochemist Winnie Richards) to microorganisms that technicians release to consume the noxious Nyodene D cloud and the gleaming new medical equipment at Autumn Harvest Farms that is to diagnose Jack's condition—are eventually revealed to be unworthy of investment and hope. Indeed, the novel's ending is an indictment of faith in technology as a cure for all that ails humankind, shot through with quintessential DeLillo irony: "The miracle vitamins, the cures for cancer, the remedies for obesity." Yet, in *White Noise* as well as *Americana* (as throughout DeLillo's work), the genuine need for redemption exists despite the misplaced faith that accompanies it; this persists in *Underworld*.

3 THE OTHER SIDE OF *PARADISE*: TONI MORRISON'S (UN)MAKING OF MYTHIC HISTORY

1. See Menand, Allen, Kakutani, and Bent, respectively, and also Gates.
2. By these I mean what someone such as Stephen Ambrose has done for World War II: cast it all into a heroic antirevisionist mould that satisfies the dominant mythologies of American nationhood. Or consider what David McCullough has similarly done for John Adams (and by extension, the founding fathers). McCullough's rehabilitation of Harry Truman is a remarkable example of the process of mythologizing history with which *Paradise* is concerned. The runaway success of Ambrose, McCullough, and, along the same lines, of films such as *Pearl Harbor* (2001) indicates the contours of the extant ideologies and the myths they inform, which continue to circulate through popular

and political rhetoric: no matter what the historical specificities and complexities of the conflict, America is the good superhero, making the world a better and safer place to be by conquering evil wherever it rears its ugly head. President George W. Bush garnered tremendous popular support for the bombing of Afghanistan in 2001 and, subsequently, the 2003 invasion of Iraq and consequent nation building of it in America's image by deploying the rhetoric of the good American cowboy cleaning up the riffraff beyond the frontier: evoking "an old poster out West," he stated on September 17, 2001, that he wanted Osama bin Laden "dead or alive." His successful portrait of "America" as "the most decent nation . . . on the face of this Earth" in contrast to the now-infamous "axis of evil" of Iraq, Iran, and North Korea reinforced the good/bad dichotomies that capture the popular imagination and characterize the arc of traditional American history from the Puritans to the present, which Morrison takes up in *Paradise*.

3. That Morrison imagined *Beloved*'s Sethe from the story of the escaped slave Margaret Garner, who, in fact, tried to kill her children when the slave catcher descended upon her home in an effort to take her and her family back into slavery, is well established. The murder, in *Jazz*, of Dorcas by Joe and the ensuing attempt by Violet to desecrate Dorcas's corpse at the funeral is based upon a picture that, like the story of Margaret Garner, Morrison found while she was editing *The Black Book*, an "'anecdotal' collection of clippings and snapshots published while she was an editor at Random House in an attempt to document another unknown side of African American history." The picture showed a "young woman in a coffin who refused to be medically attended and to mention the name of the lover who shot her so that he could get away" (Tally 15).

4. On the historical contexts more generally, see Tally, especially 31–54.

5. "The history of the Negro in America is the history of America written in vivid and bloody terms; it is the history of the Western Man writ small. It is the history of men who tried to adjust themselves to a world whose laws, customs, and instruments of force were leveled against them" (74).

6. Because Morrison (like Frances E. White, whom Dalsgård cites in reference to this point) "is concerned with the way African Americans are engaged in the construction of a national identity on the basis of an historical master narrative," Dalsgård argues that Morrison destabilizes "(African) America's past" (237–38); I employ Dalsgård's useful denotation of "(African) American"—where appropriate to my argument—along this same line.

7. On the relationship of polyphonic narration to memory in *Beloved*, *Jazz*, and *Paradise*, see Lehmann.

8. Tally offers another, historicized explanation of these babies that is equally plausible: "Jeff, however, had married Sweetie just after he

came back from [Vietnam] and there are references to his contentions with military authorities.... Jeff's complaint before the administration is never specified, but the fact that he is ignored and frustrated may point to the government's reluctance to admit than [*sic*] exposure to Agent Orange causes malformation in off-spring" (26–27). As is not uncommon in *Paradise*, the reader is left to consider various contextual possibilities for the answer to this riddle.

9. The task of a genealogy, according to Foucault, is "to expose a body totally imprinted by history and the process of history's destruction of the body" ("Nietzsche" 83).

10. Crawford explores endowing the idea of "pure" blackness with transcendence in *Paradise*.

11. See Hine for a discussion of this in relation to black women's history particularly.

12. In her essay "The Site of Memory," Morrison claims that "a very large part of my own literary heritage is the autobiography," particularly slave narratives. See the essay for Morrison's description of literary archaeology and its involved processes of research, memory, imagination, and truth telling, especially 111–113.

4 A POLITICS OF TRUTH AND THE TRANSNATIONAL COMM(UNITY) OF ABOLITIONISTS: MICHELLE CLIFF'S *FREE ENTERPRISE*

1. Historian Lynn Hudson details several sources that validate Pleasant's testimony identifying herself as "the party who furnished John Brown with most of his money to start the fight at Harper's [*sic*] Ferry and who signed the letter found on him when he was arrested" (Pleasant quoted in Hudson 60). Moreover, her "request that the words 'She was a friend of John Brown' be printed on her gravestone was honored in 1965 when the San Francisco Negro Historical and Cultural Society placed a marker bearing the phrase on her grave in Napa, California" (Hudson 66). Elsewhere Pleasant asserts, "I never regretted what I did for John Brown and for the cause of freedom for my race" (quoted in Bibbs 4). NB: Since my original research for this essay, Hudson's dissertation has been published: *The Making of "Mammy Pleasant": A Black Entrepreneur in Nineteenth-Century San Francisco* (Urbana and Chicago: U of Illinois P, 2002). All the citations to Hudson herein are from the dissertation as noted.

2. Although Cliff adds, "When [Brown] was leading the raid" on Harpers Ferry, Pleasant "was down south dressed as a man trying to organize slaves to tell them that there was going to be an insurrection and they were supposed to rise up," Hudson explains that Pleasant's financing Brown, participating with him at the Chatham convention, and purchasing four plots in Chatham, Canada (as a refuge for the slaves who would rebel, free themselves, and escape from the United

States as part of the raid on Harpers Ferry) has more historical credence than does her inciting the Southern slaves for rebellion while
posing as a jockey, which Cliff references here ("Art of History";
Hudson 58–66, 70).

3. Thus *Cloudsplitter* asserts the causal truth of its argument: "If
[Brown] was sane, then terrible things about race and human nature,
especially here in North America, are true. If he was insane, then
other, quite different, and perhaps not so terrible things about race
and human nature are true" (7). Banks moves the reader to con-
cur irrefutably with the former logic, in part by profoundly evoking
the "beast" of slavery as definitively "evil": the "vision of the fate
of our Negro brethren" as the Brown family saw it. Deep into the
night, for example, they communally read aloud from a "very popular [book] amongst abolitionists," which is authentic, still in print,
and excerpted in *Cloudsplitter: American Slavery as It Is: Testimony
of a Thousand Witnesses*. After thus taking in its horrific accounts,
"[Father's] face was the face of a man who had been gazing at fires,
who had roused the attendants of the fires, serpents and demons hiss-
ing back at the man who had dared to swing open the iron door and
peer inside. We all knew what Father had seen there. We had seen it,
too" (67, 75).

4. Giles's essay, "Transnationalism and Classic American Literature," is
part of the January 2003 *PMLA* Special Issue, "America: The Idea,
The Literature," a representative articulation of the changing field of
American studies in relation to which this book is significantly situated. In his introductory essay, Djelal Kadir exhorts, "America, even
in the United States, is a heteronomy that, demographically diverse
and culturally plural, complicates [the] unitary identity construct" of
"the United States of America" (20–21).

5. From the first words of Tituba's tale to her trials in Salem, the novel
emphasizes Puritan complicity in the atrocious African slave trade.
"Abena, my mother, was raped by an English sailor in the deck of
Christ the King," Tituba begins. "I was born from this act of aggres-
sion. From this act of hatred and contempt" (3). The tension implicit
in the contradiction between the ship's name and the rank sins of its
sailors produces a bitter irony that recurs in a decidedly Puritan vein
when, 20 years later, Tituba and her husband, John Indian, board
their first ship in Barbados, bound for the New England colonies.
They have been sold to an infamous Boston reverend, whose "ruthless
violen[t] cutting words" greet them: "On your knees, dregs of hell!
I am your new master! My name is Samuel Parris. Tomorrow...we
leav[e] aboard the brigantine Blessing" (36). Thus Condé graphically
links the Puritans to the brutal Middle Passage and slave trade and
likewise roots the Salem witch trials to it as well.

6. Condé's most flagrant anachronism is that of Tituba's influential
encounter with Hester Prynne—of Nathaniel Hawthorne's *The*

Scarlet Letter (1850)—in jail, following her conviction in the Salem witch trials. To achieve this meeting between the fictional Prynne and the historical-fictional Tituba, Condé not only shifts the setting of *The Scarlet Letter* from 1640s Boston to 1692 Salem but also gives Hester a late-twentieth-century feminist vocabulary and consciousness, which empowers both her and Tituba. She chides Tituba, "You're too fond of love, Tituba! I'll never make a feminist out of you!" (101).

7. To elicit her testimony, Condé's inquisitors, four men wearing "black hoods, with holes for their eyes" bind, beat, and rape Tituba, demanding that she "denounce [her] accomplices! Good and Osborne and the others!" (91). This vicious scene undermines the historical document that Condé then inserts into the novel; the deposition rather appears as evidence of Tituba's manipulated—and thus silenced—voice:

"And what would they have you do?"
"Kill her with a knife."
"How did you go?"
"We rode upon sticks and were there presently."
"Do you go through the trees or over them?"
"We see nothing but are there presently."

* * *

It went on for hours. I confess I wasn't a good actress. The sight of all these white faces lapping at my feet looked to me like a sea in which I was about to drown. (106)

8. Julia Alvarez, *In the Name of Salomé* (2000); *Life and Debt* (Dir. Stephanie Black, 2001); Christina Garcia, *Dreaming in Cuban* (1992); Jamaica Kincaid, *A Small Place* (1988); Paule Marshall, *Daughters* (1992); Toni Morrison, *Tar Baby* (1981); Esmeralda Santiago, *When I Was Puerto Rican* (1993); and *Buena Vista Social Club* (Dir. Wim Wenders, 1999)—and a previous concert and ensuing albums of the Buena Vista Social Club—just to name a few.

9. Remarkably, in Julie Dash's 1991 film *Daughters of the Dust*, a boy traces the same cosmogram in the sand. Through its focus on a Gullah community on the Sea Islands of Georgia at the dawn of the twentieth century who, as a result of their isolation, created and maintained a distinct, imaginative, and original African American culture, the film conceptualizes a critical remembrance of the African diaspora. Through the mise-en-scène of the film, the past, present, and future of the Gullah community interpenetrate—a fusion of narrative times and space that the cosmogram evokes and represents.

10. Few scholars have devoted an entire essay or chapter to *Free Enterprise*; a scattering of authors devote a few pages to it in articles that focus on the earlier works. Meryl F. Schwartz briefly considers *Free Enterprise* among Cliff's "political awakening novels" but argues, "To date, Michelle Cliff's most sustained analysis of political development is in her first two novels, *Abeng* (1984) and

No Telephone to Heaven (1987)" (290). Nada likewise centers on *No Telephone to Heaven* with reference to *Abeng*; her 37-page chapter devoted to Cliff includes five pages on *Free Enterprise* that discuss orality and strategic passing in the novel. Chancy and Garvey both include the novel in comparative analyses; Chancy compares it to *Amour, Colère et Folie*, by Haitian writer Marie Chavet, to examine the Caribbean female exile; and Garvey addresses novels by Paule Marshall and Caryl Phillips to consider treatments of African American identity and the African diaspora. See Kekeh-Dika, Pollock, and Johnson for other considerations of the novel.

11. See, e.g., Ashcroft, Griffiths, and Tiffin, eds., The Empire Writes Back: Theory and Practice in Post-Colonial Literatures (1989); Kaplan and Pease, eds., Cultures of United States Imperialism (1994); King, ed., Postcolonial America (2000); Schmidt and Singh, eds., Postcolonial Theory and the United States (2000); Schwarz and Ray, eds., A Companion to Postcolonial Studies (2000); and Schueller and Watts, eds. Messy Beginnings: Postcoloniality and Early American Studies (2003).

12. One wonders if Cliff is being consciously orientalist here, with her description of Eastern peoples as "oriental and surreptitious"; if Annie, the character to whom this recollection ostensibly belongs, is the one being orientalist, her prejudice is not indicated elsewhere in the novel. Cliff, however, despite "moving toward a conception of affiliation" based on "political enthusiasms" rather than "on origins," betrays essentialist biases, both in her fiction and in her depiction of writing by "people of color": "We're able to be freer, more experimental because we're not faithful to Western forms as much as white, Western writers are. We have a different sense of time and space, and we have more access to a dream life" ("Interview" 617). Clearly, these claims are subject to skepticism, given that many Western writers also experiment with time and space and "have access to a dream life" (from Miguel de Cervantes and Sigmund Freud to modernist writers such as Marcel Proust, Gertrude Stein, and William Faulkner, for example).

13. Chronotopicity is particularly germane to African American diasporic studies because the interrelation of the space of the Atlantic Ocean and the temporal history of cultural migrations is foundational to the concept of diaspora. Gilroy, in *The Black Atlantic*, also uses chronotopicity as a focus for his study of the two-way cultural traffic of the African diaspora; and, similar to this moment in *Free Enterprise*, Gilroy proposes "the image of ships in motion across the spaces between Europe, America, Africa, and the Caribbean as a central organising symbol for this enterprise" (4). Bahktin originally coined the chronotope in his essay, "Forms and Time and Chronotope in the Novel": the chronotopicity of "poetic images conceived as an image of temporal art...represents spatially perceptible phenomena in their movement and development [and] serve[s] for the assimilation of

actual temporal (including historical) reality, that permit the essential aspects of this reality to be reflected and incorporated into the artistic space of the novel" (252).

14. The time-lag emphasizes "the relation between the temporality and meaning in the *present* of utterance, in the performativity of a history of the present; in the political struggle around the 'true.'...This opens up a spatial movement of cultural representation which I shall call a 'time-lag': an iterative, interrogative space produced in the interruptive overlap between...synchronicity and caesura or seizure (not diachronicity)" ("Postcolonial" 57–59).

15. Along with McHale, Diane Elam, Linda Hutcheon ("flagrant anachronism"), and others identify postmodern fiction in part by "creative anachronism" (McHale, *Postmodernist Fiction*, 90).

16. Her court case *Pleasant v. The North Beach and Mission Railroad Company* helped ensure that blacks in San Francisco gained the right to ride on public transportation almost 100 years before that right was won nationally; the case secured damages for discrimination and set a precedent in the state supreme court (Bibbs 1–4, 6). The title "The Mother of Civil Rights" appears in the official San Francisco memorial to Pleasant at the intersection of Bush and Octavia Streets. The African American newspapers *Pacific Appeal* and the *Elevator* and, in the San Francisco mainstream press, the *Bulletin*, *Examiner*, and *Call* chronicle her charity to African American churches and organizations of her day. The historical Pleasant seems most remembered by and in San Francisco, where she became a local celebrity. In addition to the San Francisco newspapers I cite, most of the sources to which my research on Pleasant led were available only through institutions in the greater San Francisco area, including the Sonoma County Library (Bibbs); San Francisco State University (*Mary Ellen Pleasant: A Television Play*, by Helen C. Jones); and the Bancroft Library at the University of California Berkeley, which supplied me with a program copy from Pleasant's Memorial Service.

17. Of the genesis of *Free Enterprise*, Cliff says, "I wanted to write a novel about Mary Ellen Pleasant because few know about her and she's a very important historical figure." This book "is about the history that's been lost to us of people who resisted, that there was a movement in this country of armed resistance." When John Brown was arrested, "they found a note from her on him saying, 'The axe is laid at the foot of the tree,' and something like 'if you need more money then I will provide it.' We have physical evidence that she was part of this thing and yet nothing is remembered." She's been "portrayed historically," Cliff continues, as a madam "called 'Mammy'" and "a voodoo queen." Yet, in Cliff's words, she was "a revolutionary." "Most of my work has to do with revising: revising the written record, what passes as the official version of history, and inserting those lives that have been left out" ("Art of History" 65, 71).

18. In *Almanac of the Dead*, Leslie Marmon Silko records the verifiable history of families of southwestern Indians and Mexicans amassing fortunes by drug- and arms-trafficking across the US/Mexican border. Think also, e.g., of the Italian and Irish Mafias, particularly in the early part of the twentieth century, and the more recent prominence of the Korean and Chinese Mafias in California and elsewhere.

19. The 1791 Haitian slave revolt, for example, which began as a rebellion against slavery and French plantation owners but became a political revolution that lasted for 13 years and resulted in independence from France, inspired fear of similar revolts in other slave-holding areas of the Caribbean and the United States. During the revolution years, refugees from Haiti settled in Louisiana, bringing accounts of revolution, revolt, and retribution with them. Slaveholders in the rest of the Americas attempted to isolate Haiti to keep the idea of emancipation from spreading. See also, e.g., Brickhouse, who treats writers in the period 1826–1856 who "registered in numerous ways the various transamerican historical narratives and literary inheritances that could never be contained within [the US] 'Domestic Question'" of race and slavery.

20. Another instance of such substitution might be read in Cliff's Pleasant associating with women almost exclusively; the novel suggests that Pleasant may have shared the same sexual orientation as the author, whose lesbianism is a part of her writing and politics ("Interview" 600–605). There does not seem to be evidence to support this characterization, although evidence exists that undermines it (see Hudson 129–31; Bibbs 5, 10). Despite the fact that Cliff has undertaken the arduous task of researching the recondite history of Pleasant, she intentionally distorts and omits facts regarding Pleasant's second husband, daughter, and lifelong love relationship with Scottish merchant Thomas Bell in an effort to write lesbian desire into Pleasant's story. The same historical structures that conceal Pleasant as a (wealthy black female) historical subject would indeed conceal her as a lesbian. The suggestion of lesbian desire in *Free Enterprise*, however, seems to reveal more about Cliff's politics and Pleasant's performative strategies than Pleasant's sexuality.

21. As Bhabha's notion of a "time-lag" in relation to Morrison's *Beloved* suggests, the appropriation of alternative forms of temporality to narrate histories of marginalized—and violently deceased—peoples is not an uncommon technique among contemporary writers of color. Silko, for example, conceptualizes an indigenous temporality that is not only cyclical but also subjective, living: "The days, months, and years were living beings who roamed the starry universe until they came around again"; history is moreover spiritual. Silko writes that within "'history' resides relentless forces, powerful spirits, vengeful, relentlessly seeking justice" (313, 6).

5 TRANSNATIONAL EMPIRE AND ITS EXUBERANT
    (DIS)CONTENTS: BHARATI
    MUKHERJEE'S *HOLDER OF THE WORLD*

1. Hereafter I will abbreviate this interview "C&G."
2. Although a number of recent studies of postcolonialism elide the United States (Christine Matzke and Susanne Muhleisen, eds., *Postcolonial Postmortems* [Amsterdam and New York: Rodopi B. V., 2006]; Clara A. B. Joseph and Janet Wilson, eds., *Global Fissures: Postcolonial Fusions* [Amsterdam, New York: Rodopi B. V., 2006]; Alfred J. Lopez, ed., *Postcolonial Whiteness* [Albany: State University of New York Press, 2005], for example), there are many exceptions; see note 11 of chapter 4 for a list of several.
3. That some of our best novelists have rewritten *The Scarlet Letter* and that critics interpret still more novels as rewritings of it demonstrate the way in which Hawthorne's morbid tale of Hester Prynne continues to capture our cultural imagination and to signify in our national mythology. William Faulkner's *As I Lay Dying* (1930) and John Updike's *A Month of Sundays* (1996) are among the most striking novels that, like *Holder of the World*, explicitly rewrite aspects of *The Scarlet Letter*; Christopher Bigsby's *Pearl* (1996) is a sequel to Hawthorne's classic. Moraru and others, however, cite several additional "rewritings" of *The Scarlet Letter* that are implicit at best: Toni Morrison's *Sula* (1973) and *Beloved* (1984), Samuel R. Delany's *Neveryona* (1983), Kathy Acker's *Blood and Guts in High School* (1984), Margaret Atwood's *The Handmaid's Tale* (1985), and Updike's *Roger's Version* (1996). These novels treat themes, such as single parenthood or sex and religion, that Hawthorne's novel did, but textual evidence of their authors seeking to (re)engage *The Scarlet Letter* is scant.
4. These are actual questions students posed in sections of each of these titled courses that I taught, at a public research university in the West and at an upstate New York public teaching college, respectively. Although both courses included numerous canonical authors—from Mary Rowlandson to Melville, Thoreau, Emerson, Whitman, and more—students (in the first case at the onset of class, in response to my asking what they expected to read in such a course, and in the second case, on the course evaluations after the class's conclusion) severally bemoaned the absence of Hawthorne's most famous novel.
5. Brickhouse, however, brilliantly demonstrates that "the formation of the American Renaissance that continues to organize so many literary-historiographical narratives of the nineteenth-century United States, whether through reinscription or multiculturalist revision, might more accurately be reconfigured as a *trans*american renaissance, a period of literary border crossing, intercontinental exchange, and complex political implications whose unfamiliar genealogies we are just beginning to discern" (8–9). *Holder of the World* is certainly an

important literary-historical text that contributes to this recent discernment. Brickhouse devotes one of her five chapters to Hawthorne, uncovering "the Mexican genealogy" of "Rappaccini's Daughter," a story through which Hawthorne "boldly addressed himself...to the venerable scene of European literary history, a gesture that separated the story geographically and thematically from his earlier work." Brickhouse argues that Hawthorne's story "returns unfailingly to the very American scenes that it seems designed to escape, a dense matrix of transamerican cultural exchange and literary influence" (182).

6. Solomon's proposal letter, Beigh writes, "is reprinted in several anthologies. This modernized example comes from *Puritans Come A-Courting: Romantic Love in an Age of Severity* (University Presses of New England 1972)." Notwithstanding the ambiguity of what a "modernized example" might be, given that the letter retains Puritan syntax and phrasing, both the title and press are invented. Conversely, when in the Peabody Museum Beigh encounters the series of Mughal miniatures featuring Hannah in ornate Indian scenes, her precise account of them echoes Mukherjee's description of the Mughal miniature she encounters at Sotheby's and the Mughal aesthetic that inspired and structures her novel (*Holder* 15–19; cf. Mukherjee in Appiah, C&G 8, and "Four-Hundred-Year-Old Woman" 38).

7. Beigh is American with an Indian boyfriend, and Mukherjee is Indian-born with an American husband. (Born in Calcutta, Mukherjee acquired US citizenship in 1988; her husband is the American writer of Canadian origin Clark Blaise.)

8. The development of Newman's argument shows that Mukherjee plumbs "the space of imperial expansion and Eastern plunder, the foundation" not only of "New England fortunes, the sphere of activity of Hawthorne's own family," but also of "a major contributor to specific forms of cultural authority in America." Pointing out that "it is no accident that the frame-narrator, Beigh Masters, is a Yale graduate," Newman cites evidence to explain that "the funding history of at least one major university in the United States—Yale—has its roots in the mercantile activities and imperial politics of the East India Company. Elihu Yale...made his vast fortune as a nabob in Madras by a combination of legitimate trade and more questionable activities" (78, 80).

9. Several critics have focused on this biographical reading of the novel. See Appiah, Cincotti, Onega, Moraru, and Rajan.

10. Geldin takes Heidegger's "hyphenated conception of the being-in-the-world"—"a being in situations with others" a step further. "'Being-in' situations with others applies to the *embodied* and sentient person," says Geldin—a conception apt for Beigh's ultimate experience here in Hannah's world.

11. "Firangi" is what the seventeenth-century Indians call whites.

6 Truth-telling Fiction in a Post-9/11 World:
Don DeLillo's *Falling Man* and Julie Otsuka's
When the Emperor Was Divine

1. I refer most notoriously to the Bush administration's use and abuse of 9/11 not only in Afghanistan, Pakistan, Iraq, and Guantánamo but around the world. Mayer's *The Dark Side: The Inside Story of How the War on Terror Turned into a War on American Ideals* (New York: Anchor Books, 2008) is among nearly two dozen books published so far that document the administration's nefarious actions in the name of the War on Terror. See, among others, Eric Lichtblau's *Bush's Law: The Remaking of American Justice* (New York: Pantheon), Jacob Weisberg's *The Bush Tragedy* (New York: Pantheon), Phillippe Sands's *Torture Team: Rumsfeld's Memo and the Betrayal of American Values* (New York: Palgrave Macmillan), and Scott McClellan's *What Happened: Inside the Bush White House and Washington's Culture of Deception* (New York: Public Affairs), all published in 2008.

2. *When the Emperor Was Divine* was Iowa City's "One Community, One Book" 2005 selection. San Francisco, California, and Boulder, Colorado, chose it for their "One City, One Book" and "One Book, One Boulder" projects, respectively, in 2006; Manchester, New Hampshire, selected it for its city-wide book read in 2007; and Loyola College selected it as their "common text" in 2009. The Library of Congress reports the following cities chose the novel for their One Book Reading Promotion Projects:

Santa Barbara (California) 2005
Silicon Valley (California) 2006
Cheshire (Connecticut) 2007
Westport (Connecticut) 2004
Winnetka-Northfield (Illinois) 2006 (Adult)
Carmel (Indiana) 2004 (adult)
Johnson County (Iowa) 2005
Topeka (Kansas) 2005
St. Peter (Minnesota) 2004
Concord (New Hampshire) 2006
Centre County (Pennsylvania) 2008
Logan (Utah) 2005
Salt Lake City (Utah) 2006 (autumn/winter—fiction)
Salt Lake County (Utah) 2006
Seattle (Washington) 2005
Ipswich (Massachusetts) 2008.

At the same time, Internet research reveals that an innumerable number of unofficial book clubs have chosen to read *Emperor*; repeatedly, members recount the power of their reading experience and its resonance in the post-9/11 United States.

3. See Peterson 216n36. Lillian Baker's Dishonoring America: The Collective Guilt of American Japanese and American and Japanese Relocation in World War II: Fact, Fiction and Fallacy (Medford, OR: Webb Research Group, 1988) details the debate of the internment-denial group Americans for Historical Accuracy.

4. By contrast, the same year the US Commission was established, 1981, two seminal books on Japanese Canadian internment were published in Canada—Ann Gomer Sunahar's *The Politics of Racism: The Uprooting of Japanese Canadians During the Second World War* and Joy Kogawa's novel *Obasan*. Both draw on historical materials on internment from the Public Archive of Canada that, because of Canada's "thirty-year rule," were unavailable until the mid-1970s. Thus Peterson attributes the issue of these two books, in part, to "the wealth of information on [Canadian] internment made available in recent years," noting that "the silence and amnesia surrounding internment in Canada was in part institutionally or structurally produced" (141).

5. Due in large part to its having been made into a major motion picture, *Snow Falling on Cedars* (1994), by a white author, may still be the best-known book about Japanese internment. Critics find the film's portrait of Japanese Americans as weak and helpless without white people to rescue them from their predicament racist. *No-No Boy* (1978) and *Farewell to Manzanar* (1983), by Japanese American authors, are not nearly as well-known as either *Snow Falling on Cedars* or *Emperor*.

6. Various estimates put the number of people that, through "extraordinary rendition," the CIA has captured since 2001 at 3,000. Rendition is the process of capturing criminal suspects in another country to ultimately bring them into the judicial system. What is "extraordinary" about the CIA program in the aftermath of 9/11 is the abduction of people to transfer them to secret detention centers in other nations known to torture—what has been called "torture by proxy"—and the interminable holding them in such "black sites" without defense or trial (i.e., declaring detainees "enemy combatants" not by trial but by executive prerogative). The Detainee Treatment Act passed by Congress in 2005 eliminated habeas corpus for all detainees at Guantánamo; the Military Commission Act of 2006 prohibited "unlawful enemy combatants" from invoking the Geneva Convention. Since January 11, 2002, some 775 such enemy combatants have been detained at Guantánamo and two trials completed. Of these, 520 detainees have been released—without explanation, without trial, without apology; the United States has, that is, implicitly admitted their innocence. Some 300 detainees remain, in legal limbo ("The Freedom Files").

7. Peterson provides a helpful summary of the fact that, although internees "were never subjected to the terrors of the death camps

as Jews under Nazi control were, because the breach in democratic principles in both countries was so extreme and because racism was such an important factor in the wartime hysteria that led to internment," both those who argued for internment (in Canada) and defenders of Japanese Canadians compared internment to Nazism (214n13). Michi Weglyn, in *Years of Infamy: The Untold Story of America's Concentration Camps* (New York: Morrow, 1976), reports the startling fact that Nazis cited the US Supreme Court rulings justifying internment as part of their defense at the Nuremberg Trials (67, 75, 291n14). Perhaps the most important point to note, in Peterson's words, "is that internment became such a cataclysmic experience that some commentators alluded to Nazism and the Holocaust in order to find a way to register and articulate the trauma" (214).

8. Peterson cites Rea Tajiri's 1991 film, *History and Memory (for Akiko and Takeshige)* (Electronic Arts Intermix, New York, 1991, videocassette), an autobiographical look at internment featuring an internee's daughter, and Janice D. Tanaka's 1999 film, *When You're Smiling* (Visual Communications, Los Angeles, 1999, videocassette), which explores Sansei (third-generation) memories of internment; both reveal similar experiences of such omission. In the words of the daughter, "I had known all along that the stories I had heard were not true, and parts had been left out." A granddaughter in the latter film recognized her grandmother and aunt in slides of internment shown in a class at the University of California, Santa Cruz, realizing with a shock that she had never heard this part of her family's history (Peterson 139–40). See also Stan Yogi's essay on Sansei internment poetry for a more detailed analysis of this problem: "Yearning for the Past: The Dynamics of Memory in Sansei Internment Poetry," in *Memory and Cultural Politics: New Approaches to American Ethnic Literatures*, ed. Amritjit Singh, Joseph T. Skerrett, Jr., and Robert E. Hogan (Boston: Northeastern UP, 1996), 245–65.

9. In response to her interviewer's question, "Why do you think there aren't any well-known books on the subject" of internment, Otsuka is nonplussed: "I have no idea why that is. I always thought, while I was writing the book, there must be twenty, thirty other people out there exactly like me, writing the same story. It's the obvious story to tell. What other story would you tell if you're the daughter or son of an evacuee?" ("Conversation").

10. Truth commissions "narrow," as Michael Ignatieff puts it, "the range of impermissible lies that one can tell in public"—the lie, for example, "in the country clubs and suburban gardens of White South Africa" that "the system [of apartheid] was unsustainable, of course, but not really that bad" (20–21).

Epilogue: Looking Back Is Looking Forward

1. Many sources document the United States violating the Geneva Convention, some of which I detail in this epilogue. US treatment of detainees after 9/11 violated the following aspects of the Geneva Convention:

   "Prisoners of war must at all times be humanely treated. Any unlawful act or omission…causing death or seriously endangering the health of a prisoner of war in its custody is prohibited, and will be regarded as a serious breach of the present Convention. Likewise, prisoners of war must at all times be protected, particularly against acts of violence or intimidation and against insults and public curiosity."

   "No physical or mental torture, nor any other form of coercion, may be inflicted on prisoners of war to secure from them information of any kind whatever. Prisoners of war who refuse to answer may not be threatened, insulted, or exposed to any unpleasant or disadvantageous treatment of any kind."

   "Prisoners of war shall enjoy complete latitude in the exercise of their religious duties, including attendance at the service of their faith, on condition that they comply with the disciplinary routine prescribed by the military authorities."

   "The following acts are and shall remain prohibited…cruel treatment and torture;…Outrages upon personal dignity, in particular, humiliating and degrading treatment."

   "Individual or mass forcible transfers, as well as deportations of protected persons from occupied territory…are prohibited, regardless of their motive" (http://impeachforpeace.org/evidence/pages/torture.html).

   Although a federal judge on November 8, 2004, shut down the first American military commission since World War II, stating that the military commissions at Guantánamo are "neither lawful nor proper," and ruled that the Bush administration violated the Geneva Convention in its handling of prisoners at the Guantánamo Bay prison, a major public blow to the Bush administration came on May 29, 2009, when General David Petraeus, President Bush's onetime top general in Iraq, admitted on Fox News that the United States violated the Geneva Convention (http://www.harpers.org/archive/2009/06/hbc-90005079).

2. Senator Leahy's speech calling for the truth commission can be viewed at http://www.bushtruthcommission.com, a site for gathering signatures of support for the truth commission.

3. When asked about Leahy's proposal at a February 2009 press conference, President Obama said, "Nobody is above the law….But generally speaking I'm more interested in looking forward than looking back." Asked for the first time in April 2009 to respond to

the likelihood that Spanish prosecutors would target Bush administration officials for sanctioning torture at Guantánamo Bay, Obama
stressed again, "I'm a firm believer that it's important to look forward and not backwards" (quoted in Stein).

4. In the words of one Rwandan government official who lost 17 members of his immediate family in the genocide of 1995, "We must
remember what happened in order to keep it from happening again."
In addition to her interviews in Rwanda, to learn "the impact of
official truth-seeking, where past horrors are publicly documented
and investigated by a special commission," Patricia Hayner also heard
from many victims in El Salvador, three years after the truth commission there, who "were clear that only by remembering could they
even begin to recover"; likewise, "in South Africa, time and again, I
heard survivors say they could forgive their perpetrators only if they
admitted the full truth" (3–4). Although the difference between
thousands of individual citizens directly victimized and the current situation in the United States (in which most victims of state-
sponsored torture are foreigners) is worth noting, the damage to the
national psyche is relevant.

5. A USA TODAY/Gallup Poll taken at the end of January 2009 found
that nearly two thirds of Americans surveyed said there should be
investigations into allegations that the Bush administration tortured
detainees and wiretapped US citizens without warrants. Given the
subsequent attention generated by Senator Leahy's proposal for a
truth commission the following month, this number is now likely
higher. Indeed, zazzle.com sells a T-shirt that reads, "Mr. Obama,
I have news for you: Looking back *IS* looking forward"; underneath
this statement, the shirt bears Obama's red, white, and blue circle
"hope" logo from his presidential campaign—but the bottom red
curve "drips," suggesting the unaccounted-for bloodshed that stains
his presidency. Below this, the shirt reads, "INVESTIGATE and
PROSECUTE the Bush cabal! (or it *will* happen again)." The ratio-
nale on the website reads, "President Obama says he prefers to look
forward and not back. The problem is that in order to look forward
and plan for the security of our future as a nation, it's imperatively
crucial that we examine our past failures and then establish safeguards
to keep from repeating them. We MUST impose accountability upon
those who've perpetrated horrendous criminal atrocities in our name
and tarnished our standing in the world. In this regard, looking back
is indeed looking forward. Our entire criminal justice system is based
upon that very premise."

6. This video has since begun to circulate on the Internet and is available to view on the ACLU website, http://www.aclu.org/national-
security/justice-denied-video-voices-guantanamo.

7. As of December 1, 2009. Of those still incarcerated, US officials
said they intend to eventually put 60 to 80 on trial and free the

rest; http://abcnews.go.com/Politics/guantanamo-detainees-transferred-france-hungary/story?id=9217004.

8. Recalling his empathetic reading of J. M. Coetzee's *Diary of a Bad Year* (2007), in which the lead character experiences shame at learning of Guantánamo, Appiah said that at times "it takes a great writer to pen down your feelings." At such a writer's poignant expression of the truth, Appiah continued, "shame" can be "met by pride."

BIBLIOGRAPHY

Allen, Brooke. "The Promised Land." *New York Times Book Review*, Jan. 11, 1998: 6–7.

American Civil Liberties Union (ACLU) Press Release. "Obama Administration Reverses Promise to Release Torture Photos." May 13, 2009. http://www.aclu.org/national-security/obama-administration-reverses-promise-release-torture-photos.

Anderson, Benedict. *Imagined Communities: Reflections on the Origin and Spread of Nationalism*. London: Verso, 1993.

Appiah, Anthony K. "Giving Up the Perfect Diamond." Review of *The Holder of the World*, by Bharati Mukherjee. *New York Times Book Review*, Oct. 1, 1993: 7.

Arar, Maher. Interview with Terry Gross. *Fresh Air*. NPR. WHYY, Philadelphia. Sept. 17, 2008.

Ashcroft, Bill, Gareth Griffiths, and Helen Tiffin, eds. *The Empire Writes Back: Theory and Practice in Post-Colonial Literatures*. London and New York: Routledge, 1989.

"Aurangzeb." *Wikipedia*. Accessed November 2, 2006. http://en.wikipedia.org/wiki/Aurangzeb.

Bakhtin, M. M. "Forms of Time and of the Chronotope in the Novel." *The Dialogic Imagination*. Ed. Michael Holquist, trans. Caryl Emerson and Michael Holquist. Austin: U of Texas P, 1981. 84–258.

Banks, Russell. *Cloudsplitter*. New York: HarperCollins, 1998.

———. "In Response to James McPherson's Reading of *Cloudsplitter*." *Historians and Novelists Confront America's Past (and Each Other)*. Ed. Mark C. Carnes. New York: Simon & Schuster, 2001: 67–76.

Barthes, Roland. "The Discourse of History." Trans. Stephen Bann. *Comparative Criticism: A Yearbook*, vol. 3. Cambridge: Cambridge UP, 1981. 3–28.

———. *Mythologies*. New York: Noonday Press, 1957.

Baudrillard, Jean. *The Illusion of the End*. Stanford, CA: Stanford U P, 1994.

———. "The Precession of Simulacra." *Art After Modernism: Rethinking Representation*. Ed. Brian Wallis. New York: New Museum of Contemporary Art, 1984. 253–81.

Bawer, Bruce. "Don DeLillo's America." *New Criterion*, Apr. 1985: 34–42.

Benjamin, Walter. "Theses on the Philosophy of History." *Illuminations.* Ed. Hannah Arendt. New York: Harcourt Brace Jovanovich, Inc., 1968. 253–64.

Benn Michaels, Walter. "'You Who Never Was There': Slavery and the New Historicism, Deconstruction and the Holocaust." *Narrative* 4.1 (January 1996): 1–16.

Bennett, Tony. "Texts in History: The Determinations of Readings and Their Texts." *Post-structuralism and the Question of History.* Ed. Derek Attridge, Geoff Bennington, and Robert Young. Cambridge: Cambridge UP, 1987. 63–81.

———. *Outside Literature.* London: Routledge, 1990.

Bent, Geoffrey. "Less Than Divine: Toni Morrison's *Paradise.*" *Southern Review* 35.1 (Winter 1999): 145–49.

Berkhofer, Robert. "The Challenge of Poetics to (Normal) Historical Practice." *The Postmodern History Reader.* Ed. Kenneth Jenkins. New York: Routledge, 1997. 139–57.

Bertman, Stephen. *Cultural Amnesia: America's Future and the Crisis of Memory.* Westport, CT: Praeger Publishers, 2000.

Bhabha, Homi K. *The Location of Culture.* New York: Routledge, 1994.

———. "Narrating the Nation." Introduction to *Nation and Narration.* Ed. Homi K. Bhabha. New York: Routledge, 1990. 1–7.

———. "Postcolonial Authority and Postmodern Guilt." *Cultural Studies.* Ed. Lawrence Grossberg, Cary Nelson, and Paula A. Treichler. New York: Routledge, 1992. 56–68.

Bibbs, Susheel. *Mary Ellen Pleasant 1817 to 1904: Mother of Human Rights in California.* San Francisco: Bibbs, 1996.

Bodnar, John. *Remaking America: Public Memory, Commemoration, and Patriotism in the Twentieth Century.* Princeton, NJ: Princeton UP, 1992.

Borges, Jorge Luis. *Collected Fictions.* Trans. Andrew Hurley. New York: Penguin, 1998.

Brickhouse, Anna. *Transamerican Literary Relations and the Nineteenth Century Public Sphere.* Cambridge: Cambridge UP, 2004.

Bryan, Sonya. "Morrison Gives Revealing Lecture at UB." Review of *Paradise* manuscript lecture by Toni Morrison. Apr. 24, 1997. http://cityhonors.buffalo.k12.ny.us/city/rsrcs/eng/morrev.html.

Buell, Lawrence. "Hawthorne and the Problem of 'American' Fiction: The Example of the Scarlet Letter." *Hawthorne and the Real: Bicentennial Essays.* Columbus: Ohio State UP, 2005. 70–87.

Callinicos, Alex. *Against Postmodernism: A Marxist Critique.* New York: Palgrave Macmillan, 1990.

Caruth, Cathy. "Introduction." *Trauma: Explorations of Memory,* Ed. Cathy Caruth. Baltimore: Johns Hopkins Press, 1995: 151–157.

Chancy, Myriam J. "Exile and Resistance: Retelling History as a Revolutionary Act in the Writings of Michelle Cliff and Marie Chauvet." *Journal of Caribbean Studies* 9.3 (Winter 1993–Spring 1994): 266–292.

Chen, Tina. "Towards an Ethics of Knowledge." MELUS: The Journal of the Society for the Study of the Multi-Ethnic Literature of the United States 30.2 (Summer 2005): 157–73.

Cincotti, Joseph A. "Same Trip, Opposite Direction." *New York Times Book Review*, Oct. 1, 1993: 7.

Cliff, Michelle. "The Art of History: An Interview with Michelle Cliff." With Judith Raiskin. *Kenyon Review* 15.1 (Winter 1993): 57–71.

———. *Free Enterprise*. New York: Plume, 1993.

———. "An Interview with Michelle Cliff." With Meryl F. Schwartz. *Contemporary Literature* 34.4 (Winter 1993): 595–619.

———. Letter to the author. June 6, 1999.

Condé, Maryse. *I, Tituba, Black Witch of Salem*. Charlottesville: Rector and Visitors of the University of Virginia and Caraf Books, 1992.

———. "Interview with Ann Armstrong Scarboro." Afterword of *I, Tituba, Black Witch of Salem*. 198–213.

Cowart, David. "For Whom the Bell Tolls: Don DeLillo's *Americana*." *Contemporary Literature* 37.4 (1996): 602–19.

Crawford, Margo N. "Transcendence Versus the Embodiment of Racial Abstraction in Novels by William Faulkner, Toni Morrison, and John Edgar Wideman." Diss., Yale University, 1999.

Cummins, John. *The Voyage of Christopher Columbus: Columbus' Own Journal of Discovery Newly Restored and Translated*. New York: St. Martin's Press, 1992.

Dalsgård, Katrine. "'The One All-Black Town Worth the Pain': American Exceptionalism, Historical Narration, and the Critique of Nationhood in Toni Morrison's *Paradise*." *African American Review* 35 (Summer 2001): 233–48.

D'Antonio, Michael. "Atomic Guinea Pigs." *New York Times Magazine*, Aug. 31, 1997: 38–43.

de Certeau, Michel. *The Writing of History*. New York: Columbia UP, 1988.

DeLillo, Don. "The American Absurd." *Harper's Magazine*, Feb. 2004, 32–34.

———. *Americana*. New York: Penguin, 1971.

———. "Don DeLillo: The Art of Fiction CXXXV." Interview by Adam Begley. *Paris Review* 128 (1993): 274–306.

———. *Falling Man*. New York: Scribner, 2007.

———. *Great Jones Street*. Boston: Houghton Mifflin, 1973.

———. "In the Ruins of the Future: Reflections on Terror and Loss in the Shadow of September." *Harper's Magazine*, Dec. 2001, 32–40. *Guardian*. Dec. 22, 2001: 1–7. http://www.guardian.co.uk/books/2001/dec/22/fiction.dondelillo.

———. "An Interview with Don DeLillo." Kevin Connolly. *Conversations with Don DeLillo*. Ed. Thomas DePietro. Jackson: U of Mississippi P, 2004: 25–39.

———. *Libra*. New York: Penguin, 1988.

———. "Notes Toward a Definitive Meditation (By Someone Else) on the Novel 'Americana.'" *Epoch* 21.3 (1972): 327–29.

DeLillo, Don. "'An Outsider in This Society': An Interview with Don DeLillo." By Anthony DeCurtis. *South Atlantic Quarterly* 89.2 (1990): 281–304.

———. *Players*. New York: Knopf, 1977.

———. "The Power of History." *New York Times Magazine*, Sept. 7, 1997, 60–63.

———. "Seven Seconds." Interview with Ann Arensberg. *Conversations with Don DeLillo*. Ed. Thomas DePietro. Jackson: U of Mississippi P, 2004. 40–46.

———. *Underworld*. New York: Scribner, 1997.

———. *White Noise*. New York: Viking, 1984.

Derrida, Jacques. *Of Grammatology*. Baltimore: Johns Hopkins UP, 1976.

Doxtader, Erik. *With Faith in the Works of Words: The Beginnings of Reconciliation in South Africa, 1985–1995*. East Lansing: Michigan State UP, 2001.

Dyess, William E. *Bataan Death March: A Survivor's Account*. Lincoln: U of Nebraska P, 2002.

Eagleton, Terry. *Literary Theory: An Introduction*. Oxford: Basil and Blackwell, 1983.

Elias, Amy. *Sublime Desire: History and Post-1960s Fiction*. Baltimore: Johns Hopkins UP, 2001.

Ermarth, Elizabeth Deeds. *Sequel to History*. Princeton, NJ: Princeton UP, 1991.

Eysteinsson, Astruadur. *The Concept of Modernism*. Ithaca, NY: Cornell UP, 1991.

Felman, Shoshana. "Education and Crisis, or the Vicissitudes of Teaching." *Testimony: Crises of Witnessing in Literature, Psychoanalysis, and History*. Shoshana Felman and Dori Laub. New York: Routledge, 1992. 1–56.

Fitzpatrick, Kathleen. "The Unmaking of History: Baseball, Cold War, and *Underworld*." *UnderWords: Perspectives on Don DeLillo's Underworld*. Ed. Joseph Dewey, Stephen G. Kellman, and Irving Malin. Newark, NJ: U of Delaware P, 2002. 144–60.

Foley, Barbara. *Telling the Truth: The Theory and Practice of Documentary Fiction*. Ithaca, NY: Cornell UP, 1986.

Foucault, Michel. "Nietzsche, Genealogy, History." *The Foucault Reader*. Ed. Paul Rabinow. New York: Pantheon Books, 1984. 76–100.

———. *Power/Knowledge: Selected Interviews and Other Writings, 1972–1977*. Ed. Colin Gordon, trans. Leo Marshall Gordon, John Mepham, and Kate Soper. New York: Pantheon Books, 1980.

"The Freedom Files: Torture and Unlawful Imprisonment." Brave New Films, LLC. Dir. Robert Greenwald. 2007. http://www.aclu.tv.

Friedlander, Saul, ed. *Probing the Limits of Representation: Nazism and the "Final Solution."* Cambridge, MA: Harvard UP, 1992.

Friedman, Susan Stanford. "Making History: Reflections on Feminism, Narrative, and Desire." *The Postmodern History Reader*. Ed. Kenneth Jenkins. New York: Routledge, 1997. 231–36.

Frow, John. *Marxism and Literary History*. Cambridge, MA: Harvard UP, 1986.

Fussell, Paul. *Thank God for the Atom Bomb*. New York: Ballantine Books, 1990.

Gallagher, Carole. *American Ground Zero: The Secret Nuclear War*. Cambridge, MA: MIT Press, 1993.

Garvey, Johanna K. "Passages to Identity: Re-Membering the Diaspora." *Black Imagination and the Middle Passage*. Ed. Maria Diedrich, Henry Louis Gates, Jr., and Carl Pedersen. Oxford: Oxford UP, 1999. 255–70.

Gates, David. "Trouble in 'Paradise.'" *Newsweek*, Jan. 12, 1998, 62.

Gates, Henry Louis, Jr. "'Ethnic and Minority' Studies." *Introduction to Scholarship*. Ed. Joseph Gibaldi. New York: MLA, 1992. 288–302.

Gauthier, Marni. "Better Living Through Westward Migration: Don DeLillo's Inversion of the American West as 'Virgin Land' in *Underworld*." *Moving Stories: Migration and the American West, 1850–2000*. Ed. Scott E. Casper, Nevada Humanities Committee Halcyon Series 23. Reno: U of Nevada P, 2001. 131–52.

Gendlin, Eugene. "Beyond Postmodernism: From Concepts through Experiencing." *Understanding Experience: Psychotherapy and Postmodernism*. New York: Routledge, 2003. 100–115.

Geras, Norman. "Language, Truth and Justice." *New Left Review* 209 (1995): 110–35.

Giles, Paul. "Transnationalism and Classic American Literature." *PMLA* 118.1 (Jan. 2003): 62–77.

Gilroy, Paul. *The Black Atlantic: Modernity and Double Consciousness*. Cambridge, MA: Harvard UP, 1993.

Grossman, Lev. "Amnesia the Beautiful." *TIME*. Mar. 21, 2004. http://www.time.com/time/magazine/article/0,9171,603222,00.html

Gruesz, Kirsten Silva. "In These Transamerican Times." Symposium: Rethinking Americas Studies: Hemispheric Perspectives. University of Chicago, Nov. 18, 2005.

Hall, Stuart. *The Hard Road to Renewal*. London: Verso, 1988.

Hantke, Steffen. "Lessons in Latent History." Review of *Underworld*. *Alt-X Electronic Book Review* 7 (Summer 1998). http://www.altx.com/ebr/reviews/rev7/r7han.htm.

Harlow, Barbara. "From Prison to Pretoria: Ruth First at the TRC." *The University and the Prison Forum*. University of Colorado, Boulder, November 2, 2000.

Harvey, David. *The Condition of Postmodernity: An Enquiry into the Origin of Cultural Change*. Cambridge, MA: Blackwell, 1990.

Hatamiya, Leslie T. *Righting a Wrong: Japanese Americans and the Passage of the Civil Liberties Act of 1988*. Stanford, CA: Stanford UP, 1993.

Hawthorne, Nathaniel. "The Custom-House." *The Scarlet Letter and Other Tales of the Puritans*. Ed. Harry Levin. Boston: Houghton Mifflin, 1960. 5–47.

Hayner, Priscilla B. *Unspeakable Truths: Facing the Challenge of Truth Commissions*. New York: Routledge, 2002.

Himmelfarb, Gertrude. "Telling It as You Like It: Postmodernist History and the Flight from Fact." *The Postmodern History Reader.* Ed. Kenneth Jenkins. New York: Routledge, 1997. 158–74.

Hine, Darlene Clark. "Lifting the Veil, Shattering the Silence: Black Women's History in Slavery and Freedom." *The State of Afro-American History: Past, Present, and Future.* Ed. Darlene Clark Hine. Baton Rouge: Louisiana State UP, 1986. 223–49.

Hitchens, Christopher. "Morrison's True West." *Vanity Fair,* Feb. 1998, 144–45.

Hudson, Lynn M. "When 'Mammy' Becomes a Millionaire: Mary Ellen Pleasant, an African-American Entrepreneur." Diss., Indiana University, 1996.

Hutcheon, Linda. *Narcissistic Narrative: The Metafictional Paradox.* Waterloo, Ontario: Wilfrid Laurier UP, 1980.

———. *A Poetics of Postmodernism: History, Theory, Fiction.* New York: Routledge, 1988.

Ignatieff, Michael. "Introduction." *Truth and Lies: Stories from the Truth and Reconciliation Commission in South Africa.* New York: New Press, 2002: 15–21.

Jaffer, Jameel. Opening Remarks. "Reckoning with Torture: Memos and Testimonies from the 'War on Terror.'" ACLU and PEN American Center. The Cooper Union, New York, New York. Oct. 13, 2009.

Jaffrey, Zia. "Toni Morrison: The Salon Interview." *Salon,* Feb. 2, 1998. http://www. salon.com/books/int/1998/02/cov_si_02int3.html.

Jameson, Fredric. *Postmodernism, or the Cultural Logic of Late Capitalism.* Durham, NC: Duke UP, 1991.

"Justice Denied Video: Voices From Guantánamo." ACLU Video, 2009. http://www.aclu.org/national-security/justice-denied-video-voices-guantanamo.

Johnson, Erica L. "Ghostwriting Transnational Histories in Michelle Cliff's *Free Enterprise.*" *Meridians: Feminism, Race, Transnationalism* 9.1 (2009): 114–39.

Johnston, John. "Superlinear Fiction or Historical Diagram?: Don DeLillo's *Libra.*" *Modern Fiction Studies* 40.2 (Summer 1994): 319–42.

Kadir, Djelal. "Introduction: America and Its Studies." *PMLA* 118.1 (Jan. 2003): 9–24.

Kakutani, Michiko. "'Paradise': Worthy Women, Unredeemable Men." Review of *Paradise* by Toni Morrison. *New York Times,* Jan. 6, 1998. *New York Times on the Web*: http://nytimes.com/books/98/01/04/daily/morrison/book/review/rt.html.

Kammen, Michael. *Mystic Chords of Memory.* New York: Knopf, 1991.

Kaplan, Amy. "Left Alone with America: The Absence of Empire in the Study of American Culture." *Cultures of United States Imperialism.* Ed. Amy Kaplan and Donald Pease. Durham, NC: Duke UP, 1994. 3–21.

Kaplan, Amy, and Donald Pease. *Cultures of United States Imperialism.* Durham, NC: Duke UP, 1994.

Kekeh-Dika, Andree-Anne. "*Free Enterprise*: Writing the Americas as Crossroads." *GRAAT: Publication des Groupes de Rechereces Anglol-Americaines de l'Universite Francois Rabelais de Tours* 27 (2003): 267–75.

King, Richard C., ed. *Postcolonial America*. Chicago: U of Illinois P, 2000.

Kristof, Nicholas D. "Rejoin the World." Op-ed. *New York Times*, Nov. 2, 2008. http://www.nytimes.com/2008/11/02/opinion/02kristof.html.

Lanzmann, Claude. "The Obscenity of Understanding: *An Evening with Claude Lanzmann*." In Caruth, *Trauma: Explorations of Memory*. 200–220.

LaCapra, Dominick. *History and Criticism*. Ithaca, NY: Cornell UP, 1985.

Laub, Dori, and Shoshana Felman. "Bearing Witness, or the Vicissitudes of Listening." *Testimony: Crises of Witnessing in Literature, Psychoanalysis, and History*. Shoshana Felman and Dori Laub. New York: Routledge, 1992. 57–74.

Lehmann, Elmar. "Remembering the Past: Toni Morrison's Version of the Historical Novel." *Lineages of the Novel*. Ed. Bernhard Reitz and Eckart Voigts-Virchow. Trier, Germany: Wissenschaftlicher, 2000: 97–203.

Lentricchia, Frank. "Libra as Postmodern Critique." *South Atlantic Quarterly* 89.2 (1990): 431–53.

Lenz, Günter H. "Border Cultures, Creolization, and Diasporas: Negotiating Cultures of Difference in America." *Negotiations of America's National Identity*. Ed. Roland Hagenbüchle and Josef Raab, in cooperation with Marietta Messmer. Vol. 2. Tübingen, Germany: Stauffenburg, 2000. 362–86.

Lewis, R. W. B. *The American Adam: Innocence Tradition and Tragedy in the Nineteenth Century*. Chicago: U of Chicago P, 1955.

Lipsitz, George. "Myth, History, and Counter-Memory." *Politics and the Muse: Studies in the Politics of Recent American Literature*. Ed. Adam J. Sorkin. Bowling Green, OH: Bowling Green State UP Popular Press, 1989. 161–78.

Lukács, Georg. *The Historical Novel*. Trans. Hannah and Stanley Mitchell. Lincoln: U of Nebraska P, 1983.

Lyotard, Jean-Francois. *The Postmodern Condition: A Report on Knowledge*. Minneapolis: U of Minnesota P: 1984.

McClure, John. "Postmodern Romance." *Introducing Don DeLillo*. Ed. Frank Lentricchia. Durham, NC: Duke UP, 1991. 99–116.

McHale, Brian. *Constructing Postmodernism*. London: Routledge, 1992.

———. *Postmodernist Fiction*. London: Routledge, 1987.

Menand, Louis. "The War Between Men and Women." *New Yorker*, Jan. 12, 1998, 78–82.

Messmer, Merietta. "Towards a Declaration of Interdependence; or, Interrogating the Boundaries in Twentieth-Century Histories of North American Literature." *PMLA* 118.1 (Jan. 2003): 41–55.

Minow, Martha. *Between Vengeance and Forgiveness: Genocide and Mass Violence*. Boston: Beacon Press, 1998.

Mohanty, Satya. "Why I Am Not a Strategic Essentialist." Lecture, Cornell School of Criticism and Theory. Cornell University, July 1, 2003.

Monroe, Becky L., Policy Counsel. *The Constitution Project.* "Statement of the Constitution Project Submitted to the Senate Judiciary Committee." Hearing on "Getting to the Truth Through a Nonpartisan Commission of Inquiry." Mar. 4, 2009. 1–2.

Moraru, Christian. "Purloining the Scarlet Letter: Bharati Mukherjee and the Apocryphal Imagination." *He Said, She Says: An RSVP to the Male Text.* London: Farleigh Dickinson UP, 2001. 253–66.

Morrison, Toni. *Beloved.* New York: Knopf, 1988.

———. *Jazz.* New York: Knopf, 1992.

———. *Paradise.* New York: Knopf, 1998.

———. *Playing in the Dark: Whiteness and the Literary Imagination.* New York: Vintage, 1990.

———. "*Profile of a Writer: Toni Morrison.*" Dir. Alan Benson. Ed. Melvyn Bragg. R. M. Arts. Home Vision, 1987. Videocassette.

———. "The Site of Memory." *Inventing the Truth: The Art and Craft of Memoir.* Ed. William Zinsser. Boston: Houghton Mifflin, 1987. 101–24.

Mukherjee, Bharati. *The Holder of the World.* New York: Fawcett Columbine, 1993.

———. "Holders of the Word: An Interview with Bharati Mukherjee." With Tim Chen and S. X. Goudie. *Jouvert: A Journal of Postcolonial Studies* 1.1 (1997): 104 paragraphs.

———. "A Usable Past: An Interview with Bharati Mukherjee." With Shefalil Desai and Tony Barnstone. *Manoa: A Pacific Journal of International Writing* 10.2 (1998): 130–47.

———. "A Four-Hundred-Year-Old Woman." *The Writer on Her Work.* Ed. Janet Sternberg. Vol. 2. New York: W. W. Norton, 1991. 33–38.

———. "Naming Female Multiplicity: An Interview with Bharati Mukherjee." With Francisco Collado Rodríguez. *Atlantis* 17.1–2 (May–Nov. 1995): 293–306.

Myers, B. R. "A Reader's Manifesto." *Atlantic Online,* July/Aug. 2001, 1–21. http://www.theatlantic.com/doc/200107/myers.

Nada, Elia. *Trances, Dances, and Vociferations: Agency and Resistance in Africana Women's Narratives.* New York: Garland Publishing, 2000.

Newman, Judie. "Spaces In-Between: Hester Prynne as the Salem Bibi in Bharati Mukherjee's *The Holder of the World.*" *Borderlands: Negotiating Boundaries in Post-Colonial Writing.* Amsterdam: Rodopi, 1999. 69–87.

Norris, Christopher. "Postmodernizing History: Right-wing Revisionism and the Uses of Theory." *The Postmodern History Reader.* Ed. Kenneth Jenkins. New York: Routledge, 1997. 89–102.

OLC Vaughn Index #97. Central Intelligence Memo to DOJ Command Center for Dan Levin. December 30, 2004: 1–18. http://www.aclu.org/accountability/released.html.

Onega, Susan. "Postmodernist Re-Writings of the Puritan Commonwealth: Winterson, Ackroyd, Mukherjee." *Intercultural Encounters – Studies in English Literatures* (1999): 439–66.

Otsuka, Julie. *When the Emperor Was Divine.* New York: Anchor Books, 2002.

———. "A Conversation with Julie Otsuka." Interview with Kawano. *Bold Type*, Feb. 2009. http://www.randomhouse.com/boldtype/0902/otsuka/interview.html.

Palmer, Bryan. "Critical Theory, Historical Materialism." *The Postmodern History Reader.* Ed. Kenneth Jenkins. New York: Routledge, 1997. 103–14.

Parkinson Zamora, Lois. *The Usable Past: The Imagination of History in Recent Fiction of the Americas.* Cambridge: Cambridge UP, 1997.

Patell, Cyrus R. K. "Emergent Literatures." *The Cambridge History of American Literature.* Vol. 7, *Prose Writing, 1940–1990.* Ed. Sacvan Bercovitch. Cambridge: Cambridge UP, 1999. 539–675.

Peterson, Nancy J. *Against Amnesia: Contemporary Women Writers and the Crises of Historical Memory.* Philadelphia: U of Pennsylvania P, 2001.

Pollock, Mary. "Positioned for Resistance: Identity and Action in Michelle Cliff's *Free Enterprise.*" *Sharpened Edge: Women of Color, Resistance, and Writing.* Ed. Stephanie Athey. Westport, CT: Praeger, 2003. 203–18.

Ponzanesi, Sandra. "Diasporic Narratives @ Home Pages: The Future as Virtually Located." *Colonies, Missions, Cultures in the English Speaking World: General Comparative Studies.* Tübingen, Germany: Stauffenburg, 2001. 396–406.

Porter, Carolyn. "What We Know That We Don't Know: Remapping American Literary Studies." *American Literary History* 6 (1994): 466–526.

Price, David W. *History Made, History Imagined: Contemporary Literature, Poiesis, and the Past.* Urbana and Chicago: U of Illinois P, 1999.

Rajan, Gita. "Fissuring Time, Suturing Space: Reading Bharati Mukherjee's *The Holder of the World.*" *Generations: Academic Feminists in Dialogue.* Ed. Devoney Looser and Ann E. Kaplan. Minneapolis: U of Minnesota P, 1997. 288–308.

Rosenbaum, Alan S. *Is the Holocaust Unique? Perspectives on Comparative Genocide.* Boulder, CO: Westview Press, 2001.

Rosenzweig, Roy, and David Thelan. *The Presence of the Past: Popular Uses of History in American Life.* New York: Columbia UP, 1998.

Rowe, John Carlos. "Nineteenth-Century United States Literary Culture and Transnationality." *PMLA* 118.1 (Jan. 2003): 78–89.

Rushdie, Salman. "Step Across This Line: An Evening with Salman Rushdie." Distinguished Speaker in the Humanities Series. Ithaca College, New York. Nov. 2, 2003.

Schmidt, Peter, and Amritjit Singh. *Postcolonial Theory and the United States.* Jackson: UP of Mississippi, 2000.

Schueller, Malani Johar, and Edward Watts, eds. *Messy Beginnings: Postcoloniality and Early American Studies.* New Brunswick, NJ: Rutgers UP, 2003.

Schwarz, Henry, and Sangeeta Ray, eds. *A Companion to Postcolonial Studies.* Hoboken, NJ: Wiley-Blackwell Press, 2000.

Schwartz, Meryl F. "Imagined Communities in the Novels of Michelle Cliff." *Homemaking: Women Writers and the Politics and Poetics of Home.* Ed. Fiona Barnes and Catherine Wiley. New York: Garland, 1996. 287–311.

Silko, Leslie Marmon. *Almanac of the Dead.* New York: Penguin, 1991.

Singh, Amritji, Joseph T. Skerret, Jr., and Robert E. Hogan, eds. *Memory, Narrative, and Identity: New Essays in Ethnic American Literatures.* Boston: Northeastern UP, 1994.

Slotkin, Richard. *Gunfighter Nation: The Myth of the Frontier in Twentieth-Century America.* Norman: U of Oklahoma P, 1992.

———. *Regeneration Through Violence: The Mythology of the American Frontier, 1600–1800.* New York: HarperPerennial, 1973.

Smith, Henry Nash. *Virgin Land: The American West as Symbol and Myth.* New York: Vintage, 1950.

Spivak, Gayatri Chakavorty. *The Spivak Reader.* Ed. Donna Landry and Gerald MacLean. New York and London: Routledge, 1996.

Sommer, Doris. *Proceed with Caution, When Engaged by Minority Writing in the Americas.* Cambridge, MA: Harvard UP, 1999.

St. George, Robert Blair. *Possible Pasts: Becoming Colonial in America.* Ithaca, NY: Cornell UP, 2000.

Stein, Sam. "Obama on Spanish Torture Investigation: I Prefer to Look Forward." *Huffington Post,* Apr. 16, 2009.

Steiner, Wendy. "Postmodern Fictions, 1970–1990." *The Cambridge History of American Literature.* Vol. 7, *Prose Writing, 1940–1990.* Ed. Sacvan Bercovitch. Cambridge: Cambridge UP, 1999. 425–530.

Tally, Justine. *Paradise Reconsidered: Toni Morrison's (Hi)Stories and Truths.* FORECAAST: Forum for European Contributions in African American Studies. Hamburg: Lit Verlag, 1999.

Talmadge, Eric, and Associated Press. "GIs Frequented Japan's 'Comfort Women.'" *Washington Post,* Apr. 25, 2007.

Tanner, Tony. "Afterthoughts on Don DeLillo's *Underworld.*" *Don DeLillo.* Bloom's Modern Critical Views. Ed. Harold Bloom. Broomall, PA: Chelsea House Publishers, 2003. 129–147.

Trouillot, Michel-Rolph. *Silencing the Past: Power and the Production of History.* Boston: Beacon Press, 1995.

Vidal, Gore. *Imperial America: Reflections on the United States of Amnesia.* New York: Nation Press, 2004.

Wald, Priscilla. "Minefields and Meeting Grounds: Transnational Analyses and American Studies." *American Literary History* 10.1 (Spring 1998): 199–218.

Wallace, Molly. "'Venerated Emblems': DeLillo's *Underworld* and the History-Commodity." *Critique: Studies in Contemporary Fiction* 42.4 (Summer 2001): 367–83.

White, Hayden. *Figural Realism: Studies in the Mimesis Effect.* Baltimore: Johns Hopkins UP, 1999.

———. *Tropics of Discourse: Essays in Cultural Criticism.* Baltimore: Johns Hopkins UP, 1978.

Whitman, Walt. *Leaves of Grass*. Boston: Thayer and Eldridge, 1860.

Wright, Richard. *White Man: Listen! Lectures in Europe, 1950–56*. New York: Harper Perennial, 1995.

Wong, Sau-ling. *Reading Asian American Literature*. Princeton, NJ: Princeton UP, 1993.

Zeleny, Jeff. "Obama Tries to Block Release of Detainee Photos." The Caucus. *New York Times*, May 13, 2009. http://thecaucus.blogs.nytimes.com/2009/05/13/white-house-wants-a-delay-in-the-release-of-detainee-photos/.

Žižek, Slavoj. "The Joint Out of Time – The Temporality of the Trauma in Psychoanalysis." Persistence of Exile Lecture Series. The Center for Humanities and the Arts. University of Colorado, Boulder. Sept. 23, 2000.

INDEX

internment of Japanese Americans,
14, 152, 219n7; mythic history
and, 155, 164; official apology
for, 4, 181; silence and, 167–170,
172, 174–175; trauma of,
172–176, 177. *See also* Japanese
Americans; *When the Emperor Was
Divine* (Otsuka)
interpretation, 74–75, 93, 121,
195n18; of Mesopotamian
cosmogram, 118; Patricia's
genealogy and, 89–90
interrogation techniques, 181, 183,
187–188
"In the Ruins of the Future"
(DeLillo), 161
Iran Holocaust denial conference,
1, 151
irony, 189; in *Americana,* 202n2,
207n18; in *Holder,* 122;
situational, 171, 180; in *White
Noise,* 207n18
Islam, 139–140
Issei men (first-generation Japanese
immigrants), 14, 170–171, 176;
testimonies of, 180
Iwo Jima battle, 45, 204n7

J. Alfred Prufrock, 49, 205n11
Jamaica *(Free Enterprise),*
105–107
Jameson, Frederic, 28–29, 37,
142–143, 198n10;
postmodernism and, 4, 18–19,
30–31; temporality and, 196n2
Japanese Americans, 218n5;
children of, 168, 219n8;
collective rejection of, 164; Issei,
14, 170–171, 176, 180; Nisei,
167, 177. *See also* internment of
Japanese Americans; *When the
Emperor Was Divine* (Otsuka)
Japanese Canadian relocation, 165,
218n4, 219n7
Japanese Imperial Army, 151, 183;
Bataan Death March and, 44–47,

204n8; comfort women and, 14,
192n5, 195n19
Jazz (Morrison), 71, 208n3
Jews, 1, 104, 110–111, 191n1,
219n7
JFK assassination, 50–54, 158,
205n12; seclusion following, 162;
uncertainty and, 160–161. *See also*
Kennedy, John F.; *Libra*
(DeLillo)
John Hathorne *(Holder),* 126
Johnston, John, 51
"Justice Denied Video: Voices from
Guantánamo," 188
Justin *(Falling Man),* 156, 162

Kadir, Djelal, 103
Kaplan, Amy, 15, 102, 103
Kazakhstan *(Underworld),* 63;
Kazakh Test Site, 58
Keith Neudecker *(Falling Man),*
156, 157–160, 163–164
Kennedy, John F., 42, 49, 161–162;
assassination of, 50–54, 158,
160–161, 162, 205n12; *Libra*
and, 50–54; Zapruder film and,
51–52, 205n13
Kogawa, Joy, 165, 218n4
Kolodny, Annette, 103
Korematsu, Fred, 167, 192n4
Korematsu v. United States (1944),
167
Kristof, Nicholas, 184

Lacan, Jacques, 37
LaCapra, Dominick, 40, 198n8
landfills, 59, 61, 65. *See also* waste
Land of Look Behind, The (Cliff),
102
language, 38, 188, 198n6; biblical,
72, 81–83, 84; in *Holder,* 147;
JFK assassination and, 53; mythic
history and, 41; power and, 76;
reality and, 30; of testimony, 181;
therapeutic, 168; in *Underworld,*
63–64